Writers of Italy Series

General Editor
C.P. Brand
Professor of Italian
University of
Edinburgh

8

PIRANDELLO

© Olga Ragusa 1980
Edinburgh University Press
22 George Square, Edinburgh

ISBN 0 85224 373 1

Set in Monotype Bembo
by Speedspools, Edinburgh
and printed in Great Britain by
Clark Constable Ltd
Edinburgh

Robert C. Betz

1980

Edinburgh University Press

Luigi

PIRANDELLO

An approach to his theatre

OLGA RAGUSA

*

Contents

Preface

The very abundance of Pirandello's production, the variety of genres, the disciplines straddled, the constant re-use of his own materials, the as yet incomplete documentation of his activity, the apparent abstruseness and controversial nature of his 'philosophy' – all this presents a challenge to the writer entrusted with an introductory study of his work. The partisanship that divided his audiences in his lifetime continues today between those who accept what Croce called his 'radical pessimism' and those who reject it, those who recognize in him an uncompromising censor of all established values and those who see him instead as politically acquiescent and even reactionary. There are those who judge him not only a great theatrical innovator but a great writer (one of the prime poetic imaginations of the age of Proust and Joyce, Kafka, Musil, and Thomas Mann) and those who claim on the contrary that he has no style and but a handful of worn ideas repeated over and over again – ideas that are variations on the metaphysical problem of reality and illusion or being and seeming, and on its analogues in psychology and drama: the self and the role, the face and the mask.

I have tried to solve the problem of superabundant material by focusing on Pirandello's theatre or, in the words of the Nobel Prize citation, on 'his bold and brilliant renovation of the drama and the stage'. It is this aspect of his work that has won him the place he enjoys in school curricula and in the culture of the theatre-goer and the general educated public. Balanced between the diachronic and the synchronic – between how the works 'happened' and how they face the reader today – this study of Pirandello is not encyclopaedic but selective. It is not a 'Pirandello Handbook' and is not intended as a substitute for a direct reading of the texts. What may to some appear an excessive 'telling of stories', an exaggerated attention to the letter of the text, is in all cases intentional. As far back as 1921 Tilgher warned that 'Pirandello's plays are usually extremely difficult to tell' because what matters in them is not the action but the *process* by which the characters gain insight into and explain to others 'the spiritual position which they have reached and at which they have stopped'.

Reviews of the plays show what difficulties critics had and continue to have in following Pirandello's expositions, in getting the crucial *antefatto* [preceding action] straight, and in making the protagonists say everything but no more than they were actually meant to say. It has been my effort to avoid the trap into which so many critics of Pirandello have fallen, that of competing with his characters in sophistry and paradox. 'Among so many "mirrors" and under so many "masks", the poet's "true face", so similar to the man's, the one that all wish to discover, has remained to almost all hidden', reads a recent assessment of Pirandello criticism. Not to complicate but to clarify was my aim in this study, and I hope that in its constant care to misrepresent Pirandello as little as possible and in its exploration of certain inescapable contexts, it will contribute to a fuller and more accurate understanding of his work.

It is with pleasure that I take the opportunity to express my gratitude to Professor C. P. Brand, General Editor of the series, for his patient and understanding acceptance of the delays that punctuated the incubation of my essay, and for his intelligent and careful reading of the manuscript.

O. R., *New York, June* 1980

NOTE. Throughout the text quotations from Pirandello's works are in Italian followed by their English translation, while quotations from secondary sources are given in translation only. All translations into English are the present writer's unless otherwise indicated. Titles of Pirandello's works, whether book-length or not, are in italics. All titles are cited in the original in the text and are accompanied by their English version in the Index.

Introduction

Virtually all aspects of Pirandello's activity have engaged the attention of critics and scholars. I use the word 'activity' advisedly, in order to underline from the beginning the difference that must perforce exist between the study of the work of a playwright as distinguished from that of a poet or novelist. A playwright's work is not finished when he has produced a literary text, for that text must, as it were, be made to come alive in a performance. Of course Pirandello was not only a playwright but also a poet, a novelist and a short story writer, but there can be no doubt that he owes his place in the history of modern Italian literature to his achievement in drama. The Nobel Prize, which he won in 1934, singled out 'his bold and brilliant renovation of the drama and the stage' as meriting specific distinction. No work on twentieth-century drama can ignore him. In Francis Fergusson's words: '"After Pirandello" – to take him symbolically rather than chronologically – the way was open for Yeats and Lorca, Cocteau and Eliot'. In an even more comprehensive perspective Robert Brustein calls him 'the most seminal dramatist of our time'. Brustein sees Pirandello as anticipating the existential anguish of Sartre and Camus, Beckett's portrayal of the disintegration of the personality and of the isolation of modern man, Ionesco's war on language; and he sees him as foreshadowing O'Neill, Pinter and Albee in their approach to the conflict of truth and illusion, Thornton Wilder and Jean Anouilh in their use of the interplay between actors and characters, and Jean Genet in his concept of man as a role-playing animal. In the history of Italian drama Pirandello is linked not only to his contemporaries (Chiarelli, Antonelli, Enrico Cavacchioli, Bontempelli, Rosso di San Secondo) in a movement to which Silvio D'Amico has given the unusually expressive and appropriate name of *Teatro dei fantocci* (puppet theatre), but to successors as varied as Ugo Betti, Diego Fabbri and Eduardo De Filippo as well.

But if it is in the perspective of the life of the theatre that Pirandello's contribution can best be understood, there is another and equally compelling reason for continued interest in his work. In essays and poems, in his long and short narrative, and of course in his plays,

Pirandello expressed a view of man and his place in the world that can be considered emblematic for his own day and which still rings true for our own. In one of his frequent statements of self-definition he wrote: 'Teatro serio il mio. Vuole tutta la partecipazione dell'entità morale – uomo. Non è teatro comodo. Teatro difficile, diciamo teatro pericoloso. Nietzsche diceva che i greci alzavano bianche statue contro il nero abisso, per nasconderlo. Sono finiti quei tempi. Io le scrollo, invece, per rivelarlo....È la tragedia dell'anima moderna' (from a 1936 interview, reprinted in Pietro Mignosi, *Il segreto di Pirandello*, Milan 1937) [Mine is a serious theatre. It requires the total participation of that moral entity – man. It is not a comfortable theatre. It is a difficult theatre, even a dangerous one. Nietzsche used to say that the Greeks raised white statues against the black abyss in order to hide it. Those times are gone. I shake them, instead, in order to reveal it.... It is the tragedy of modern man]. Seriousness of intention, moral outrage, the refusal to compromise, to be soothed; disillusionment, pessimism, the accent on the dark side of things, on what is out of harmony in the universe; the rage to be heard, to be heeded, with a perverse pleasure in everything that has shock value (from unconventional, paradoxical views of society to impatience with the accepted routine of the stage) – these are some of the attitudes that characterize Pirandello's work. They are attitudes that do not leave reader or spectator indifferent but have the power of inducing a direct subjective response that may translate itself into troubled repulsion as readily as into warm partisanship. Not all of Pirandello's critics have been favourable to him, not all of his spectators and readers have been attracted by the 'black abyss'. It is well to look at their reservations for they tell us much about the difficulties he had in affirming himself.

Croce, Italy's intellectual leader during the first half of the twentieth century, was harsh in his assessment. For him the early Pirandello is no more than an epigone, his practice of *verismo* mechanical, with none of the poetic feeling of the Neapolitan regionalist Di Giacomo or the Sicilian novelist and short story writer Verga, and none of the faith in science that marked De Roberto's and Capuana's brand of naturalism. As for Pirandello's later work, which Croce dates from *Il fu Mattia Pascal*, he finds it even less meritorious: 'occasional, artistically successful fragments, drowned out or disfigured by a convulsive and inconclusive philosophizing. Neither genuine art nor philosophy, checked by a fault in conception from developing in either direction.' Not one of Pirandello's works escapes Croce's sharp critique: they are at best derivative and repetitious, at worst stupid and pretentious, none is 'beautiful'.

In his anthology of Italian literature since unification, Gianfranco Contini, as respected and influential now as Croce was in his day, is equally negative in his judgment. Pirandello's scepticism and pessimism are not the products of robust, rigorous thinking and he cannot therefore be compared with Leopardi or Schopenhauer. His relativism is 'elementary', his language undistinguished, reflecting the colourless usage of the Roman middle class, the bureaucrats of the 'new' Italy at the turn of the century. He is a 'sophist', not a writer who gives expression to existential anguish. His essays on literary and theoretical subjects – and here Contini, the philologist, joins hands with Croce, the philosopher, who repeatedly attacked Pirandello's essay on humour – are unscientific and unscholarly, the work of a dilettante and not of a professional.

The criticism of Croce, Contini and others who share their views derives from a variety of sources but it is also rooted in a deep distrust of the theatre in general, the consequence of an age-old suspicion of its morality and of the traditional bias in favour of poetry. In this respect it is instructive to see what Italian writers and intellectuals thought of the theatre in the years when Pirandello was starting out on his career. Ugo Ojetti's 1895 series of interviews, *Alla scoperta dei letterati*, can serve as a guide. According to Ojetti, almost no one had a good word to say for the theatre. Verga, for instance, is reported as saying: 'I have written for the theatre, but I certainly don't think it a form superior to the novel. Indeed, it is an inferior and primitive form.' Enrico Annibale Butti, himself a playwright, is quoted as follows: 'As a work of art which must be represented, the theatre has such mechanical drawbacks that it cannot be placed high on the aesthetic scale. Moreover, it will always be humiliated by its natural judge, the crowd.' Scarfoglio, a leading Neapolitan journalist, expressed his opinion thus: 'Tragedy is dead. As far as I'm concerned, comedy no longer has any reason for existing.... Now we have the novel which is a superior and richer form of art.' Giacosa, remembered today exclusively for his plays, also denigrated the theatre as a 'truly inferior form of art'. Camillo Antona-Traversi, playwright and drama critic, likewise preferred the novel to the theatre: 'The novel, being more extended and freer, is inevitably superior to the theatre. Since its public is not gathered together, the crowd does not disturb the spirit of the different individuals that compose it: the quiet reader, ready for his reading, is more receptive, more friendly, freer

to understand and appreciate the artist.' Only Marco Praga dissented:
'In general I disdain the novel. It is an inferior form to drama which
is more difficult to compose and of greater effectiveness on the
public.'

Many of these formulations are strikingly close to ideas expressed
by Pirandello himself on many different occasions. Some of the early
essays especially readily come to mind. *L'azione parlata* (1899) is an
attack on those *professionisti di teatro*, opportunistic craftsmen not
artists, who approach the writing of a play as they would the demonstration of a thesis; and it makes a plea for 'spoken' dramatic dialogue
to replace the florid, literary 'written' language of D'Annunzio then
triumphant on the Italian stage. In *Illustratori, attori e traduttori* (1908)
Pirandello sees the actor as no different from the illustrator or the
translator in his inevitable transformation – and hence misrepresenta-
tion – of the original he tries to interpret. *Teatro siciliano?* (1909)
grapples with a problem very much alive in the days of *verismo*: the
impasse faced by the realistic theatre caught between the logical
claims for the use of dialect to reflect a regional setting, and the re-
quirements of the box office which made it imperative for an audience
in Rome, or Milan or Turin to be able to understand what was going
on. 'Il teatro è l'arte della scopa' [The theatre is the art of the broom-
stick] is reported to have been one of Pirandello's favourite sayings.
By which he meant what Antona-Traversi meant in the passage cited
above, that in contrast to the novelist's, the dramatist's brush strokes
are rough, that he must strive for immediate effect while the novelist
can count on the reader's more sustained and repeated attention, on
reflection and meditation. In one sense the whole of Pirandello's
development can be seen as a progressive moving away from his
initial rejection of the theatre in its late nineteenth-century guise ('Io,
se Dio m'assiste, non scriverò mai né commedie, né drammi' [I, so
God help me, shall never write plays nor dramas], he wrote to a friend
in 1909) to his full and aggressive championing of *his* theatre – *his*
theatre, and not the theatre *qua* theatre, because his theatre turned out
to be the medium best designed – and carefully nurtured and per-
fected by him – to be the vehicle for his ideas. These are the ideas that
he described in the Preface to *Sei personaggi* as 'i travagli del mio
spirito' [the pangs of my spirit], which happen to be also the pangs of
his characters, and (for a well-defined historical period at least, if not
for all time) the pangs of men in general: 'l'inganno della comprensione reciproca fondato irrimediabilmente sulla vuota astrazione delle
parole; la molteplice personalità d'ognuno secondo le possibilità

d'essere che si trovano in ciascuno di noi; e infine il tragico conflitto immanente tra la vita che di continuo si muove e cambia e la forma che la fissa, immutabile' (MN, I, 60) [The deception of mutual understanding founded on the empty abstraction of words, man's multiple personality corresponding to the possibilities of being that are found in each of us, and finally the inherent tragic conflict between life which is continually moving and changing and form which fixes it, immutable].

But what affected Pirandello's reception even more than the contemporary scepticism about the theatre as an art-form was the fundamental malaise experienced by so many readers and spectators in coming face to face with his 'radical pessimism', as Croce termed it. Here it is no longer a question of evaluation but one of assent or rejection that involves not particular aspects of his work but its impact, its possible *moral* impact, in its totality. In other words, a work of art, any work of art, is not a self-contained object to be judged only in relationship to other works of art. It has also a social dimension – it can influence life – and indeed its representation of life is part and parcel of its possible effect on the world, and for this too it must be judged, and indeed inevitably *is* judged. For Croce, the works of *decadentismo* (the turn-of-the-century movement that set art apart and above the ordinary concerns of men and to which Pirandello in many respects belongs), 'perhaps reflect the psychic conditions of the present-day world, with its lack of faith in and derision of the ideals that have always sustained mankind and indeed constitute its humanity... with its general lowering and humiliating of spiritual forces', but these works achieve neither 'aesthetic nor poetic truth' nor 'philosophical truth'. The view of the world they reflect is, in other words, partial and unilateral and fails to take into consideration the positive aspects of man's activities, his capacity to make the world go round *in spite of* what is wrong with it. For Croce, whose ideal for art as well as for life is that of classical equilibrium, of the golden mean, the very extremism of a position such as Pirandello's would rob it of its validity and render it socially dangerous, a possible incitement to *abulia* or to anarchy, the two sides of alienation.

Of course, it is precisely because it belongs to the literature of alienation, because it represents an antidote to self-satisfied optimism, to the social imperatives (as Henry Furst has put it) of 'efficiency, a high standard of living, safety first', because it bears witness to the sense of psychological disintegration and of the collapse of accepted values experienced by a whole class in the first part of the century, because of

its rejection of logic and its acceptance of the irrational that Pirandello's work has been recognized as belonging so much to its time and
as foreshadowing so thoroughly the even more brutal contrasts of our
own.

1. World View and Theoretical Statements

What are the historical and cultural factors that must be borne in mind in order to understand Pirandello's pessimism and to lay the foundation for an introduction to his theatre? Before seeking an answer to this question, it is important to record the basic biographical facts. After that, it will be our purpose to examine some of the theoretical statements that early in his career portrayed his view of the world. These statements appear in essays such as *Arte e coscienza d'oggi* and *L'umorismo* where they are presented directly, or in novels or short stories such as *Il fu Mattia Pascal* and *La tragedia di un personaggio* where they appear indirectly within a context of fiction. The close relationship between the two worlds, the world of every-day reality and the world of fiction, is one of the earmarks of Pirandello's work, and it is not surprising that we should find it exemplified here at the very beginning of our discussion.

Pirandello was born near Agrigento, on the southern coast of Sicily, in 1867. His father was a mine owner, a descendant of traders who had come from Liguria in the eighteenth century. His mother belonged to a family that on the local level had been deeply involved in Italy's struggle for unity and independence, the Risorgimento. The second of his parents' six children, Pirandello received the conventional education of the well-to-do child in the provinces and was destined for the study of law. From his teens, however, he showed a preference for literature: two manuscript notebooks of poetry date back to 1883. In 1887 he transferred from the University of Palermo to the University of Rome, where his study of literature proved to be as short-lived as his study of law had been. Because of an act of insubordination he was expelled from the University of Rome and he moved to the University of Bonn which was famous for its tradition in the study of philosophy and where a new discipline, Romance philology, was just beginning to take root. Pirandello earned his doctorate in 1891 with a dissertation written in German on the dialect of his native region, *Laute und Lautentwickelung der Mundart von Girgenti*.

The first period of his life can be considered to have come to a close in 1892-3, when he settled in Rome and, aided by a monthly allow-

ance from his family, began seriously to turn his attention to writing.
At that time he already had two collections of poetry in print (*Mal
giocondo*, 1889 and *Pasqua di Gea*, 1891), had translated Goethe's
Roman Elegies (published in 1896) and written his own *Elegie renane*
(published 1895), and had contributed a number of articles on linguistic and literary subjects to the reputable Florentine review, *Vita nuova*.
His association in Rome with artists and writers, most of them transplanted Sicilians like himself, plunged him into the intellectual life of
the capital and prepared the way for his first success, the serialization
in 1904 of *Il fu Mattia Pascal* in the pages of *Nuova antologia*. *Nuova
antologia* was Italy's leading literary review and counted among its
contributors such outstanding writers as Verga, D'Annunzio, Fogazzaro, Carducci and Pascoli. Between 1893 and 1904 Pirandello published (in addition to the works already listed) the narrative poem
Pier Gudrò (1894), a fourth verse collection, *Zampogna* (1901), the
novelette *Il turno* (1902), four collections of short stories (*Amori senza
amore*, 1894; *Beffe della morte e della vita*, 1902; *Quand'ero matto*, 1902;
Bianche e nere, 1904), his first full-length novel, *L'esclusa* (1901), many
scattered articles and stories, and his first play, the one-acter *L'epilogo*
(1898; later retitled *La morsa*). He had turned from poetry to prose
upon the advice of his friend and fellow-Sicilian, Luigi Capuana
(1839–1915), probably the most important Italian literary animator
and 'militant critic' (i.e., of contemporary works) of the second half
of the nineteenth century. Pirandello had married the daughter of one
of his father's business associates in 1894 and by 1899 he was the father
of three children (two sons and a daughter). A disaster in a mine in
which his father's capital and his wife's dowry were invested cut off
his income in 1903 and forced him to turn his writing into a financially
profitable activity and to stabilize his position at the *Regio Istituto
superiore di Magistero femminile*, where he had been teaching grammar,
composition and style since 1898.

In 1908 Pirandello published his essay on humour, *L'umorismo*, and
a collection of other essays, *Arte e scienza*, the two works which won
him a permanent position at the *Magistero*. Until 1916 he continued to
write mainly novels (*I vecchi e i giovani*, 1909; *Suo marito*, 1911, later
retitled *Giustino Roncella nato Boggiòlo*; *Si gira...*, 1915, later retitled
Quaderni di Serafino Gubbio operatore) and short stories (the collections
La vita nuda, 1910; *Terzetti*, 1912; *Le due maschere*, 1914; *La trappola*,
1915; *Erba del nostro orto*, 1915 date from this period), although there
was also an occasional play (*Lumíe di Sicilia* was performed in 1910;
Cecè published in 1913), and still another collection of poetry (*Fuor di*

chiave, 1912). In 1915 his first three-act play, *Se non cosi*...(later retitled *La ragione degli altri*), was performed in Milan; a year later it was the turn of *Pensaci, Giacomino!* and *Liolà*, both written not in Italian but in Sicilian dialect. In 1916 Italy was already at war: Pirandello's sons had enlisted and both became prisoners of war. Anxiety about their well-being was now added to the long-standing concern over his wife, whose mental illness, which had first manifested itself in 1903–4, would eventually (1919) make it necessary for her to be interned in a nursing home. Between 1917 and 1921, while he continued to publish short stories (*E domani, lunedì*..., 1917; *Un cavallo nella luna*, 1917; *Berecche e la guerra*, 1919; *Il carnevale dei morti*, 1919 are the collections that belong to these years), he wrote and had performed twelve new plays: *Cosi è (se vi pare)*, *Il berretto a sonagli*, *La giara*, and *Il piacere dell'onestà*, all in 1917; *Il giuoco delle parti*, *Ma non è una cosa seria*, and *La patente*, in 1918; *L'innesto*, *Tutto per bene*, and *L'uomo, la bestia e la virtù* in 1919; *La signora Morli, una e due* and *Come prima, meglio di prima* in 1920. In 1921 *Sei personaggi*, first a failure and then a spectacular success, opened the way for Pirandello's international reputation. The London and New York performances of *Sei personaggi* and the Paris performance of *Il piacere dell'onestà* took place in 1922 and made theatrical history. Also in 1922 a new edition of his short stories was begun under the collective title *Novelle per un anno* by which they were to become famous.

Pirandello took his first trip abroad as an acclaimed and controversial playwright in 1923; he attended the Pitoëff production of *Sei personaggi* in Paris and was guest of honour at a 'Pirandello Season' at the Fulton Theatre in New York. Between 1921 and 1923 he had written and seen performed *Enrico IV*, *Vestire gli ignudi*, *La vita che ti diedi*, and three one-act plays, *All'uscita* (first published in 1916), *L'uomo dal fiore in bocca* and *L'altro figlio*. In 1924 he would complete his last novel *Uno, nessuno e centomila*. The more frequent and more intense contacts with theatrical life, both in Italy and abroad, made him eager to try his hand at directing and producing. Like others he hoped that the new regime (Mussolini had just come to power) would support the arts and recognize the propaganda value of a strong and prestigious Italian avantgarde theatre, patterned on the State Theatres in existence in other countries. His Company, the Teatro d'Arte di Roma, which was founded in 1924 and gave its first performance on 4 April 1925 in the newly remodelled Teatro Odescalchi in Rome, enjoyed government sponsorship though it did not attain the status of state theatre. The programme of the première, which included Pirandello's one-act play, *Szgre del Signore della nave* and Lord Dunsany's *The Mountain Gods*, illustrates the double purpose of the Company, the performance of Pirandello's own plays and of others chosen by him. During the next three years Pirandello and his Company toured tirelessly, performing in the principal cities of Italy as well as in London, Paris, Berlin, Dresden, Cologne, Bonn, Budapest, Vienna and Prague, among others, and in Argentina and Brazil (1927). At the same time Pirandello's plays were being performed in translation in every major city of Europe and North America and as far away as South America and Japan. Proof that his theatre was no longer thought of as regional or national in its appeal but that it had come to belong to the world is the fact that some of his plays had their premières (in translation) outside Italy: *Diana e la Tuda*, 1926, in Zurich; *Lazzaro*, 1929, translated by Scott-Moncrieff, in Huddersfield; *Questa sera si recita a soggetto*, 1930, in Koenigsberg; *Sogno (ma forse no)*, 1931, in Lisbon; *Quando si è qualcuno*, 1933, in Buenos Aires; *Non si sa come*, 1934 in Prague; *La favola del figlio cambiato*, 1934, in Braunschweig. In 1925 Marta Abba had become the leading actress of the 'Teatro d'arte': Pirandello wrote *Diana e la Tuda*, *L'amica delle mogli* (1927), *La nuova colonia* (1928), *Lazzaro*, *Come tu mi vuoi* (1930), *Trovarsi* (1932), and *Quando si è qualcuno* specifically for her.

Pirandello's first contact with the motion picture world occurred in 1920 when *Ma non è una cosa seria* was turned into a film by Arnaldo Frateili and Augusto Camerini. Among others of his works adapted to the new medium during his lifetime were *Il fu Mattia Pascal* in a French version by Marcel L'Herbier (1925), *Enrico IV* in a German version with Conrad Veidt in the main role (1926), *Come tu mi vuoi* [As you Desire Me] in the famous Hollywood version with Greta Garbo (1932), *Il viaggio*, *La rosa* and *Lo scaldino* (all 1921) from the short stories of the same name, and *La canzone dell'amore* (1930) from the short story *In silenzio*. In 1929 he collaborated with Adolf Lantz on the script for a German film based on *Sei personaggi*, which was never produced, and in 1933 he wrote the screen play, *Gioca, Pietro!* (in collaboration with his son, Stefano Landi), which became the film *Acciaio*. Pirandello's total involvement with the performing arts is also reflected in the transformation of the one-act play *La giara* into a ballet with music by Alfredo Casella (1924) and of *Liolà* into a three-act opera with music by Giuseppe Mulè (1935). *La favola del figlio cambiato* was set to music by Malipiero, and in 1928 Pirandello wrote the scenario for a pantomime, *La salamandra*, for which the avant-garde writer Massimo Bontempelli provided the music.

In addition to the Nobel Prize Pirandello was honoured by nomination to membership in the 'Accademia d'Italia' (1929) and by the presidency of the 'Convegno Volta sul teatro drammatico' sponsored by the Academy in 1934. He died in 1936 leaving his last play, *Igiganti della montagna*, unfinished.

These facts of Pirandello's life will serve as points of reference throughout the discussion of his works and be expanded or added to as the occasion requires. It is well to remember, however, that Pirandello considered them of little interest in themselves. When in 1924 his rising reputation was accompanied by frequent articles and interviews, he wrote for a Roman periodical: '...nella mia vita non c'è niente che meriti di essere rilevato: è tutta interiore, nel mio lavoro e nei miei pensieri che...non sono lieti' (SPSV, 1246) [there is nothing worthy of note in my life: it is a completely inner life, concentrated in my work and in my far from cheerful thoughts].

Whereas it is possible to divide Pirandello's life into periods and to study these in relation to one another within the view of a progressive development, it is more difficult to deal in a similar way with his 'ideas'. As Mario Pomilio writes in *La formazione critico-estetica di Pirandello*: 'From the beginning the signs of a fracture are present that Pirandello will later only get into more deeply....His vision of the world is completely 'given' [in the French meaning of the word] from the start....' The 'beginning' Pomilio is referring to is the essay *Arte e coscienza d'oggi*, and because Pirandello's vision of the world – as distinct from his works and yet as embedded in his works – is in itself so important that the critic cannot ignore it, we shall turn to it now by way of this essay.

Arte e coscienza d'oggi was written in 1893 and published in the Florentine review *La nazione letteraria*. Pirandello had returned from the University of Bonn and was laying the foundation of his literary career in Rome. A letter of February 1893 documents the intense activity of those days. It lists twenty-one titles of short stories, novels, verse collections, and plays which he had already written or was in the process of writing but for which he had as yet found no publisher. The novel *L'esclusa*, written in that same year, was not published till 1901. In a blurring of the boundaries between art and life so characteristic of Pirandello, it contained a chapter, later omitted, in which one of the characters, the lawyer and politician Gregorio Alvignani, expressed ideas very similar to those of *Arte e coscienza d'oggi*, often using the very words of the essay. In the revised version of the novel only the title of the essay remains, as the title of one of Alvignani's own lectures.

Arte e coscienza d'oggi is a topical, journalistic piece, not dissimilar from those that date back to Pirandello's student days. As a self-contained work it lacks the incisiveness and directness of the later Pirandello, its development being somewhat obscured by the juxtaposition rather than concatenation of the subjects dealt with. It has never been translated, nor did Pirandello himself reprint it. It is an excellent index, however, to the 'cultural baggage' with which he entered upon the literary scene. Moreover, the pessimism engendered by his awareness and sympathetic understanding of the *fin de siècle* crisis through which he was living is paradoxically replaced at the end by an affirmation of the autonomy of art which foreshadows – if we look ahead – the composition of *Sei personaggi*, a play whose very 'form' proclaims not only the equality of art with life, but its actual superiority.

The point of departure of the essay is a lecture given by Ruggero Bonghi, a dominant public figure in the years immediately preceding and following Italian unification but who by the 1890s represented all that was conservative and backward looking in the Italy of his day. In the words with which Bonghi had ended his lecture (entitled significantly *Questa fin di secolo*) Pirandello recognizes some of what he felt were the characteristic signs of the time: a passionate disdain of science, the sense of helplessness engendered by the results of modern philosophical inquiry, and the desire to return to the simple faith of the past. After having cited Tolstoy, Bourget, Fogazzaro and Verlaine as contemporary examples of writers who had in various ways rejected the solutions offered by science and philosophy and turned to the comforts of religion, Pirandello pithily concludes, 'Lo spirito moderno è profondamente malato, e invoca Dio come un moribondo pentito' [The modern soul is seriously ill and like a contrite sinner on his deathbed invokes God]. And expressing his own lack of belief in the existence of God adds, 'Mi fa bensí meraviglia che si chiami Dio quel che in fondo è bujo pesto' (SPSV, 867) [I am surprised only that the name God is given to what is fundamentally pitch darkness].

From this introduction Pirandello passes directly to consider the recent contributions of psychiatry to the diagnosis of the ills that beset the modern artist. His life-long interest in abnormal psychology thus preceded by many years the tragic personal experience of his wife's illness and had its roots instead in the discussion of the problems encountered by the contemporary artist in his relationship to society.

The books Pirandello refers to by name are Max Nordau's *Entartung* (1892–3), better known by its French title *Dégénérescence*, in which Symbolists, Pre-Raphaelites and other poets of Decadence are studied as clinical cases of physical and psychological deterioration; B. A. Morel's *Du Délire panophobique des aliénés gémisseurs* (1871), a more strictly medical discussion of a specific type of mental derangement; and Cesare Lombroso's famous *Genio e follia* (1864). As illustrations of the deleterious effects of contemporary conditions on art, he cites the works of the Portuguese poet Guerra Junqueiro and of the Italian painters Edoardo Gioja, Edoardo Cortese, Franco Lojacono and Aristide Sartorio. (Pirandello was himself a painter, and passed his talent on to one of his sons.) In Junqueiro's poetry 'nessun pensiero riesce a concretarsi, a coordinarsi' [no thought succeeds in concretizing and coordinating itself], he writes. Of the painters, he says, one is obviously affected by hysterical amblyopia, another by the inability to focus, a third cannot perceive perspective, while the beautiful landscapes of the fourth produce in the viewer a feeling of melancholy so profound that Pirandello is led to muse on the enmity with which men have come to look on nature. Incapable of wresting nature's secrets from it, men despise themselves and the earth, 'che pur ogni anno per noi si rinnova e pare che per noi voglia celar le rughe coi fiori. L'uomo strappa quei fiori e s'incorona di spine. "Non son fatte per noi le primavere"' (SPSV, 1869) [which yet every year renews itself for us and seems to want to hide its wrinkles from us with flowers. Man pulls up those flowers and crowns himself with thorns. 'Spring is not made for us'] – he writes in one of the striking images with which he was throughout his life to fix his intuition of the human condition. Here the pessimistic note is reminiscent of Leopardi in its formulation and of Nietzsche in its implied contrast between the harmonious coexistence of man and nature in antiquity and their disjointedness since the advent of Christianity. Nature cannot give knowledge but only love, Pirandello says, in an early statement of what, in the only counteraction of pessimism he permits himself, is to become the essence of his ethical 'message'.

The central portion of the essay describes the modern, scientific conception of the universe as a living machine and reviews some of the efforts made by philosophers to explain it. Again, there is no systematic exposition but rather what might be called a layman's presentation of cosmological models and a poet's cautionary tale which tells of the encounter between contemporary Everyman and a positivist philosopher. Two views of the universe and of man's place in it are opposed: one in which science has indeed assigned man a 'melancholy place' in nature; the other in which once upon a time the earth was 'the navel of a boundless universe'. (In the 'Second Foreword' to *Il fu Mattia Pascal* Copernicus will be named as the author of the change.) As is usual with him, Pirandello entrusts the expression of his ideas to striking images, alternately playful and pathetic. Thus in the days when the sky, the sun, the stars turned continually around the earth, 'honest mortals with their hands clasped across their stomachs' could sit peaceably and enjoy the wonderful spectacle that God had created for them: 'La luna a quei tempi scendeva lentamente sul mare agitato, il mare se la sorbiva come un grosso torlo d'uovo, e l'onesto mortale batteva le mani ed esclamava: —Sì, questa scena è fatta bene!' (SPSV, 869) [In those days the moon set slowly above the surging sea, the sea would swallow it as though it were the giant yolk of an egg, and the honest mortal would clap his hands and exclaim, 'Yes, this scene has been fashioned well!'] But what is the case now? What has become of man, 'questo re dell'universo' [this king of the universe]? 'Ahi povero re! Non vi vedete saltar dinanzi Re Lear armato d'una scopa in tutta la sua tragica comicità? Di che farnetica egli?' (SPSV, 870) [Alas, poor man! Can't you just see King Lear, armed with a broomstick, jump before you, in all his tragic comicality? What is he raving about?] This man, dispossessed and humiliated, exiled from what was once his kingdom, searching to know why he has lost his erstwhile status, meets up with a philosopher, someone who has about him 'that particular air of the priest of a new, very rational religion'. But the various materialistic, rational explanations of the universe which the philosopher proposes – Laplace's cosmology, Darwin's morphology, Spencer's biology, Berthelot's chemical synthesis – leave Everyman unsatisfied. Even Spencer's ethics (*Principles of Ethics* was published in 1892–3), which Pirandello discusses at some length, are in the end rejected.

In the third, last and longest section of the essay no scientist or philosopher is mentioned by name but considerable space is given over to two fictional representations of awareness of the deep crisis that had developed in modern society. One of the scenes is from Max Nordau's novel *Die Krankheit des Jahrhunderts* (1887), the other from Ibsen's play *Pillars of Society* (1882). In both, opposing views of the social problem created by the conditions of industrial workers are dramatically portrayed in the words of characters who state their 'reasons'. A recurring pattern in Pirandello's later theatrical works is exactly this: the delimitation of a space within which 'la ragione degli altri' [the others' point of view] (and the expression will become the title of one of his plays) can be told and heard. This set situation is prefigured here both in the illustrations chosen (in both scenes the spotlight is on a spokesman) and in the manner (absence of introduction or stage-setting) in which the cited passages interrupt Pirandello's own exposition of the 'tramenío vertiginoso che da tutti i lati ci preme, urta e logora' (SPSV, 878) [dizzying bustle that presses upon us from all sides, jostling us and wearing us down].

In his exposition of the 'straordinaria confusione' that reigns among old and young alike, Pirandello emphasizes the disillusionment left in the wake of scientific progress, with the resultant return to God of some and the parallel but diametrically opposite flight of others into absolute relativism (*un volgar fenomenismo* is the expression). Especially unfortunate are the young. Born at the time of Italy's struggle for independence, they grew up amid the constant debates on political and philosophic issues that accompanied the new government's search for stability. (Pirandello's description of that period as 'quando i padri piú che all'amore intendevano a far la guerra' (SPSV, 873) [when their fathers were more intent on making war than making love] has indeed a curious ring for those who lived through the anti-war demonstrations of the 1960s!) Sickly of constitution, educated without any over-all directive plan, they could muster no real enthusiasm, but became neurotic and world-weary, oppressed by a sense of the inanity of life. Obviously Pirandello, who was born in 1867, is speaking of his own generation, though not of course in every detail of himself. As a matter of fact, anyone wishing to see how Pirandello, this least autobiographical and yet most subjective of writers, *did* write of himself should turn to the autobiographical fragment that dates from the same year as *Arte e coscienza d'oggi* and was later published with the title *Frammento d'autobiografia*: 'Io dunque son figlio del Caos' [I then am the child of Caos], it begins, but Caos being the name of the locality where he was born, this grandiose statement turns out to be no more than the first fact that the biographical fragment contains. Conversely, for a frankly fictionalized version of the observations made in this part of *Arte e coscienza d'oggi*, the work to read is the historical novel *I vecchi e i giovani*: its action takes place between 1892 and 1894 and its setting is divided between Pirandello's birthplace Girgenti, and Rome, his habitual residence from 1893. The three works taken together not only reinforce one another as documents for Pirandello's biography but show how indissolubly intertwined fiction and reality are in his imaginative universe.

One final aspect of *Arte e coscienza d'oggi* should be mentioned: the embryonic statement of Pirandello's poetics that it contains. There is first of all the fleeting appearance of a hypothetical *poeta umorista* who could find material for his poetry in the contrast between what was once man's central position in the universe and what is now his dispossessed status of 'poveretto smarrito per lo spazio' (SPSV, 870) [poor little man lost in space]. There is then the bald assertion, in face of the positivist's presentation of solutions to the mystery of life, that 'Nessuna conoscenza, nessuna nozione precisa possiamo aver noi della vita; ma un sentimento soltanto e quindi mutabile e vario' (SPSV, 871) [we can have no knowledge, no precise notion of life, but only a feeling of it, changeable and varied]. And there are finally the concluding paragraphs in which Pirandello rejects the demands being made of art that it should turn away from subjectivity (i.e., from the various alienations described by the psychiatrists and social commentators mentioned at the beginning) and that it should champion instead the various democratic movements of the time and the 'triumphs' of science. Art, Pirandello believes, cannot be produced on order; it is 'il polso della vita' [the pulse of life] and must be born 'spontaneamente dal sentimento' [spontaneously from feeling]. At the moment men perceive life (have consciousness [*coscienza* (an important Pirandellian word)] or awareness of it) as 'un sogno angoscioso...una battaglia notturna...una mischia disperata' [a nightmare...a nocturnal war... a desperate battle], in which thousands of banners appear only to disappear again amid the continual clash of discordant voices. The art of the present cannot help reflecting this 'agitazione continua' [continuous agitation], this feverish rush in search of an answer. What may come in the future is another matter. And in a final sentence that contrasts so sharply with what has gone before that one can only wonder what he really means, Pirandello states categorically, 'Siamo certamente alla vigilia d'un enorme avvenimento' (SPSV, 880) [We are surely on the eve of a momentous event]: as at other crucial points in history so now too a genius unafraid of the gathering storm may arise to create 'il libro unico, secolare' [the unique, eternal work] 'that other times too have known'.

Some of the ideas of *Arte e coscienza d'oggi* reappear ten years later and reached a much wider audience in the fictional context of *Il fu Mattia Pascal*, the novel that first made Pirandello's name known outside Italy. The essay identifies a situation of crisis in contemporary society and illustrates its harmful effects especially on the artist. In the novel the crisis affects everyone and a solution to it is suggested on one level by don Eligio Pellegrinotto, the librarian of the *comune* of Miragno, who encourages Mattia Pascal to write the story of his strange life; and on another by Anselmo Paleari, the retired civil servant who is the landlord of Adriano Meis (*alias* Mattia Pascal) in Rome and who has developed a 'philosophy' to cope with it. *Lanterninosofia* (philosophy of the little lantern) is discussed at length in chapter XIII of the novel and is already adumbrated in the 'Second Foreword'. It is in many respects a precursor of *L'umorismo*, Pirandello's most important theoretical statement, and for this reason merits our attention here.

Il fu Mattia Pascal is the autobiography of a man (Mattia Pascal) who is accidentally thought to have committed suicide and who seizes the opportunity to opt out of an unhappy marriage and to start life anew. Under the assumed name and identity of Adriano Meis he first spends some time travelling and then settles down in Rome where he becomes deeply entangled in the affairs of the family with whom he rooms. He falls in love with the gentle Adriana, Paleari's daughter, and tries to save her from the unwholesome environment created by her father's addiction to theosophy and her brother-in-law Papiano's dishonest designs. He fails in the attempt and finds himself obliged to contrive a second 'suicide' in order to save Adriana from the unhappiness of her liaison with his fictitious self, which could under no circumstances lead to marriage. As Mattia Pascal once more, he returns home to his wife and mother-in-law. But during his two-year absence his wife has remarried and she is now the mother of a child. Mattia accepts the new reality that the passage of time has created, and in yet another change becomes the still living late Mattia Pascal. In 1918 Pirandello thoroughly revised the original (1904) text of *Il fu Mattia Pascal* and in a new edition in 1921 added as a postscript an article he had recently written. This postscript, 'Avvertenza sugli scrupoli della fantasia', comparable to the Preface to *Sei personaggi*, must now be considered an integral part of the novel. The story of Mattia Pascal thus lies between two forewords and a postscript, which provide it with a rather complicated frame.

The 'Second Foreword' repeats the contrast described in *Arte e coscienza d'oggi* between geocentric and heliocentric views of the universe, but presents the Copernican revolution not simply as the general cause for man's sense of his insignificance and the consequent disorientation in his values but specifically as the reason why a novel can no longer be written as once it used to be. Mattia, who has decided to tell the story of his life in spite of his disdain for books and their

non-readers, is advised by don Eligio Pellegrinotto to model himself
on the many assorted books that they have found among those
bequeathed to the library back in 1803. But who, objects Mattia,
would read 'una narrazione minuta e piena d'oziosi particolari' [a
detailed narration full of insignificant details] now that the earth is
rotating and man, no longer 'dressed as a Greek or Roman', is no
longer imbued with the sense of his own dignity and importance?
Who cares whether '*Il signor conte si levò per tempo, alle ore otto e mezzo
precise....La signora contessa indossò un abito lilla con una ricca fioritura di
merletti alla gola....Teresina si moriva di fame....Lucrezia spasimava
d'amore...*' (TR, I, 323, Pirandello's italics) [The Count rose early, at
eight-thirty precisely....The Countess wore a lilac-coloured dress,
richly adorned with lace at the neck....Teresina was dying of
hunger....Lucrezia was desperately in love....]. Our stories have
become the 'stories of worms', whether they concern individuals or
the masses of men. A disaster – the eruption of a volcano on a distant
island, for instance – has as much importance, Mattia concludes in one
of Pirandello's images of the downgrading of man, as the roasting of a
thousand worms.

The examples of narrative *topoi* should not deceive us. Pirandello is
not speaking about subject matter here. It is not the social context of
some contemporary narrative that he is objecting to, nor is he in-
dicating a preference for regional rather than urban or cosmopolitan
settings. Rather, he is saying here what he will repeat with greater
seriousness and directness in the Preface to *Sei personaggi*, that he does
not belong to the class of writers Aristotle called historical, but to the
philosophical. He describes the two groups as comprising those who
are satisfied with portraying figures, events, or landscapes for the
sheer pleasure of doing so, and those for whom figures, events and
landscapes are significant only if they are imbued 'd'un particolar
senso della vita' [with a particular sense of life] that gives them universal meaning. Thus if for Mattia the strangeness of his experiences is
sufficient reason for his recounting them, for Pirandello the story must
be framed within a larger intention, an intention, as a matter of fact,
which will not become completely clear until he writes *L'umorismo*,
the treatise not accidentally dedicated in 1908 'Alla buon'anima.di.
Mattia Pascal.bibliotecario' [To the Late.Mattia Pascal.Librarian].
For if on the one hand *Il fu Mattia Pascal* is an amusing book about a
bungling Peter Schlemiel, the eternal outsider, on the other it is the
ironist's answer to the failure of science to provide a satisfactory ontological explanation of the universe.

This failure is the historical background against which we define Pirandello as a writer, and it is also the background for *lanterninosofia*. And *lanterninosofia*, like the better known *filosofia del lontano* [the philosophy of remoteness] (Dr Fileno's invention in the short story *La tragedia di un personaggio*, 1911), is a fictional version of *umorismo*. Both are attempts at philosophy – the inventions of a poiētēs – on the part of characters who far from being philosophers (that is, trained speculative thinkers) are laymen attracted by a variety of notions with which they seek to assuage their existential anguish and which, by the way, Pirandello himself labelled 'specious'. Though we shall attempt to show shortly that *L'umorismo* is more than the scholarly exercise of a dilettante, it is understandable that confusions should have arisen from the implied analogy between Pirandello author of *L'umorismo* and Dr Fileno author of *La filosofia del lontano* or Anselmo Paleari author of *Lanterninosofia*. Such confusions offended Croce's fine sense of logical distinction and in his 1909 review of *L'umorismo* he wrote: 'Pirandello's fault is to confront philosophy in the same way in which men confront ordinary, every-day matters, each individual thinking that he understands the terms being used and that he is entitled to have his say'. But this lack of professionalism which irked Croce can also be looked upon with sympathy, as it is in our own do-it-yourself age in which the efforts of the amateur are more frequently applauded than derided.

Lanterninosofia, though not yet named, makes its appearance in the 'Second Foreword' during a discussion between don Eligio and Mattia on men's failure to have destroyed their illusions. 'La provvida natura' [provident nature], says don Eligio, has given men short memories as a permanent means for restoring their illusions. And Mattia finds an illustration for don Eligio's observation in the municipal regulation which in order to save money forbids street lamps from being lit on the full-moon nights marked in the calendar. If it then turns out that these nights are cloudy, the citizens of Miragno are left in the dark but their conviction that in spite of the Copernican revolution man is still the centre of the universe and that moon, stars and sun continue to shine for him has been vindicated. Darkness – with or without its opposite, light – is a constantly recurring image-symbol in Pirandello. And it is appropriate that in chapter XIII Anselmo Paleari should explain 'Lanternosophy' to Adriano Meis while the latter is recuperating from an eye operation in the dark. Just as it is appropriate that the 'miracles' of the supernatural should a little later (in chapters XIII and XIV) be revealed during a séance, again in the dark. Traditionally, physical blindness was thought to free men from the contingent and enable them to tap transcendent truth. This is not the case in Pirandello. The woman veiled in black who can neither be seen nor see and who appears in order to solve another mystery at the end of *Così è (se vi pare)*, brings no stable truth with her but only a paradox built on shifting sands.

Like 'The Philosophy of Remoteness' and, as a matter of fact, like Christianity itself, 'Lanternosophy' is a consolatory philosophy which in Paleari's view should be able to comfort Adriano by showing him that his darkness is only an illusion. Paleari begins by making a distinction that Pirandello himself made more than once. Recasting into figurative language what in *Arte e coscienza d'oggi* is the straightforward statement that man has no knowledge of life but only the feeling of it, Paleari points out that men differ from trees because trees have life but no feeling, while men feel themselves alive and mistake this inner feeling for reality. Not content with enjoying nature they have anthropomorphized it and projected their feelings onto its component parts. Thus to a tree the earth, sun, air, rain and wind are not things different from it, not things potentially friendly or harmful to it. But men have endowed earth, sun, air and wind with changing moods similar to their own which must be propitiated. It is at this point that the image of the lighted lantern reappears. No longer an ordinary street-lamp it is now the little, lighted lantern that Paleari imagines each man carrying about with him, the externalization of his inner feelings, by which he is to find his way: each man has his lantern. Outside the circle of light cast by the lantern there is utter and fearful darkness, a darkness that like the light itself would not exist if the lantern were not lit – if, that is, men were trees, feelingless objects, and not men. But as long as the lantern is kept lit, the shadows are as real as the light. Thus men create their illusions in the midst of 'la notte perpetua' [eternal night].

But Illusion (Pirandello personifies it by writing it with a capital 'I') is a shopkeeper who sells coloured glass, the parable continues, the lanterns are of different colours, and at the different seasons in men's lives one or the other colour may predominate. This is also true for the different periods in history. And it is here that Paleari's explanation moves from the one-to-one relationship of man and his illusions to the centripetal pull of the time in which he lives. For in addition to the little lanterns there are also the big ones, the super lights, which stand for the consensus reached in any period regarding such abstract notions as Truth, Virtue, Beauty, or Honour: the red super light of pagan virtue, the 'depressing' violet light of Christian virtue. In stable periods, when all is well, the light of the big lanterns shines bright and steady, fed by the feeling of the collectivity. When the unity of that feeling wavers, however, and contradictory feelings emerge, as happens in transitional periods, the lights flicker and die down. And in even more troubled times, when even the *idea* of consensus is lost, fierce gusts of wind may blow out the big lanterns altogether, leaving the little ones, the *lanternini*, hurrying and scurrying madly, in full disarray, bumping into one another, or clustering together in little groups, 'come le formiche che non trovino più la bocca del formicajo, otturata per ispasso da un bambino crudele' (TR, I, 485–6) [like ants that can no longer find the entrance to their ant hill, blocked up by the whims of some cruel child].

It is in a period such as this that Paleari – sharing Pirandello's feeling regarding his own times – feels that he is living: 'Gran bujo e gran confusione! Tutti i lanternoni, spenti' [Deep darkness and great confusion! All the big lanterns are out]. The confusion of the moment that Pirandello had amply illustrated in *Arte e coscienza d'oggi* ten years before ('il sorgere improvviso delle piú bizzarre baracche in questa internazionale fiera della follia' (SPSV, 875) [the sudden appearance of the strangest booths in this international fair of folly] is not further detailed here, but the interplay of light and darkness – that is, the question of faith and belief – is looked at more closely.

To whom should we turn, asks Paleari. To retrace one's steps is out of the question. The stock of consecrated oil for feeding the votive lights of faith is gone. And Pirandello quotes a few lines from Niccolò Tommaseo's *La lampana* [*sic*], thus revealing one of the sources for the light imagery that almost runs riot in this passage. (I say one of the sources and not *the* source, for I should hesitate to give a literary precedent greater weight in Pirandello's creative imagination than an image from everyday experience such as the *scala da lampionajo* [lamplighter's ladder] on which we first meet don Eligio Pellegrinotto perched in his library in the 'Second Foreword'.) In *La lampana* Tommaseo, a late Romantic writer who had not lost his faith, speaks of *his* lamp burning brightly, straining upward towards the sky: he is confident that it will continue to burn later too, on his grave, and that others will be able to come and relight their own spent lamps from it. But in Humbertine Italy, Paleari reminds Mattia, only 'poveri vecchi, povere donne, a cui mentì la vita' [poor old people, poor women, whom life disappointed] continue to visit the churches. Only they seek to nourish their lamps so they will have light at least until they

die. Or so, at any rate, it seems to Pirandello who felt no sympathy for
the clergy and derided, as we saw in *Arte e coscienza d'oggi*, the sudden
mystic yearnings of some of his contemporaries. But the disdain he
felt for the latter does not destroy the sympathy he feels for the 'poor
old people' just mentioned. For them he has compassion, as can be
seen from the legend-like short story of 1901, *Il vecchio Dio*, in which
God the Father appears to one such bent old man on a hot summer day
in an empty church in Rome. The child-like, genuine devotion of
what – like the pensioner in *Il vecchio Dio* – were essentially victims of
social change evokes 'scornful commiseration' not from Paleari or
Pirandello but from 'certi altri, invece, che si credono armati, come
tanti Giove, del fulmine domato dalla scienza, e, in luogo di quelle
lanternucce, recano in trionfo le lampadine elettriche' (TR, I, 487)
[certain others, instead, who think that Jove-like they are armed with
thunderbolts tamed by science and who carry their electric light bulbs
around with them triumphantly in place of those little lanterns].

But if it is impossible to turn to the overbearing self-assurance of
science – the steady glow of the electric bulb – and it is equally impossible to turn to the undermined certainties of traditional religion –
the flickering light of each man's lantern – what course is left? What
is the 'corrective', the remedy to which one can turn? Readers of *Il fu
Mattia Pascal* already know by this point in the novel what help
Paleari had found. As for Pirandello, he, too, had by 1904 found a
remedy – let us call it, for the sake of brevity, a kind of Romantic
irony – but he had not yet given it the name by which it would henceforth be known.

Much has been written on *umorismo*, very little on the importance of
the occult in Pirandello's work. Paleari's remedy for what Dr Fileno
calls 'the public and private calamities', the *lanternino dal vetro rosso*
which is now lit in Adriano's sick room, introduces us to the latter
subject and invites us to explore it with some attention. It plays, I
believe, a crucial role in the genesis of the concept of the character
without an author, a subject studied thoroughly by Leone De Castris
in *Storia di Pirandello* but without reference to this aspect of it.

Paleari had been attracted to his new tenant, Adriano Meis, from
the first, and as a sign of his esteem had shown him his library as
though to a fellow-scholar (chapter X). Among the books, mostly on
philosophy and science (that is on serious not frivolous subjects), there
is one section that surprises Adriano. Pirandello lists the titles: *La Mort
et l'au-delà, L'Homme et ses corps, Les Sept Principes de l'homme, Karma,*

La Clef de la Théosophie, ABC de la Théosophie, La Doctrine secrète, Le Plan Astral – works which Giovanni Macchia has shown to have all been featured in the catalogue of Publications Théosophiques, a turn-of-the-century Parisian publisher. The first thing Adriano learns from these books is that the dead are neither souls that have moved into the heareafter nor bodies in decomposition. They are beings that now dwell on a different level of consciousness.

In *La casa del Granella*, a short story published the year after *Il fu Mattia Pascal*, the lawyer Zummo who is presented with a case involving a haunted house turns to a similar body of material and learns from it that a new religion is emerging: spiritualism or, to be more precise, spiritism. (In the word *spiritism*, 'spirit' in the sense of 'ghost' is more readily apparent than in *spiritualism*, which has often been used instead of it.) In this case, too, Pirandello sets forth the documentation for a 'conversion' from a rational and scientific explanation of the universe (be it geo- or heliocentric) to the recognition of the presence in it of an irreducible mystery. Zummo starts out by reading 'una storia sommaria dello Spiritismo, dalle origini delle mitologie fino ai dí nostri, e il libro del Jacolliot su i prodigi del fachirismo' (N A, I, 313) [a summary history of Spiritism from the origins of mythology to the present and Jacolliot's work on the wonders wrought by fakirs]. (Pirandello does not identify the author of the history; Louis Jacolliot was a scientific popularizer.) These are followed pell-mell by a whole roster of names known to late nineteenth-century cultists of the supernatural. Contrary to the list in *Il fu Mattia Pascal* the literature referred to here is not limited to theosophy but encompasses the work of physicists, chemists, psychologists, physiologists, anthropologists and psychiatrists – all originally sceptical, positivist scientists who had become convinced in the course of their experiments that psychic phenomena do exist. Of the names cited by Pirandello it may be sufficient to mention Sir William Crookes, the British physicist who in the 1870s and 1880s alienated the scientific community by research into mediumship; Johann Karl Friedrich Zöllner, professor of astrophysics at Leipzig and an enthusiastic exponent of spiritualism; Charles Richet, professor of physiology at the Sorbonne, Nobel Prize winner, and coiner of the term *metapsychique* (the French equivalent of parapsychology); and the greatest of them all, Allan Kardech [*sic*], invoked by Zummo as the new messiah in the course of his impassioned peroration in court. Kardech, who had changed his name from Denizard Rivail to mark his reincarnation and 'birth' to spiritualism, was the author of *Livre des esprits* (1857), in which are laid down

the foundations of the new doctrine, a doctrine also propagated by
the long-lived *La Revue spirite* which is still published today.

The titles and names cited point to a comprehensive though no
doubt superficial acquaintance with the field, for included are the
basic works of what might be called its three component strands:
spiritism (the origins of which go back to the experiences of the Fox
family in a haunted house in Hydesville, New York, in 1847), *theosophy* (associated more particularly with Mme Blavatsky and her
circle, and their connection with the 'secret science' of the East), and
the medical or paramedical *study of psychic or psychological phenomena*.
Under the latter heading fall manifestations such as telepathy and
clairvoyance, or, more generally, personality disturbances such as
those described by the French experimental psychologist Alfred Binet
in his *Les Altérations de la personnalité* (1892), a work first mentioned
by Pirandello in his 1900 essay *Scienza e critica estetica*. (In *Arte e coscienza d'oggi*, it should be noted, abnormal psychology was discussed
in connection with contemporary artists, a quite different context
from the one in which it appears here.)

Pirandello was, of course, not interested in this body of material as
a practitioner (although table-turning, like photography, was very
much a hobby with his friend Capuana). He did not espouse one as
against any other theory. Hence, a very rapid exposition of a kind of
generalized doctrine, emphasizing the features most useful for the
analysis of his works, is all that is needed here. Basic to the beliefs of
Kardech, for instance, is a view of man as consisting of three principles: a physical body, the vehicle for the manifestations of the individual during his passing through this life; a fluid body, which
makes possible certain paranormal manifestations in the living (such
as the physical phenomena connected with the activities of mediums)
and enables the dead (who continue to have the fluid body for at least
part of their 'evolution' to a different level of existence) to communicate with the living; and a spirit indestructible and perfectible. Or,
put differently, with the help of a dictionary definition, spiritism or
spiritualism is the belief that the human personality continues to exist
after death and can communicate with the living through the agency
of a medium or psychic. Thus, death merely means a change in wave-
length for those who die, and the medium is able to perceive radia-
tions, frequencies, or vibrations that cannot be sensed by the ordinary
person.

Specific aspects of the occult are present in different combinations
and with varying intensity in Pirandello's works. The one-act *mistero*

profano (non-sacred mystery play) *All'uscita* (1916) is probably the most directly dependent on a formulation of the relationship between this world and the other similar to Kardech's. The cast of characters distinguishes between 'Apparitions' and 'Aspects of Life' (as *Sei personaggi* will later distinguish between actors and characters) and two of the Apparitions, as they meet at a cemetery gate, discuss the nature of their state of being almost as though they were summarizing spiritist or theosophic doctrine. Apparitions of another kind – not the playful ghosts clamouring for attention in *La casa del Granella*, nor yet the unquiet, disembodied spirits continuing to linger on earth in *All'uscita* – have a role in Pirandello's last play, *I giganti della montagna*. One act of this 'myth' was published as a self-contained work in 1931 with the significant title *I fantasmi*; the third act, left unfinished at Pirandello's death, takes place in 'L'arsenale delle apparizioni', a setting suggestively translated by Marta Abba as 'The Ghost Supply Room'. The apparitions that materialize in *I giganti della montagna* are the results of man-made, theatrical magic. In *La vita che ti diedi* still another kind of manifestation of the supernatural occurs: 'someone' moves a chair in front of a desk on the empty, dark stage, 'an invisible hand' raises the curtain at the window: 'Chi sa che cose avvengono, non viste da nessuno, nell'ombra delle stanze deserte dove qualcuno è morto' [Who knows what things happen, unseen by anyone, in the shadow of empty rooms where someone has died], Pirandello writes parenthetically in a stage direction in Act II. In *Sei personaggi* Madama Pace 'appears', enticed by the scene, the setting of her daily life, prepared for her by the Father. Compared with 'inventions' (in the classical rhetorical sense of the word) such as these, the use of the supernatural to further the plot of *Il fu Mattia Pascal* is slight indeed.

Paleari, we have seen, finds consolation in 'Lanternosophy', a view of the world which recognizes the existence and the importance of illusion in human life. He also finds release in lighting 'un certo lanternino col vetro rosso' [a certain little lantern with red glass] from time to time. This is the 'lantern' by whose feeble light the chaotic and funny scene of the séance is set up, with its comic cast of characters, its slaps and kisses exchanged in the dark, and the messages sent by the spirit Max through Signorina Caporale, another lodger in Paleari's household, whom he is hoping to turn into a first-rate medium. When Adriano had first heard of these séances, he had wondered why Paleari, given his merciless derision of mankind's willingness to be fooled by the lantern each man carries around with him, should have wanted to light a second lantern. 'Correttivo!' Paleari had explained.

'Un lanternino contro l'altro!' [It's a remedy! One lantern against the other!]. And Adriano had soon given up arguing with him for he recognized that this was a question of faith, 'Fede', which according to Maestro Alberto Fiorentino (Don Eligio interjects in a footnote, suddenly reminding the reader that he too has been present at Mattia's storytelling all this time), 'è sustanzia di cose da sperare, e argomento e prouva di non appariscienti' (TR, I, 489) [Faith is the substance of things to be hoped for, the argumentation for and proof of things that are not visible].

Faith is of course something Pirandello lacked, whether we think of it in terms of belief in the transcendent truths of religion or content ourselves with convictions of doubtful respectability such as spiritism and theosophy which both religion and science viewed with suspicion and rejected. Although, as we have seen, Pirandello appropriated some of the notions that *fin de siècle* interest in the occult had put into circulation, he did not embrace theosophy nor did he find in occultism as such an answer to or an escape from his sense of loss. Images of loss – of the diminution of man, the downgrading of the planet earth, the disappearance of God – abound in the early Pirandello. In *Arte e coscienza d'oggi* we have seen man crowning himself with thorns, lost in space, the raving King Lear waving a broomstick; the earth 'un atomo astrale...una trottoletta volgarissima' [a star-atom...a cheap little top] one day hurled off by the sun; the contemporary historical moment 'an international fair of follies'. In *Il fu Mattia Pascal* man is compared to an ant that can no longer find the entrance to the ant-hill that is the world because of the wilful act of a cruel child (i.e., God); men are proudly carrying electric light bulbs around with them, or else are hurrying and scurrying around madly, colliding with one another, gathering together for a moment only to scatter again in confusion and anguish; the earth is 'un'invisibile trottolina, cui fa da sferza un fil di sole...un granellino di sabbia impazzito che gira e gira e gira' (TR, I, 323) [a tiny, invisible top whipped on by a ray of sun...a crazed grain of sand that goes round and round and round]. In letters to his sister, written when he was barely twenty, *before* leaving Sicily, Pirandello spoke of men as 'poveri ragni che per vivere hanno bisogno d'intessersi in un cantuccio la loro tela sottile...povere lumache che... han bisogno di portare a dosso il loro guscio fragile...poveri molluschi che vogliono tutti la loro conchiglia in fondo al mare' [poor spiders who to live must spin their thin webs in some corner...poor snails who...must carry their fragile shells on their backs...poor molluscs who are yearning for their conches at the bottom of the sea];

he described life as 'un'enorme pupazzata' [a huge puppet show], and
the earth seen from the distance as reduced to the size of a lemon
(Giudice, 93–4). In *L'umorismo*, in what is an obvious reworking of
'Lanternosophy', Prometheus (man) is shown as having become
finally aware that 'Giove (God) non è altro che un suo vano fantasma,
un miserevole inganno, l'ombra del suo stesso corpo che si projetta
gigantesca nel cielo, a causa appunto della fiaccola ch'egli tiene accesa
in mano' (SPSV, 156) [Jupiter is nothing but a vain phantasm of his
(i.e., an idea, a figment of his imagination), a miserable deceit, the
shadow of his own body projected gigantically against the sky, there
indeed *because of* the torch he holds lit in his hand].

A perception of man, world, and God such as this can be countered
only by an act of will, by making virtue out of necessity, creating distance between the self and the world, finding a stoic response to
cosmic despair. 'It's a remedy! One lantern against the other', Paleari
had answered Adriano Meis when asked why he should want to add
one more illusion to all those, big and small, already running rampant
in the world. And it seems a statement peculiarly at home in the novel
which exemplifies on so many levels what Oscar Büdel has called a
'view of human life and actions as an immanent doubling process'.
'Console yourself...resign yourself', the Author in *La tragedia di un
personaggio* urges Dr Fileno, suggesting that he should have recourse
to his own 'Philosophy of Remoteness' so as to gain perspective on his
disappointment over being a still-born character: viewed through the
small lens of the telescope what is large and present instantly becomes
small and distant. 'Guarda le cose anche con gli occhi di quelli che non
le vedono piú! Ne avrai un rammarico, figlio, che te le renderà piú
sacre e belle' (NA, II, 1138) [Look at things also with the eyes of those
who can no longer see them! You will feel such regret for them, my
son, that they will become more sacred and beautiful for you], with
these words the recently dead mother comes back to comfor her son
in *Colloqui coi personaggi* (1915). And what elsewhere, in the more
trivial concerns of ordinary situations, is the statement of *la ragione
degli altri* [the others' point of view], is broadened here to include
'existences' in both this world and another one. 'Non credere pertanto
che la mancanza d'ogni illusione e d'ogni speranza mi perda' [Do not
think, however, that the absence of all illusions and hope will destroy
me], Pirandello had written to his sister in one of the letters mentioned
earlier, showing once again how far back the crystallization of not
only his basic interests but also his basic attitudes goes.

Pirandello's personal answer to the sense of loss and torment we have been delineating was the self-absorption with which he threw himself into his work – his acceptance of the challenge made over and over by his characters that he should identify with them (the Italian reflexive verb *immedesimarsi* is especially strong in expressing this idea) to the point of permitting himself to be 'possessed' by them. To understand the nature of this 'possession' fully seems to me so important for mastery of his meaning at many crucial points in his work that a perhaps overly long presentation of a virtually unknown passage may be justified.

The passage occurs in the first edition of *Il fu Mattia Pascal* as published serially in *Nuova antologia* and then issued in book format, and it has only recently come to light again thanks to Giovanni Macchia's critical edition of Pirandello's novels. It came at the beginning of chapter v and was later replaced by the single sentence: 'La strega non si sapeva dar pace' ['The witch couldn't resign herself'], the witch being 'quella donna esecrabile' [that abominable woman], Mattia's mother-in-law, the widow Pescatore. The passage begins by referring to a book which the first-person narrator had just read: 'Ho letto testé in un libro che i pensieri e i desideri nostri s'incorporano in un'essenza plastica, nel mondo invisibile che ne circonda, e tosto vi si modellano in forme di esseri viventi, la cui apparenza corrisponde all'intima loro natura. E questi esseri, non appena formati, non sono più sotto il dominio di chi gli [*sic*] ha generati, ma godono d'una lor propria vita, la cui durata dipende dall'intensità del pensiero o del desiderio generatore' (TR, I, 1010) [I have just now read in a book that our thoughts and desires become embodied in a plastic essence in the invisible world that surrounds them, and forthwith take on the shapes of living beings whose appearance corresponds to their intimate nature. And these beings, as soon as they are formed, are no longer under the control of their generating maker but enjoy a life of their own, whose duration depends on the intensity of the generating thought or desire]. Fortunately, the passage continues, the thoughts of most people are so vague that the beings formed by them have but the briefest of existence. But the constant repetition of the same thought or idea strengthens their ability to survive and in turn to produce again those thoughts and ideas that nourish them: 'Chi dunque insista e batta costantemente su un desiderio, viene a crearsi come un camerata invisibile, legato a lui dal proprio pensiero, quasi un cagnolino incatenato, senz'obbligo di museruola ed esente di tassa' [Whoever concentrates and constantly harps on a desire, thus, comes to create for himself something like an invisible comrade, almost a chained pet dog who is not required to wear a muzzle nor to have a licence]. So much for the quasi-externalization or 'materialization' of their ideas and desires by which as by an invisible wall men are surrounded.

Underlying the second part of the passage is familiarity with practices of primitive magic and witchcraft. Mattia remarks that he read in the same book that when a man's thoughts and desires concern not himself but someone else, the resultant beings travel with lightning rapidity towards this other person in order to discharge the power with which they have been endowed. Thus the widow Pescatore's anger at having been tricked by Mattia in her plans for her daughter, her evil thoughts, her ferocious desires had turned into terrible demons, infernal creatures that were now surrounding him, Mattia, making his life impossible and preparing the further sequence of misadventures that constitutes the *Bildungsroman* aspect of the novel. It is, of course, of great significance that in the sentence that replaces this passage in the definitive edition of *Il fu Mattia Pascal* the whole cluster of notions we have been delineating has been subsumed into what appears to be the purely figurative use of the word *witch* as an abusive epithet: 'La strega non si sapeva dar pace'.

Macchia believes that he has identified the direct source for this passage – the book referred to – in C. W. Leadbeater's *The Astral Plan* (London 1897), translated into French as *Le Plan Astral – premier degré du Monde invisible, d'après la Théosophie* and published by the same Paris publisher already mentioned in connection with Paleari's library. Macchia's quotations from *Le Plan Astral* are sufficiently close to what Pirandello wrote to show that in this case too – as Rauhut has shown for Marchesini's *Le finzioni dell'anima* (1905) and Binet's *Les Altérations de la personnalité* (1892), and Andersson for Séailles' *Le Génie dans l'art* (1883) – Pirandello had simply taken what he needed where he found it without bothering to acknowledge his debt. (But the writer of fiction is not really expected to footnote his sources!) In addition Macchia quotes from another work of Leadbeater's, this one written in collaboration with Annie Besant, *Thought-Forms* (1905), translated into French as *Les Formes-Pensées*. The passage quoted by Macchia likens the novelist's 'construction' of characters to the formation of beings that result, as described above, from recurrent feelings and ideas. Leadbeater and Besant write that, once created, these 'marionettes' (characters, beings) are set in motion by the writer's will so that the novel's plot starts playing itself out before his eyes. However, they observe, men, because of their erroneous concept of reality, find it difficult to understand 'how these mental images can actually exist'. We shall have to return to this point in the course of our discussion later. But it must be apparent even now how central these ideas, derived from the literature of the occult, are to Pirandello's concept of artistic creativity and its embodiment especially in his best-known play *Sei personaggi*. Interestingly enough, a sense of the consistency – the physicality – of fictional characters similar to Leadbeater's, Besant's and Pirandello's runs through much of what actors and directors thought of their craft in the 1920s: Charles Dullin, for instance, in the chapter 'Naissance et vie des personnages', in his *Souvenirs et Notes de travail d'un acteur* (1946).

Filosofia del lontano and *lanterninosofia* are in many respects but a step removed from *umorismo*. *L'umorismo*, the essay on humour, is probably one of the most frequently invoked and least often read-in-its entirety of Pirandello's works. A few of its formulations have become by-words in Pirandello criticism: one or two of its passages are quoted with unfailing regularity. But as a self-contained work it has proved puzzling, apparently a hybrid which belongs neither in the category of philosophical works such as Bergson's *Le rire* (1899) nor among the literary genres from which Pirandello derives his fame. In reviewing it in 1909 Momigliano attributed what he considered its shortcomings (its prolixity, digressions, 'absence of concise and crystalline form') to its not being 'an organic whole', but a collection of articles. And indeed, as is well known, it was put together hastily from a course that Pirandello held at the *Istituto superiore di Magistero* in Rome, when he was competing for a permanent appointment in that institution. No doubt in order to add to his academic publications, he permitted some of the chapters, either in part or in their entirety, to appear as independent articles almost simultaneously with the book.

Before 1908, Pirandello had already written two important essays related to the subject matter of *L'umorismo*: *Un preteso poeta umorista del secolo XIII*, and *Alberto Cantoni*, later retitled *Un critico fantastico*. In the first, published in *La vita italiana*, 15 February 1896, and virtually forgotten until it was included much later in *Saggi, poesie, scritti varii*, he had disputed the appropriateness of Alessandro D'Ancona's use of the epithet *umorista* to characterize the thirteenth-century burlesque poet Cecco Angiolieri. (As a matter of fact, in the very first paragraph of *L'umorismo* Pirandello quotes D'Ancona in order to make an initial distinction with respect to the term humorism: 'But for us, Angiolieri is not only a burlesque writer, but also, and more properly, a humor-

ist'.) The second had been written as an introduction to Alberto
Cantoni's posthumous novel *L'Illustrissimo* when it first began to
appear in serial form in *Nuova antologia*, on 16 March 1905, shortly
after the prestigious periodical had opened its pages to *Il fu Mattia
Pascal*. As *Un critico fantastico* it was later included in the volume *Arte e
scienza*, published like *L'umorismo* in 1908 to further Pirandello's
academic career. But Pirandello had also written on Cantoni much
earlier, in 1893, when he reviewed his novella *L'altalena delle antipatie*
in the short-lived Roman periodical *Folchetto*. At that time he was
already acquainted with Cantoni's novel *Un re umorista* (1891), which
he considered one of the few original works in modern Italian literature: 'Ma è proprio noto a tutti, come dovrebbe essere, questo capo-
lavoro del Cantoni che s'intitola *Un re umorista*? Molti, forse piú per
la speciosità del titolo che per averlo letto, lo ricordano e ne parlano;
ma se esso fosse noto veramente, starebbe per consenso unanime tra le
poche opere culminanti della letteratura italiana contemporanea, tra
le poche piú originali ed espressive di tutta quanta la nostra letteratura
moderna' (SPSV, 385) [But is this masterpiece of Cantoni's, *Un re
umorista*, really known to everyone as it should be? Many remember it
and speak of it, but perhaps more because of the speciousness (having
the ring of truth or plausibility but actually fallacious – present writer's
gloss) of the title than because they have read it. For if it were really
known it would belong by unanimous consent among the few
crowning works of contemporary Italian literature, among the few
most original and expressive works of all our modern literature]. We
shall return to Cantoni shortly, but it is interesting to note at once
that in a bibliography of critical works which runs to several thousand
and is constantly being added to, the place of Cantoni in the development of Pirandello's thought and art has barely been touched upon.

When Pirandello published *L'umorismo*, his interest in the subject
went back at least fifteen years. We do not know for certain whether
he actually attended the lecture course on the aesthetics of the comic
and the tragic which the philosopher Theodore Lipps held during his
student days at Bonn nor whether he actually wrote the essay on the
Romantic writer Ludwig Tieck (1773–1853) which he is reported to
have composed at that time, but Lipps' *Komik und Humor: Eine
psychologisch-ästhetische Untersuchung* (1898) is cited more than once in
L'umorismo, and Tieck is referred to apropos the meaning given to the
word in German romantic circles. Pirandello's university training in
Romance Philology had acquainted him with the methods of positivist historical research and he had read widely in contemporary criti-

cism and scholarship. This background accounts for the particular structure of *L'umorismo* and places the essay within a well-defined genre category, that of the critical study, thesis, or dissertation. If it is true, as Illiano and Testa write in the introduction to their recent integral translation of *L'umorismo* (1974) that the work is 'a lively mosaic of argumentation and polemics, critical insights, penetrating analysis, and finally a profound poetic exposition of life, all of which clearly establish an organic relationship between the essay itself and the rest of Pirandello's work', it is also true that it is a work of scholarship and that it belongs not only with Pirandello's other works but generally with studies on the various aspects of the comic. The fact that it has not yet found its proper place in that literature may be attributed, in part at least, to Pirandello's choice of the anomalous and ambiguous *umorismo* over other terms which he could have chosen to name that 'eccezionale e speciosissima espressione d'arte' [exceptional and most specious art form] with which, in his own words, the essay deals.

L'umorismo is divided into two unequal parts, of which the first, the longer one, has been largely ignored by Pirandello critics, while the second has attracted the lion's share of attention. So much so, for instance, that when excerpts from the essay were first translated into English (*Tulane Drama Review*, Spring 1966), they were all selected from part II, thus passing over the historical and literary contexts and the lively illustrations used by Pirandello in part I and leaving only dry abstractions and often difficult-to-follow and easy-to-refute ratiocinations. Part I is divided into six chapters which discuss in turn the word *umorismo* itself, whether or not humorism is an exclusively modern attitude and literary phenomenon, whether it is restricted to the literatures of the north of Europe, and how it figures in Italian literature. The longest chapter is the fifth, a veritable essay on Italian chivalric poetry, with a magnificent *coda* on the genetic relationship between the character of Don Quixote and its author Cervantes. Even the most cursory glance at the table of contents, then, reveals that *L'umorismo* has a structure and is not simply an agglomeration of occasional articles, a fact made explicit by a statement at the beginning of chapter II that certain subjects must be dealt with before coming to the heart of the matter, that is, before turning to the question 'Che cosa è l'umorismo?' which opens part II of the essay. Chapters III, IV, and V all begin in the same manner (and so does chapter I) by referring to the opinion or observation of some other critic or historian who has written on the same subject: Alessandro D'Ancona, Hippolyte Taine,

Giacomo Barzellotti, and Ferdinand Brunetière. Chapter VI opens with a disclaimer: it is *not* Pirandello's intention to write a history of humorism amongst the Latin peoples, especially the Italians. In part II the sub-sections, none of which have chapter titles, all start with expressions such as 'Vediamo dunque...Teniamoci a questo...Per spiegarci la ragione....Da quanto abbiamo detto finora....' [Let us see then....Let us pursue this point further....To try to understand the reason....On the basis of what we have said so far] – expressions each of which emphasizes the logical structure of a discourse whose purpose is to convince the reader of the truth of what is being said through the marshalling of adequate demonstration or proof.

A glance at the broad range of secondary sources used by Pirandello reinforces this view of *L'umorismo* as a work of scholarship. There are first of all the works of contemporary scholars and critics, those that Wellek deals with in the volume on the late nineteenth century in his *A History of Modern Criticism*. To the ones just mentioned should be added Fernard Baldensperger, Enrico Nencioni, Louis Cazamian, Giorgio Arcoleo, Guido Muoni, Ettore Romagnoli, Arturo Graf, Carducci, Ruggero Bonghi, and the most important of all, Francesco De Sanctis. On a different level are such classics of romantic aesthetics as Schiller's *Über die aesthetische Erziehung des Menschen* and *Über die naive und sentimentalische Dichtung* (referred to by way of Victor Basch's 1902 *La Poétique de F. Schiller*), and a rapid survey of post-Kantian idealism from Hegel, Herder and Fichte to F. Schlegel and Tieck. And there is a third set of references in which particular works – the sonnets of Cecco Angiolieri, the sonnets of other comic poets from Berni to Belli, Pulci's *Morgante*, the *Orlando furioso*, Pascarella's modern mock epic *La scoperta dell'America*, *Don Quixote*, *I promessi sposi*, *Tristram Shandy*, Leopardi's *Operette morali*, and several Italian works from Giusti's 'Sant'Ambrogio' to Panzini's *La lanterna di Diogene* – are looked at more or less closely, frequently, it would appear, at the suggestion of one of the secondary sources Pirandello consulted, at other times to sketch in the outlines of that presence of humorism in Italian literature which it is one of Pirandello's purposes to establish. In part II the theorist most often referred to is Lipps, but there is also the addition of a new kind of secondary source, the psychological studies of Marchesini and Binet – all in all, a significant and revealing constellation of choices.

To evaluate these sources adequately and to try to establish what each may have contributed to Pirandello's theory would require a sequence of particular analyses by specialists in different areas beyond

the scope of the discussion here. We should note however how wide
ranging and varied Pirandello's readings were and especially how
natural and unselfconscious was his passing from one literary and
linguistic tradition to another in a perspective which is European and
not national and which can also be described as interdisciplinary.
When in 1923 Pirandello took his first trip to Paris, to be followed in
the remaining years of his life by more and more frequent trips abroad
to stage his own and others' plays and eventually to be present at the
filming of some of his works, he was in a sense only resuming – after
the lapse of thirty years – that journey beyond the boundaries of Italy
begun, in a rather exceptional move for an Italian student in 1889,
when he transferred from the University of Rome to Bonn.

Exactly what Pirandello brought back from his student days in
Bonn has never been satisfactorily established. Italian cultural life was
for a good part of the twentieth century characterized by xenophobia,
by a deep-seated distrust of Romanticism, and by distrust and ignorance of German Romanticism in particular. These limitations, together with the exclusion of drama (not classical tragedy) from
serious critical work on literature, created that barrier of reservations
and incomprehensions around Pirandello that continues to colour
Pirandello scholarship even today. Outside Italy, where xenophobia
did not operate, what was and is known of Pirandello either comes
directly *via* Italian sources (hence the same emphases and omissions as
in Italy) or is confined almost exclusively to the most visible aspect of
his best known play: the theatrical setting of *Sei personaggi*. This situation would tend to explain why in a work such as D. C. Muecke's
The Compass of Irony (1969) references to Pirandello deal only with
his use of the convention of the play-within-the-play, while the context of Muecke's argument would more obviously seem to call for a
discussion of *L'umorismo*. Or why Pirandello is barely mentioned in
Wayne Booth's *A Rhetoric of Irony* (1974), that far-ranging exploration of a term so 'imperialistic' (in Booth's words) as to have come to
cover 'just about everything there is'.

In chapter 1 of part 1 of *L'umorismo* Pirandello examines the word, first
to distinguish the Italian *umore* from the English *humour* ('temper' or
even 'melancholy'), and then, passing from the 'word' to the 'thing',
to try to define its meaning. He is naturally more interested in the
'thing' than in the 'word', brushing aside, as D'Ancona had done, 'the
stewards of the language' who would pretend that 'in Italian we must
be resigned not to name the "thing" because we do not have the

"word"'. Pirandello is even ready to admit that there would be no
harm in using another word if this were necessary to signify the 'thing'
less equivocally. The word he specifically chooses is *ironismo*, and we
shall have to bear it and two other terms that Pirandello might have
chosen in mind as we look at the theoretical content of *L'umorismo*,
and at the 'philosophy' it expounds, more closely. The two other
terms are *critic[a] fantastic[a]* (from the title *Un critico fantastico* given
to the essay on Cantoni in 1908) and *grottesco* (from an article *Immagine
del 'grottesco'* published in *L'idea nazionale* in 1920).

In *Un critico fantastico* or more precisely in the 1905 introduction to
Cantoni's *L'Illustrissimo*, the word *umorismo* appears about a third of
the way through, almost as an afterthought. The essay begins with the
anecdote of the illiterate peasant naive enough to think that the right
kind of eyeglasses will without more ado enable him to read. The
anecdote, which elsewhere (*Teatro nuovo e teatro vecchio*, 1922) satirizes
Italian imitation of fashions in drama imported from France, serves
here to make the more basic distinction between originality and imitation in general, or, in terms of the Italian tradition, between subser-
vience to and rejection of the norms and precepts of rhetoric, which,
Pirandello writes, were supposed to teach the poet how to 'construct'
a work of art as though it were a logical argument: 'E appunto alla
Retorica si deve se tutte o quasi le opere della nostra letteratura hanno,
nella loro paziente diligenza, nella loro rigorosa compostezza, un'aria
di famiglia, che sconsola. Non ci sono come nella letteratura inglese,
per esempio, tra un autore e l'altro, abissi d'anima, originalità per-
spicue di forme, di vedute, di concezioni. Quasi tutta la letteratura
nostra sta come in un casellario: nel casellario della Retorica...' (SPSV,
367) [Precisely to Rhetoric do we owe it if all or almost all our works
of literature have – in their patient diligence, their rigid dignity – a
family air among them that is discouraging. There are neither deep
differences in consciousness between one author and the other, nor
outstanding originality in form, view, or conceptions, as there are in
English literature for instance. Almost all our literature can be pigeon-
holed, in the pigeon-holes of Rhetoric...]. Pirandello's characterization of the inhibiting effects of rhetoric (i.e., Renaissance aesthetics,
the legacy of the *Cinquecento*), his contrasting the imaginative literature of the North with the tradition-bound classicism of the South,
echo the terms of the polemic concerning Romanticism which had
raged almost a century earlier, down to the very virulence with which
the paragraph ends: 'E per tanti secoli della nostra letteratura noi
assistiamo alla sfilata d'un innumerevole armento di scimmie inna-

morate che vanno, sospirose, in pellegrinaggio alle chiare, fresche e
dolci acque del cantore di Laura' (SPS V, 368) [And for many centuries
of our literature we witness the parade of a countless herd of love-sick
monkeys on a pilgrimage to the clear, fresh and sweet waters of the
singer of Laura].

If imitation is to be the touchstone of success for the writer, Pirandello's argument runs, then why write? 'Perché ridire con voce
minore ciò che altri han detto con maggior voce? esser ombra e non
persona? aver dentro un pappagallo invece di un'anima?' [Why
repeat in a weaker voice what others have said with a stronger one?
Why be a shadow instead of a person? Have a parrot inside you
instead of a soul?], he asks in the figurative language typical for him in
moments of deep emotional involvement. No, 'Retorica' must be
replaced by 'Critica' and 'Carattere', the two ingredients Italian
literature lacks but with which Cantoni was in Pirandello's opinion so
exceptionally endowed. The invention of the figure 'Critica', a quasi-
personification which here joins 'Retorica', may well have been suggested to Pirandello by Cantoni's couple, 'Humour classico' and
'Humour moderno'. Cantoni imagines these two – 'un bel vecchio
rubicondo e gioviale' [a pleasant, handsome, chubby old man] and
'un ometto smilzo e circonspetto, con una faccia sdolcinata e motteg-
giatrice' [a thin, wary man with a mocking, maudlin expression] – as
having met one day at the foot of Donizetti's statue in Bergamo to
engage in a discussion of the comic. In some respects a forerunner of
the much more 'fleshed-out' personification 'Fantasia' in the Preface
to *Sei personaggi*, 'Critica' no doubt derives also from the designation
'novelle critiche' by which Cantoni referred to those of his stories in
which discussion of aesthetic problems proceeds hand in hand with
the creation of a fictional microcosm. From 'novelle critiche' to
'critico fantastico' it is but a step, but the term is so important for
Pirandello that he stops to define it: 'un critico che non si serve dei
procedimenti della critica, bensí di quelli dell'arte...dunque un *umorista*'. I have chosen not to translate here for the sake of maintaining the
very sensation of the rapid flow of Pirandello's thought which in spite
of the heavily assertive and conclusive *dunque* has by no means come
to a definitive resting place. Indeed, three paragraphs later we reach
the same point, though this time we arrive at it from the opposite
direction: 'Ogni vero umorista è, dunque,...un critico *sui generis*:
fantastico, come ho già detto, e capriccioso' [every humorist is
therefore...a critic *sui generis*; imaginative, as I've already said, or
whimsical]. *Umorista* and *critico fantastico* are thus interchangeable

synonyms for Pirandello, and it is interesting to speculate whether if the language had offered him an 'ism' from the root that gives *fantasy*, *fantastic* and *phantasm* ('fantasismo' perhaps?) he might not have preferred it to *umorismo*.

We have already indicated that at the beginning of *L'umorismo* Pirandello did indeed examine another word ending in 'ism' as a possible substitute: 'E piú d'uno, per non passar da buffone, per non esser confuso coi centomila umoristi da strapazzo, ha voluto buttar via la parola sciupata, abbandonarla al volgo, e adottarne un'altra: *ironismo, ironista*. Come da umore, umorismo; da ironia, ironismo' (spsv, 21) [And more than one person, so as not to be considered a clown, not to be confused with the thousand and one run-of-the-mill humorists, has thought of throwing out the worn-out word, abandoning it to the crowd, and choosing another one: *irony, ironist*. As humour gives humorism, so irony, ironism]. In what could almost pass as a gloss on this passage, Giudice points out that there was something ambiguous in the word *umorismo* in the very Roman environment in which Pirandello used it, for it was associated with the work of the journalists, writers, and illustrators who published in *Il Travaso delle idee*, the satirical weekly that caricatured contemporary life, 'sforzandosi', as Pirandello himself puts it, 'di far ridere piú o meno sguajatamente a ogni costo' [making every effort to evoke more or less coarse laughter at any cost]. In spite of this connotation, however, Pirandello remained attached to the term, and argued against the use of *irony* in its place.

He had two reasons for doing so. One related to irony as a rhetorical figure, the other to the concept of irony as developed by F. Schlegel and Tieck from the subjective idealism of Fichte. As a rhetorical figure, irony implies a 'fictitious contradiction' between what is said and what is meant. As for philosophical irony, in the post-Kantian universe it became the force that, according to Tieck, made it possible for the writer to dominate his subject-matter – a subject-matter that, according to F. Schlegel, irony reduces to 'a perpetual parody, a transcendental farce'. In its rhetorical sense, irony is fundamentally different from humorism, Pirandello continues, because in humorism the contradiction is not fictitious but essential. Philosophically, irony does have some affinity with humorism, but only if Schiller's words on the *Spieltrieb* in his *Über die aesthetische Erziehung des Menschen* are taken literally, as F. Schlegel took them. Pirandello paraphrases Schlegel: '…per il poeta l'ironia consiste nel non fondersi mai del tutto con l'opera propria, nel non perdere, neppure nel momento del patetico, la coscienza della irrealtà delle sue creazioni, nel non essere lo zimbello dei fantasmi da lui stesso evocati, nel sorridere del lettore che si lascerà prendere al giuoco e anche di sé stesso che la propria vita consacra a giocare' (SPSV, 24) [...for the poet irony consists in never merging completely with his work, in never losing – not even in the moment of pathos – the awareness of the unreality of his creations, in never being the stooge of the phantoms called forth by him, in smiling at the reader who permits himself to be drawn into the game and at himself who devotes his life to playing]. But this is not the whole story of humorism, Pirandello concludes, as can be seen from the example of Manzoni who never doubted objective reality and indeed condemned his own masterpiece in the name of historical truth. Nor, we could add, is this humorism if we take Pirandello himself as an example, for to him *immedesimarsi* (=*fondersi*) [to identify with]) is the very key to artistic creation, and for him – as we have already pointed out and shall have occasion to repeat – his characters, his *fantasmi*, are often more real than persons of flesh and blood. As for the function of art, it was no more hedonistic (playful rather than serious) for Pirandello than it had been for Manzoni. *Irony* cannot be substituted for *humorism* because in it there is something mocking and mordant, two attitudes which are foreign to the humorist who, like Manzoni or Pirandello, is more often motivated by compassion.

Grottesco is the third word related to *umorismo* which should be examined. Pirandello published *Immagine del 'grottesco'* in the Rome daily *L'idea nazionale*, 18 February 1920, and followed it a few days later with a companion piece, *Ironia*. At the beginning of the latter he says explicitly that he is continuing to speak of the 'grotesque' but that this time he is doing so in a serious vein. There comes next the almost *verbatim* repetition of a little more than a page from chapter v of *L'umorismo* on the relationship between the illusion created by art and the illusion created by the senses (SPSV, 80–2), and a freer transposition and reworking of the concluding pages of chapter I on, as Pirandello states, that older version of the contemporary 'grotesque', the transcendental farces of German Romanticism (SPSV, 22–4). Topical allusions to 'i più significativi grotteschi moderni' show that the two 1920 articles were prompted by the vogue of the Theatre of the Grotesque after the 1916 success of Chiarelli's *La maschera e il volto*. But actually the two articles would more properly be placed with *L'umorismo* than under the rubric 'Scritti sul teatro' where we find them in Lo Vecchio-Musti's volume of Pirandello's essays.

Just as *Un critico fantastico* opens with an anecdote, so *Immagine del* '*grottesco*' opens with a fable. It concerns two little almond trees that had spent the winter slumbering, both appearing to be dead. Come spring, only one of them bursts into bloom, its branches shining with what look like a hundred fluttering butterflies. But after heavy rain a few days later, the tree stands stiff and barren, only a yellow leaf here and there still clinging to its branches. The other tree instead has blossomed. But, oh!, what a surprise and what a burst of laughter when it is discovered that the 'blossoms' are hundreds of little white snails: 'Tutti i rami scontorti di quell'alberello morto s'erano incrostati, rabescati di bianche lumachelle, schiumate or ora dalla terra grassa, dopo l'acquata tempestosa' (SPSV, 991) [All the crooked branches of that little dead tree had become encrusted, covered with arabesques of little white snails that had just then 'foamed up' from the fertile earth after the storm and rain]. And 'fiorito cosí per burla' [having blossomed thus as a joke], the tree seems to be saying to the other one that *it* is alive now while the other is dead, that *it* has flowered as best it could.

The story is followed by Pirandello's commentary, the first part of which is concerned with the reaction of laughter to the plight of the tree, while the second applies the metaphor of the fable to art. It is significant that Pirandello does not share in the laughter but identifies instead with what the tree must have felt when it 'bloomed' in that way: 'non era poi molto allegro fiorir cosí' [it was after all not very cheerful to bloom in that way]. In other words, Pirandello passes from what in *L'umorismo* he calls *avvertimento del contrario* [the perception of the incongruous] to *sentimento del contrario* [the sense, i.e., feeling, of the incongruous]. For the little white snails, he explains, were neither intended to seem real flowers nor to be fake flowers, they were simply what they were: evidence that the tree was dead and that that 'blossoming' was laughing at itself by thus creating the illusion of life. That kind of laughter, born of disenchantment, is of course not happy but sad, and to echo it with mockery is to have missed its meaning, to have remained, that is, at the stage of *avvertimento del contrario* instead of having moved on to the next stage, *sentimento del contrario*. Actually, Pirandello adds, both trees had been victims of illusion, the first having been lulled into blooming by the fine spring weather that preceded the storm, the second having believed that it could hide 'la triste nudità dei rami' [the sad nakedness of its branches] (the gnarled, contorted branches of the almond tree) in the iridescent slime of the snails. Translated into aesthetic terms, the two kinds of flowering, the natural and the artificial – the 'alberetti che fioriscono

per famiglia' [the trees that bloom for family gardens] and the 'alberetti stravaganti' [the fantastic, eccentric little trees] – stand for the conventional bourgeois plays that were the run-of-the-mill theatrical fare
of the day and the new plays of the Theatre of the Grotesque. Pirandello ends the article by pointing out that 'la stravaganza è anch'essa
contagiosa' [eccentricity too is contagious] and that there have now
been so many of the artificial trees that one has grown tired of them.

   Immagine del 'grottesco' offers a companion piece to, a perhaps more
subtle version of what has become the most famous passage in
L'umorismo, the paragraph in part II which analyzes the process by
which a humoristic view of the world is achieved. The anecdote of
Un critico fantastico and the fable of *Immagine del 'grottesco'* are paralleled
in *L'umorismo* by the *exemplum* of the 'vecchia signora, coi capelli
ritinti, tutti unti non si sa di quale orribile manteca, e poi goffamente
imbellettata e parata d'abiti giovanili' (SPSV, 127) [old lady, her hair
dyed, all sticky we know not with what vile pomade, clumsily made-
up and adorned in youthful finery]. Upon first catching sight of her,
observes Pirandello, seeing her so different from what a respectable
old lady should look like, we laugh. But upon thinking about her, if
we realize that she may feel no pleasure in 'decking herself out like a
parrot' but is only doing so to try to hold the love of a much younger
husband, we can no longer laugh as before. To the *avvertimento del
contrario* has been added the *sentimento del contrario* and, Pirandello
concludes his demonstration, the mark that distinguished the comic
from the humoristic.

   Umorismo, ironismo, critic[a] fantastic[a], grottesco form a nexus in
Pirandello's thinking and much of his speculative energy was directed
to trying to isolate the precise meaning of each: a task rendered particularly difficult by the long history of the interrelation of the
different comic impulses between the opposing poles of irrational
vision and social accommodation. The most personal of the four
expressions is *critic[a] fantastic[a]*. The two terms that compose it are
at odds with one another and it thus reflects or 'imitates' that 'feno-
meno di sdoppiamento nell'atto della concezione' [phenomenon of
doubling in the act of artistic conception], that 'erma bifronte, che
ride per una faccia del pianto della faccia opposta' [double-faced
herm that laughs on one side about the tears shed on the other], that
'demonietto che smonta il congegno dell'immagine, del fantoccio
messo su dal sentimento' (SPSV, 373) [little demon that takes apart the
mechanism of the image, of the puppet put together by feeling],
which are some of the expressions Pirandello uses to try to explain

humorism. The other – and larger – part of the 'definition' consists in a sequence of examples, a phenomenology of literary representations of the *stato d'animo* [state of mind, mood] that constitutes humorism. The vignette of the old lady is followed immediately by a passage from *Crime and Punishment* (a companion piece, by the way, to the passages from Nordau and Ibsen cited in *Arte e coscienza d'oggi*, see p. 14 above); by a commentary on Giusti's poem 'Sant'Ambrogio', in which the poet passes from hatred for the Austrian soldiers worshipping in Milan's old church to compassionate understanding of their plight as exiles far from home; and by an analysis of the reader's complex reaction to the ambiguously comic aspects of *Don Quixote*. Had Pirandello chosen *critic[a] fantastic[a]* instead of *umorismo* as the appropriate label for the psychological state out of which works such as these are generated and which they in turn create, he would have gained in precision, for the expression recognizes the role played by imagination (*fantasia*) – that power to transcend the immediacy of impression of the here and now – in the formation of *sentimento del contrario*.

One might wish, in some respects, that he had been able to accept *ironismo*, for his essay would then more easily have found its way into the literature on the subject. In this connection it is interesting to note D.C. Muecke's comment in his pamphlet *Irony* (1970): 'Pirandello's "humour" is close to irony, particularly to what might be called the General Irony of inevitable self-deception'. But if we go back for a moment to the very passage in which Pirandello disavows the term irony, it becomes clear that what he rejected was the idea of the author's, of his own, 'inevitable self-deception'. For he does not take that additional step which today's 'sophisticated' reader, victim of and seeker after W.C. Booth's 'infinite instabilities' would like him to take – and which F. Schlegel took in the passage referred to. Pirandello is not aware of the 'unreality of his creations' nor does he 'smile at the reader for permitting himself to be drawn into the game': the attitude of the humorist is serious, not playful or parodic. In other words, just as Pirandello does not go all the way in *consciously* placing imagination at the apex of human activity (he is unaware for instance of the macroscopic presence in his own work of the organic metaphor of Romanticism), so he does not go the whole way of Romantic irony.

Readers are often struck by how firmly Pirandello's fictions, for all the brilliant modernism with which they are given shape, are rooted in the social and psychological situations of late nineteenth-century

Europe, with, of course, the typical emphases or exaggerations that come from his Sicilian background and early experience. Thus the triangle remains the basic cause of conflict between the sexes, economic necessity the basic mainspring for men's activity, self-justification – rationalization – the basic form of self-assertion and of self-defence in an unfriendly world and an unfeeling universe. In the case of his theoretical and critical writings, too, it is obvious to what an extent his aesthetic and philosophical concepts, his scholarly and critical methodology reflect the positions and practices of his day. This in spite of his sympathy and understanding for – indeed his proselytizing in favour of – a conception of individual freedom which rejects all social conventions and roles, an attitude which was to become generally accepted only much later in this century and which explains the first thrill of recognition on the part of many readers today. It is well to remember however that Pirandello's freedom is won on a personal level, that it is an ethical and existential condition, the result of insight or conversion. It has nothing in common with the so-called freedom won by political group combat, which to Pirandello would be but a new instance of constraint and tyranny.

2. Early Narrative and Drama

No study of Pirandello's work is complete without an examination of the Sicilian component in his formation. The expression 'Sicilian component' is used here to cover not only the accident of birth, family background, and early experience, but also his beginnings as a narrative writer in the tradition of *verismo* and his early theatrical experiments in Sicilian dialect. The characteristics of Pirandello's work in terms of *sicilianità* [Sicilianism] or *meridionalità* [Southernism] have been studied primarily by Italian critics, many of them Sicilians or transplanted Sicilians, all of them aware that the strait which separates the island from the mainland is more than a narrow body of water. Pirandello's Sicilianism has also attracted the attention of readers and critics outside Italy: for them it often contains the spice of the exotic and the primitive, creating a comfortable barrier against having to take his *vision autre*, his seeing the world in its deformations and excesses, too seriously.

The history, the landscapes, the social and psychological situations of Sicily appear in their undisguised, documentary reality in many of Pirandello's works. In many others they are attenuated and generalized, no more than a colouring or glow that points back through analogy to facts and circumstances actually or potentially experienced. There are stories set in Porto Empedocle (where Pirandello's father was engaged in the mining and exporting of sulphur), Agrigento (where the young boy lived and went to school until 1881), Palermo (where the family moved after a first financial setback, where Pirandello attended secondary school, became engaged to a cousin he did not then marry, and started his university studies). But there is also (in *Questa sera si recita a soggetto*, for instance) the generic 'città dell'interno della Sicilia, dove le passioni son forti e covano cupe e poi divampano violente' [city in the interior of Sicily, where passions are strong, smoulder for a long time and then flare up violently]. And there are the completely unidentified locales of other plays: a lonely country road along a cemetery wall (*All'uscita*); a square in front of a country church, crowded with worshippers and merrymakers (*Sagra del Signore della nave*); a witch's den, a seaport café, a princely garden, in which the old tale of changeling and mother love runs its course (*La favola del figlio cambiato*); the solitary, run-down villa *La Scalogna*, 'al limite, fra la favola e la realtà' [on the boundary line between myth and reality], where a group of 'drop-outs' from society creates the magic of theatre (*I giganti della montagna*). None of these are properly speaking in Sicily and yet they suggest that setting through reference to particular beliefs, attitudes, superstitions, myths, landscapes.It is said that at the very end of his life, in the fevered state that preceded his death, Pirandello told his son that he had found the solution for his last, unfinished play: 'C'è un olivo saraceno, grande, in mezzo alla scena: con cui ho risolto tutto' [There's a Saracen olive tree, a large one, in the middle of the scene. With it I've solved everything]...the Saracen olive tree of *La giara*, of *Liolà*, of the many rural vistas of his stories, his emblem for the Sicilian countryside as the carob tree was for Verga.

Giovanni Verga (1840–1922), the great Sicilian *verista* of the last decades of the nineteenth century, was Pirandello's first literary model. A short story, *Capannetta*, published in the Sunday supplement of the Turin *Gazzetta del popolo*, 1 June 1884, is the earliest of Pirandello's prose works to have survived. It was written when he was seventeen and is, like Verga's *Nedda* (1874), a *bozzetto siciliano* [Sicilian sketch]. We do not know how it found its way to Turin, but 1884 was the year of the successful première of *Cavalleria rusticana* (the play Verga had drawn from his own short story) at Turin's Teatro Carignano – with Eleonora Duse in the role of Santuzza – and *verismo* was so-to-speak in the air. Only shortly before, Verga had published *I Malavoglia* (1881), which was a failure at its appearance, and two collections of short stories almost entirely set in Siciliy, *Vita dei campi* (1880) and *Novelle rusticane* (1883). In his review for *Corriere della sera*, 20–21 September 1880, Capuana had strongly emphasized the originality of *Vita dei campi*, an originality which he dates back to *Nedda*, whose protagonist, a poor olive picker in her torn dress, bare feet, and sun-burnt face, stood ill-at-ease among Verga's other female characters at that time, the Evas and Adeles, the Velledas and Natas of his so-called mundane and Romantic period. The novelty of *Vita dei campi*, Capuana wrote, was not only its subject-matter – epitomized in the Maras, Lolas, Jelis and Turiddus, the other lower class Sicilians who had come to join Nedda – but also in its 'art', in its successful achievement of the ideal of impersonality in storytelling. Capuana paraphrases that veritable manifesto of *verismo* which is the introductory letter to Salvatore Farina (1846–1918, journalist, critic and writer active in Milan) in Verga's short story *L'amante di Gramigna*, by writing: 'A work of art, be it short story or novel, is perfect when the affinity and cohesion of its every part is so complete that the process of creation remains a mystery, when the sincerity of its reality is so evident, its manner and reason for being so necessary, that the hand of the artist remains absolutely invisible and the work of art appears to be an actual event, as though it had *produced itself* and had matured and issued forth almost spontaneously, without bearing any trace in its living forms either of the mind in which it was conceived, or of the eyes that first glimpsed it, or of the lips that murmured its first words'.

This ideal of art, with its strong emphasis on realistic detail and the almost mystical fervour with which in contrast to Romantic practice it wishes to expunge the author from his work, informs *Capannetta* and will, as we shall see, continue to be present in Pirandello's work for the rest of his life, although often in dialectic tension with the need and desire of restoring the author. *Capannetta* is narrated impersonally in a sequence of five 'scenes', without any attempt to provide a frame. This essentially dramatic technique should not be taken as fore-shadowing Pirandello's activity as a playwright. It reflects rather Pirandello's very thorough understanding of the practice of *verismo*. For both Capuana and Verga drama had been an early temptation: when they moved to Florence in the 1860s Verga had hoped to make his mark as a playwright, Capuana became drama critic for *La Nazione*. The first discussions of French realism, *verismo's* most important source, reached them at that time: these discussions centred on painting and drama, *not* the novel. As a matter of fact, it took a good many years before the desired objectivity – the elimination of the omniscient author – made its appearance in the narrative genres. Verga's early novels and short stories all have introductory passages which define the storyteller's relation to his subject. *Nedda*, for instance, has a very elaborate introductory frame, something Verga no longer thought necessary in recognized masterpieces such as *Cavalleria rusticana* and *La lupa*, in *Vita dei campi*, or indeed *I Malavoglia*. Thus if *Capannetta* recalls *Nedda* in its genre designation of 'bozzetto siciliano', it is closer to the stories of *Vita dei campi* in narrative technique – and this shows a rather remarkable artistic intuition in a writer as young as Pirandello.

The first scene of *Capannetta* takes place at dawn, in long shot (to use a cinematic term). A servant child, barely awake, is seen coming out of a hut against the distant background of horizon, fiery-red sunrise, yellow-brown clouds, the emerald green of trees, the sea. She climbs up a cliff, sits down, begins to hum a song. Then she calls out to Zi' Jeli: he is to come, the master wants him. The scene shifts to the hut: papà Camillo, the master, is giving orders to Jeli for the morrow. Jeli has eyes only for Màlia, papà Camillo's older daughter, who has eyes only for him. Papà Camillo warns the young man. After he is gone, in a monosyllabic exchange of the greatest economy, Jeli urges Màlia to run away with him: if she doesn't he will kill her father. The third scene: it is evening, the hour established for the elopement: Jeli comes for Màlia. They leave together. Later that evening (scene IV) papà Camillo comes home, asks for Jeli; the child stammers out the truth. In one dense paragraph is described 'la collera pazza di quell'uomo' [the mad rage of that man], his setting fire to the hut to obliterate all memory of his daughter, his racing after the lovers, gun in hand. The last scene is again in long shot: red flames colour the sky, dark clouds of smoke rise from the hut. The child is watching, wide-eyed.

This is not the place for a thorough analysis of this piece, such as Franz Rauhut and Gösta Andersson have produced. It is sufficient to point out characteristics typical of *verismo* and some more particularly Verghian reminiscences. First of all, the choice of a stock situation from Sicilian country life involving family honour: in this case, we have the elopement, the planned kidnapping intended to force the girl's unwilling parents to consent to her marriage. (For another Sicilian's treatment of this same theme, it is interesting to read Rosso di San Secondo's 1911 *sintesi drammatica, La fuga,* significantly enough dedicated to Pirandello.) There are then the names of the characters: Jeli and Màlia both appear in Verga, *Jeli il pastore* being one of the *novelle* of *Vita dei campi.* Finally there is the sparse storytelling, with frequent hiatuses in the action, the idiomatic expressions patterned on popular speech, the absence of elaborate physical and psychological descriptions before the characters are shown in action – all features with parallels in Verga. What is different is the explosive, discomposed violence of the ending, the excessive 'collera pazza di quell'uomo'. In *Cavalleria rusticana* and *La lupa,* for instance, which both end in homicide, killer and victim approach the moment of death with dignity and fatalism, not with the wild grimace of papà Camillo's 'riso frenetico che si perde in un rantolo strozzato' [frenzied laughter that changes into a choked cry]. Different too is the highly pictorial and colourful rendering of nature, closer to D'Annunzio's *Novelle della Pescara* than to Verga. (We shall return to D'Annunzio later.)

In addition to recognizing a general relationship between Pirandello and Verga, critics have often stopped to analyze specific pairs of stories and plays: *La giara* and *La roba*, for instance, for the conception of property that each reveals; *Ciàula scopre la luna* and *Rosso Malpelo* because they both deal with the intolerable conditions of the sulphur miner; *Il berretto a sonagli* and *Cavalleria rusticana* for their treatment of adultery and jealousy. But there is also a direct way for finding out what Pirandello thought of his predecessor. In 1920 on the occasion of Verga's eightieth birthday he took part in the celebration held at Catania's Teatro Massimo with an address which now figures in his collected works under the title *Giovanni Verga*. Pirandello also spoke on Verga a second time, in 1931 when the Reale Accademia d'Italia, of which he had recently become a member, commemorated the fiftieth anniversary of the publication of *I Malavoglia*. The two versions of what is essentially the same text and the variants that have been published (especially for the two *exordia*) show that Pirandello encountered some difficulty not so much in what to say but in what attitude to take toward what he was saying. It was difficult, in other words, for him to divorce his own experience as a writer from Verga's. Thus the speech tells us a great deal not only about Pirandello's understanding of Verga's art but also about himself and about the place he felt he occupied in Italian literature. For these reasons it deserves the attention we shall now devote to it.

The Catania version is the more straightforward one for it starts directly with the basic problem of the critical evaluation of a work such as Verga's, highly original and unique and therefore (as Pirandello will be at pains to explain) eternal, but to all outward appearances inextricably caught up in a theoretical position, *verismo*, rooted in the intellectual needs of a specific historical moment. The second writer Pirandello mentions is Capuana, Verga's closest companion in art and Pirandello's own *maestro*, and he does so, inverting the usual judgement, to pay public homage to the novelist and short-story writer rather than the critic. Further, just as he detaches writer from movement, he detaches the single work from the genre to which it belongs. Having rejected the usual approaches of literary history, he focuses on the essential quality of Verga's work, its 'antiletterarietà' (a term virtually impossible to translate, but perhaps we could say its 'non belletristic quality'), at the opposite pole of the work of the writer who was Verga's strongest and, in terms of contemporary success, triumphant rival, D'Annunzio. This is followed by a bird's-eye view of the course of the whole of Italian literature seen as falling

into two distinct camps: 'là uno stile di parole, qua uno stile di cose'
[there a 'style of words', here a 'style of objects']. The distinction is the
one made by the sixteenth-century poet Francesco Berni in praising
the poetry of Michelangelo as against that of the Petrarchists: 'Ei dice
cose, e voi dite parole' [He speaks objects, and you speak words], and
extended by Pirandello to Dante as against Petrarch, Machiavelli as
against Guicciardini, Ariosto as against Tasso, Manzoni as against
Monti, and finally Verga as against D'Annunzio. Connected to
Verga's 'stile di cose' is his 'dialettalità', his having opted for the spoken
rather than the literary language, his being regional and therefore
authentic. It is at this point, mid-way through his speech, that Pirandello takes up the epithet 'Siciliano triste' which had been applied to
Verga, and describes in one of the strongest and most intensely felt
passages the Sicilian's instinctive fear of life: 'Tutti i siciliani in fondo
sono tristi, perchè hanno quasi tutti un senso tragico della vita, e anche
quasi una istintiva paura di essa oltre quel breve ambito del covo, ove
si senton sicuri e si tengono appartati; per cui son tratti a contentarsi
del poco, purché dia loro sicurezza. Avvertono con diffidenza il con-
trasto tra il loro animo chiuso e la natura intorno, aperta, chiara di
sole, e piú si chiudono in sé, perché di quest'aperto, che da ogni parte
è il mare che li isola, cioè che li taglia fuori e li fa soli, diffidano, e
ognuno è e si fa isola a sé, e da sé si gode, ma appena, se l'ha, la sua poca
gioia, da sé, taciturno e senza cercar conforti, si soffre il suo dolore
spesso disperato' (SPSV, 419) [All Sicilians are basically sad, because
they almost all have a tragic sense of life, and also an instinctive fear of
it beyond that narrow compass of the lair where they feel themselves
secure and keep themselves apart; so that they are inclined to be satisfied with little, as long as it gives them security. They note with
diffidence the contrast between their own closed personalities and the
nature that surrounds them, wide-open and flooded by the sun. And
they withdraw even further within themselves, distrusting the open-
ness about them, the sea that isolates them, cuts them off, leaving them
lonely and alone. Each one becomes an island to himself and enjoys
his small share of pleasures – if he has any – soberly, by himself. Alone,
silent, without seeking comfort, he suffers his often desperate un-
happiness].

We have paused on this passage because it provides an approach to
what is probably the most fascinating aspect of the speech: Pirandello's search for his own identity in the act of composing 'un solenne
discorso di celebrazione' (SPSV, 427) for which he feels himself in-
adequate and which is concerned through and through with the

definition not only of artistic but of human characteristics. This search for identity, more than the new occasion, explains, I propose, the radical redirection of the speech in 1931 when a sharply polemical tone replaced what had been essentially an eulogistic one. If we were dealing not with what is to all intents and purposes a literary essay but with a work of fiction, we might say that in the 1931 version three distinct and well-rounded characters emerge: Verga, Pirandello and D'Annunzio. D'Annunzio is Pirandello's antagonist, the butt of his polemic. Verga becomes more than he had already been in 1920 a shielding figure behind which Pirandello places his own personality without however creating any confusion between the two. What separates Pirandello from Verga is spelled out unequivocally in both versions of the speech in almost identical words: '...[il Verga] non è, né può essere, nel senso vero e proprio della parola, un umorista' (SPSV, 419, 399) [Verga is not, nor could he be, in the fundamental sense of the word, a humorist]. This is because, in contrast to Pirandello, Verga did not doubt that the world actually was what it appeared to be. Pirandello is extremely precise at this point and his words bear quoting, for the two opposite and diametrically opposed views of reality, reality as man's internal construct (the humorist's view) and reality as that which exists independent of man (the realist's view), could not be more clearly stated: 'Il mondo non è per se stesso in nessuna realtà, se non gliela diamo noi; e dunque, poiché gliel'abbiamo data noi, è naturale che ci spieghiamo che non possa essere diverso. Bisognerebbe diffidar di noi stessi, della realtà del mondo posta da noi. Per sua fortuna il Verga non ne diffida' (SPSV, 419, 399) [The world has no reality in itself except if we give it one. Consequently, if we have given it that reality, we cannot expect it to be otherwise. To do so would be to distrust ourselves, to distrust the reality that we have given the world. Luckily for him Verga did not distrust it]. So much for the basic epistemological difference between Verga and Pirandello. In terms of *lanterninosofia*, the colour of the *lanternone*, the super light of consensus, had changed: Verga's philosophical materialism had been displaced by Pirandello's idealism, and the pendulum had once more swung from Aristotle to Plato.

But what separates Pirandello from D'Annunzio is something else entirely. We pass from the abstract realm of ideas to the concrete world of historical existence. In the 1920 version of the speech Gabriele D'Annunzio (1863–1938) had first made his appearance as the opposite of Verga when Pirandello had been speaking of Verga's limited success in the second part of his career: *I Malavoglia* and *Mastro*

Don Gesualdo had had the misfortune of being published when a new movement was displacing *verismo*, a movement exemplified by Pirandello with the psychological novels of D'Annunzio (and Fogazzaro). In the 1931 version of the speech on the other hand, D'Annunzio, though not immediately mentioned by name, is present from the very beginning and he has become much more than simply the opposite of Verga. D'Annunzio, who was Verga's junior by more than twenty years, was Pirandello's almost precise contemporary. The four years that separated them had dwindled to total insignificance by 1920 and 1931; not so the difference in their literary careers. In facility and versatility D'Annunzio and Pirandello can be said to be equals: both were prolific writers who passed with ease from one genre to another. In precocity, fame and flamboyance, however, D'Annunzio was unique. His first work, the collection of poetry *Primo vere*, was published in 1879 when he was only sixteen, and was greeted as a revelation. In addition to being a man of letters he was a man of action, witness his exploits as a pilot and his expedition to free the city of Fiume during the War. He was famous – or infamous – as a lover, witness his liaison with Eleonora Duse, shamelessly exploited by him in his novel *Il fuoco* (1908). His had been, in Pirandello's words, 'una grande, o piuttosto, prestigiosa avventura letteraria, che prese tutt'a un tratto e tenne per tanto tempo gli animi in un abbaglio fascinoso' (SPSV, 415) [a great, or rather, prestigious literary adventure which suddenly seized men's minds and kept them captive in a spell-binding dazzle]. When Pirandello sought to distinguish not only Verga but himself from D'Annunzio, he could think only in absolute terms, of a contrast in manner of being, in basic identity, or in style. Such a contrast, as we have seen, had already appeared in the first version of the speech when Pirandello had divided Italian writers into those endowed with *stile di parole* and those endowed with *stile di cose*. The dichotomy is broadened in 1931 to include men in general and Italians in particular, and the whole beginning of the speech is used to drive home the difference: 'Due tipi umani, che forse ogni popolo esprime dal suo ceppo: i costruttori e i riadattatori, gli spiriti necessari e gli esseri di lusso, gli uni dotati d'uno "stile di cose", gli altri d'uno "stile di parole"; due grandi famiglie o categorie di uomini che vivono contemporanei in seno a ogni nazione, sono in Italia, forse piú che altrove, ben distinte e facilmente individuabili' (SPSV, 391) [Two human types, that perhaps every nation produces from its stock, the builders and the adaptors, the necessary beings and the beings of luxury, the former endowed with a 'style of objects' and the latter with a 'style of words', these two great families or categories of men, living contemporaneously within each nation, are in Italy, perhaps more than elsewhere, quite distinct and easily recognizable].

It is impossible to study the ramifications of these statements here, to follow Pirandello in his sharp indictment of a national preference for 'bei gesti', 'belle parole', 'passioni decorative'; in his sarcastic summary of what the superficial observer sees in Italy: 'gl'Italiani tutti perduti a vivere nei sensi, ebbri di sole, di luce, di colori, ebbri di canzoni e tutti sonatori di facili strumenti' (SPSV, 391) [Italians all living the life of the senses, intoxicated by sun, light, colour, exulting in song, each one playing some easy musical instrument]; and in his cutting characterization of Italy's 'uomini rappresentativi' [the men that best represent her] as 'immaginosi letterati dal linguaggio sonoro, e magnifici decoratori, e rievocatori delle glorie passate' (SPSV, 392) [fanciful men of letters speaking a grandiloquent tongue, magnificent adorners, and evokers of past glories]. All this opposed to the others, 'quelli che appajono di meno e giovano di piú' [those who shine less and contribute more], those endowed with *stile di cose*. Through a complicated juxtaposition and superimposition of images, which cannot be traced here, Pirandello arrives at the implicit identification of Verga's and of his own art on one hand ('la virtù nuda e forte dell'arte di uno scrittore come Giovanni Verga' [the unadorned and vigorous strength of the art of a writer like Giovanni Verga]), and of the reserve and diffidence of the Sicilian on the other as emblematic of the self-effacement necessary to the writer whose purpose it is to 'esprimere nudamente delineando le dure sagome delle cose da dire' (SPSV, 393) [say nakedly the things he has to say, outlining their harsh contours].

Our consideration of the relationship between Pirandello and Verga has taken us in chronological terms well beyond his beginnings as a writer in prose. *Capannetta*, as we have seen, was to remain for many years without companions in its genre, for in his student days Pirandello devoted himself almost exclusively to poetry. So much so that all through 1892, after he had returned from Germany and had settled down to literary life in Rome, he continued to think of himself as a poet. His change of direction is upon his own testimony usually attributed to Capuana, and it should come as no surprise that Capuana's flair for novelty, which had in the 1860s influenced both himself and Verga to abandon romantic drama in favour of the realistic novel, should in the 1890s have encouraged Pirandello to cut short his outpouring of verse. In his collected works poetry occupies almost 400 pages but it is generally deemed unoriginal in form, echoing all the major lyric voices of the nineteenth century, and interesting only for the typically 'Pirandellian' themes that it expresses. We have been introduced to some of these themes in chapter I and we shall consider others in turning now to a selection of Pirandello's narrative writings, all first published around 1900, and variously representing the genres of *romanzo*, *racconto*, and *novella*.

L'esclusa (1901; first written as *Marta Ajala* in 1893) and the contemporaneous *Il turno* (1902; first written 1895) share with *Capannetta* a distorting vision in which violence and excess play an important part. Both are set in Agrigento (the second part of *L'esclusa* shifts to Palermo) in a middle-class milieu where even a janitor may display 'la dignitosa gravità d'un notajo' (TR, I, 13) [the decorous dignity of a notary], and are teeming with characters whom Pirandello sees in their atypicalness, in their grotesqueness. *L'esclusa* begins with a scene at the dinner table of Antonio Pentàgora, father of Rocco, the husband of Marta Ajala, the outcast of the title. Antonio's sister, Sidora, is described as 'pallida e aggrottata, con gli occhi acuti adirati e sfuggenti sotto il fazzoletto di seta nera che teneva sempre in capo' [pale and frowning, her sharp, angry eyes unsteady and shifting under the black silk kerchief she always wore on her head]. Antonio's younger son, Niccolino, is 'spiritato, con la testa orecchiuta da pipistrello sul collo stralungo, gli occhi tondi e il naso ritto' [as though possessed, his head with its large bat-like ears set on an over-long neck, his eyes round, his nose straight]. Signora Popònica, an impoverished lady whom Antonio has hired to do the house work, has 'capelli color tabacco di Spagna, unti non si sa di qual manteca, gli occhi ammaccati e la bocca grinzosa appuntita' [hair the colour of Spanish tobacco, greasy with one knows not what pomade, bruised eyes, and pursed, wrinkled lips]. She comes in unsteadily on her thin little legs, wiping her hands on an old jacket of her master's which she is wearing in lieu of an apron with the sleeves tied around her middle. In anticipation of what he will write later on *avvertimento* and *sentimento del contrario*, and actually foreshadowing the vignette of the painted woman with which he will illustrate the distinction, Pirandello cannot help observing: 'La tintura dei capelli, l'aria mesta del volto davano a vedere chiaramente che quella povera signora caduta in bassa fortuna avrebbe forse desiderato qualcosa di più che il disperato amplesso di quelle maniche vuote' (TR, I, 7) [The dyed hair, the mournful expression of the face showed clearly that that poor lady fallen on evil days might perhaps have desired something more than the desperate embrace of those empty sleeves].

If the characters are outlandish, the situation they find themselves in is no less strange. On the Pentàgoras there is a kind of curse: the fate of being cuckolded is passed from father to son. Rocco is just returning home after having thrown Marta out of his own house on the suspicion – to him a certainty – of infidelity. Antonio had done the same to *his* wife, and Antonio's father before, to his. 'Te lo avevo predetto!' [I had foretold you as much!] father repeats to son.

In *Il turno* the storyteller's hand is lighter. The first chapter foregoes description of setting and characters completely. The action is at once 'spoken'. Instead of the distance of the omniscient storyteller, we have the voice of Marcantonio Raví engaged in a soliloquy which is at the same time argumentation as he tries to persuade his indignant and unbelieving neighbours that he has found a way whereby his daughter can become both rich and the wife of the penniless young man who has set his heart on her: she must first marry the wealthy septuagenarian don Diego Alcozèr, now a widower for the fourth time. 'Ragioniamo!' [Let's be reasonable!] is Marcantonio's first word. 'Se non siamo beste, proviamoci a ragionare' [If we're not dumb beasts, let's try and reason]. Reason suggests that his scheme must work: don Diego cannot have long to live. But Marcantonio is not the only extreme character in *Il turno*. Before long we meet Ciro Coppa. In one of those 'minute pedantic portraits' which will later abound in his plays Pirandello describes him as 'tozzo, il petto e le spalle poderosi, enormi, per cui pareva anche più basso di statura, il collo taurino, il volto bruno e fiero, contornato da una corta barba riccia, folta e nerissima, la fronte resa ampia dalla calvizie incipiente, gli occhi grandi, neri, pieni di fuoco' [stocky, with strong, enormous chest and shoulders that made him look even shorter, a bull-like neck, his proud dark face surrounded by a thick, short, curly and very black beard, his forehead made broader by incipient baldness, his eyes large, black, full of fire]. In comparison with the descriptions quoted from *L'esclusa* and in comparison with the description of don Diego Alcozèr just a few pages earlier in *Il turno*, this one is severe and controlled. Not so the theatrical gesture (similar to Chiàrchiaro's in the one-act play *La patente*, for instance) with which Ciro Coppa is introduced: one hand in his pocket, a whip in the other hand, which he is nervously beating against his hunting boots. A thousand times more determined than Marcantonio to bend things and people to his will, the despotic, eccentric 'madman' Ciro Coppa will be the reason why the fool-proof plan fails: the marriage between Stellina and don Diego does take place but ends in separation, and Ciro Coppa, her lawyer, marries her himself before dying of a stroke as he tries to control his uncontrollable jealousy. The young Pepè Alletto, having thus twice waited his turn, now seems close to the realization of his wish.

Critics have devoted considerable attention to *L'esclusa* and *Il turno*, principally to illustrate the undermining of the postulates of *verismo* already present in these early examples of Pirandello's work: in particular, the devaluation of 'facts' as determinants of action and judgement. 'Ma un fatto è come un sacco: vuoto non si regge', says the Father in *Sei personaggi*. 'Perché si regga, bisogna prima farci entrar dentro la ragione e i sentimenti che lo han determinato' (MN, I, 93) [But a fact is like a sack: if it's empty it won't stand up. To make it stand up you must first pour into it the logic and the feelings that have determined it]. Cause and effect are here reversed. In the Preface to *L'amante di Gramigna* Verga had written in defence of impersonality, his ideal of storytelling, that surely the reader would prefer to find himself face to face 'col fatto nudo e schietto' [with the bare, straightforward fact], without having to look for it between the lines of the book, through the lens of the writer. For Pirandello the bare, straightforward fact as such does not exist. There are only lenses. Or as Luigi Bàccolo, one of his exceptionally good early critics, put it: 'It is not with eyes such as Pirandello's that one could see the world as something to be photographed. A personality such as his does not simply accept what is. It imposes itself.'

Thus *L'esclusa* diverges from other, more or less contemporaneous realistic works. The economic motif, though present, does not have the same compelling force it has in Verga, for instance. The story of Marta is quite different from Nedda's and this difference is not only attributable to the different class to which the two protagonists belong. Marta, too, is forced to look after herself, to become a bread winner when her family is plunged into poverty. But what she must struggle against is not competition born of need or greed but social and moral prejudices which make her an outcast when she aspires to use her education by becoming a teacher just as she had been literally cast out by her husband when he suspected her of having an illicit love affair. The theme of adultery, too, which lies at the very heart of *L'esclusa*, receives a different treatment from that in the much better known *Madame Bovary* or, for that matter, in Capuana's *Giacinta* (1879, rev. ed., 1889), a novel to which *L'esclusa* has often been compared. The setting is in all three cases provincial, but the circumstances and motivations are radically different. Emma's adultery is self-indulgent, a romantic dream of escape from what she experiences as a confining environment. Giacinta's is perverse: having been brutally raped as a child, she refuses to marry the man she loves so that she may become his mistress once she is married to someone else. Marta's is, as it were, forced on her: it occurs only later when she 'acts out' the role for which she was cast when her husband rejected her for having *supposedly* been unfaithful to him. Because of Pirandello's sympathy for his courageous, self-aware, innerly independent protagonist, *L'esclusa* has also been compared to Ibsen's *A Doll's House*. But by their different endings the two works project the new-found consciousness of their respective female protagonists against two different socio-psychological configurations: Nora seeks self-realization in the world outside the home, Marta is reunited with her husband at his mother's death-bed. Finally, as has already been suggested with reference to the 'curse' that weighs on the Pentàgoras, the theme of heredity itself, from whose iron-clad laws there is no escape in the fictional universe of a Zola for example, is almost turned into a laughing matter in *L'esclusa* were it not that 'honour' plays such an important role among the appearances that must be saved in its Sicilian setting.

In 1908 when Pirandello reissued *L'esclusa* in book form, he prefixed it with a letter of dedication to Capuana in which he wondered whether the original appearance of the novel as a serial had permitted readers to recognize its novelty, the 'parte scrupolosamente nascosta sotto la rappresentazione affatto oggettiva dei casi e delle persone' [part scrupulously hidden under the completely objective representation of characters and events]. This 'hidden' part he called 'humorist', thus referring to the concept that must have been uppermost in his mind in the year of *L'umorismo*. From that point of view, 'le umili e minute rappresentazioni, che occorrono frequenti nel mio romanzo' [the humble, minute representations that are so frequent in my novel], that is, its naturalistic or veristic component, were something to be apologized for. And, indeed, Pirandello apologizes for them, in a rather contorted way it must be recognized, by contrasting the apparent chaos of nature with the intentionally controlled and co-ordinated world reflected in a work of art. In the Preface to *Sei personaggi* (1925) the rejection of *verismo* will be stated with greater self-confidence when he distinguishes between historical and philosophical writers, between those who are satisfied with telling a story for the simple pleasure of telling it and those others who have a deeper spiritual need and consider figures, events, and landscapes only if they are imbued 'd'un particolar senso della vita' [with a particular sense of life] which gives them universal value. It might, of course, be argued that there is no storytelling which is not set in an ideological framework and that nineteenth-century realism for all its striving after objectivity and impersonality was just as determined by 'a particular sense of life' as Pirandello's humoristic view was. But that is not the point at issue here. Like his retrospective estimate in the speech on Verga of his own position vis-à-vis the writers who dominated Italian literature when he first became active in it, so his comments on L'esclusa show Pirandello's need and will to define the individuality and the novelty of his art.

Still another insight into Pirandello's intentions in his early narrative is afforded by the introduction he wrote in 1915 for a reissue of Il turno. The work, which had originally appeared as a novel, was linked in this new edition with the short story Lontano (written in 1901), the two forming a diptych with the subtitle Novelle di Luigi Pirandello. Their principal merit, Pirandello wrote in the introduction, was 'la schietta vivacità della rappresentazione, al tutto aliena d'ogni intenzione letteraria' [the simple liveliness of the representation, completely independent of any literary intention] and he prophesied longer life for them than for other more mature and ambitious works of his. The prophecy has proved wrong but the fact of joint publication, the linking of what had been thought of as a romanzo with a novella – both now (in the introduction) designated as racconti – invites a closer look at what to judge by the evidence must have been a recurrent practical problem for Pirandello: the choice of genre designation for his works.

That the problem of genre has never been faced squarely in Pirandello criticism does not mean that it does not exist but rather that the twentieth century inherited the Romantic distrust of types and norms and that Italian criticism for a long time preferred analytic techniques that viewed works as the unique expressions of unique talents. But considerations having to do with 'form' in its various ramifications and connotations are pervasive in Pirandello's thinking and are extended when the occasion arises to questions of genre designation. Thus, for instance, in the Preface to Sei personaggi, where they are no more than an undercurrent in Pirandello's detailed recounting of the genesis of that work, they come to the surface beautifully, as we shall see, in the distinction he makes between the dramma and the commedia that together go to make up that play. Traces of awareness of the significance of genre designation are also apparent in early editions of his plays where in addition to the term most frequently used, *commedia* (the Italian equivalent catch-all for the English 'play'), a whole gamut is run from *tragedia* (reserved for *Enrico IV*, *La vita che ti diedi*, and *Diana e la Tuda*) to *dramma* (used for *Questa sera si recita a soggetto* and for *Non si sa come*), *mito* (*La nuova colonia* and *Lazzaro*), *apologo* (*L'uomo la bestia e la virtù*), *parabola* (*Cosí è* [*se vi pare*]), *mistero profano* (*All'uscita*), *epilogo* (*La morsa*), *dialogo* (*L'uomo dal fiore in bocca*), *rappresentazione* (*Quando si è qualcuno*), and the laconic *tre atti* of *Trovarsi*.

While there seems to be no record of Pirandello's thinking with regard to these distinctions in the area of drama, we have for narrative literature the short piece, *Romanzo, racconto, novella*, which he published in 1897 and which like *Arte e coscienza d'oggi* he did not include in his later collection of essays, *Arte e scienza*. By 1897 Pirandello had written both *L'esclusa* and *Il turno*, and had written and published a number of short stories. Some direct experience with the narrative genres may therefore be assumed to have contributed to the interests expressed in this article. But *Romanzo, racconto, novella* also reflects, as Gösta Andersson has pointed out, Pirandello's concern with the old and ever renewed *questione della lingua*. Indeed Pirandello gives as the reason for attempting to distinguish between the various types of narrative prose, his desire to contribute to the establishing of a unified Italian language in which there might be some firmer correspondence between the signifier and the signified than at present, to 'fermare questo immenso ondeggiamento della forma, del significato della parola, del valore delle espressioni' [to hold fast this great fluctuation in the shape, in the meaning of words, in the significance of expressions], which constitutes a veritable stumbling block for Italian writers, 'cosí digiuni, come spesso sono, della disciplina filologica' [so ignorant, as they often are, of the discipline of philology]. What he means by fluctuation in the meaning of words is self-evident; what he means by fluctuation in the shape of words may be less so. But to understand exactly what the neophyte philologist has in mind here it is enough to turn to another article of his, *Per la solita quistione della lingua* (1890), where he points out that Tuscan recognizes only the first of the two diphthongs (*ie*, *uo*) of written Italian (Tuscans insist on *novo* rather than the normal Italian *nuovo*, for instance); or to remember how firmly he defended the use of the semi-vowel *j* in words like *gioia* or *noia*; or, for that matter, to think of the exasperating alternative use of acute and grave accents in the different editions of his own works prepared in accordance with different house styles (*così* as against *cosí*).

As far as the meaning of the three words, *romanzo*, *racconto*, *novella*, is concerned, Pirandello defines the *novella* as the genre that deals with its subject 'synthetically', concentrating on the salient and the culminating events; the novel (*romanzo*) as the genre that gives a full, 'analytical' exposition of its subject in all its particulars and developments; and the *racconto* as either a *romanzo* or *novella* in which the story is told 'descriptively' rather than being 'represented' or *mossa in azione* [put into action], told either by the author or by one of the characters speaking in the first person. All three definitions are interesting although the third one with its emphasis on 'point of view' and on the distinction between 'telling' and 'showing' is in the light of Pirandello's own development as a writer the most suggestive. It is worth noting that Pirandello, contrary to the usual practice in distinguishing between these terms, gives no importance to length. This may well be the result of the source he is using: Niccolò Tommaseo, too, in defining a whole cluster of words grouped under *storia* (story) in both his *Nuovo dizionario dei sinonimi della lingua italiana* and his *Dizionario estetico*, is interested in more sophisticated conceptualizations than an essentially extrinsic consideration such as length would be.

With respect to the terms *racconto* and *novella*, it is well known that, as Elio Pagliarani and Walter Pedullà write in the introduction to their anthology, *I maestri del racconto italiano* (1964), the *racconto* is the genre typical of Italian prose narrative in the twentieth century while *novella* is an earlier genre, now fallen into disuse. In the perspective of the history of Italian literature Pirandello's total work represents the most radical break with naturalism and his *Novelle per un anno* the most ambitious corpus of short stories written in modern times. It may thus seem paradoxical that he should have chosen as a label for them the term most closely associated, by way of Verga's *novelle*, with naturalism. One of the reasons for this may just simply have been the force of tradition, reliance on the word most frequently used for short fiction and most firmly established. We find the clue to what may have been another reason in the 1897 article we have been considering when Pirandello links the *novella* and classical tragedy. Following in the footsteps of Tommaseo, he points out that the two genres 'condense' actions and feelings that in the natural course of events may have occurred at different and distant moments; and echoing both what Verga had said in the preface to *L'amante di Gramigna* apropos the necessary connection between the point of departure and the point of arrival of a story and what he himself will say when he defines his first one-act plays as epilogues, he emphasizes the import-ance of the concluding action in both *novella* and classical tragedy: 'La novella e la tragedia classica invece [in contrast to the novel] pigliano il fatto, a dir cosí, per la coda: e di questa estremità si contentano: intese a dipingerci non le origini, non i gradi della passione, non le relazioni di quella con i molti oggetti che circondano l'uomo, e servono a sospingerla, a ripercoterla, ad informarla in mille modi diversi, ma solo gli ultimi passi, l'eccesso insomma' [The *novella* and classical tragedy instead take the action as it were by the tail, and are satisfied with this extremity, intent on portraying not the origins, not the stages of the passion recounted, not the relationships between it and the many objects that surround men and serve to impel it, to augment, to shape it in many different ways, but only the last steps, the extreme in brief].

It is always a temptation for the critic to measure a writer's works against his poetics, against his theoretical statements of intent and technique. In this case the distinctions just referred to would seem to offer an excellent guide to an examination of Pirandello's early Sicilian narratives from a formalistic rather than thematic point of view. But when we try to apply Pirandello's definitions of *romanzo* and *novella* to *L'esclusa*, *Il turno* and *Lontano*, we quickly come to the same conclusion that Terracini reached when (with reference not to *Romanzo, racconto, novella* but to the 1906 article *Soggettivismo e ogget-tivismo nell'arte moderna*) he noted that the relationship between novels and short stories is not as clear and simple as Pirandello's distinction between 'the vast and complex' narrative form of the novel and 'the brief and synthetic' form of the *novella* would seem to imply. *Lontano* is no more 'brief and synthetic' than *L'esclusa* and *Il turno* – nor, for that matter, are *Il 'fumo'* (1901?), *Il vitalizio* (1901), or to a lesser extent *Scialle nero* (1900?), all medium-length Sicilian stories which for the convenience of discussion we can here group together.

Like *L'esclusa* and *Il turno* these four stories are set in Agrigento, Porto Empedocle and environs, though unlike the novels the point of view from which they are told is more frequently rural than urban. This is true even for *Scialle nero*, whose protagonist, a *signorina* first and then a *signora*, is subjected to the harsh laws of social decorum imposed by her lawyer-brother, which exile her from Agrigento and force her into a most unsuitable marriage with the brutish son of the tenant farmer of their land. And it is also true for *Lontano*, whose action is dominated and indeed determined by the life of the bustling seaport of Porto Empedocle and in which the country appears only obliquely as the setting for the honeymoon of the Sicilian girl Vene-rina and her sailor-husband, the Norwegian Lars Cleen. *Il vitalizio* and *Il 'fumo'* are more exclusively rural, although in both the life of the farmer is counterbalanced by another kind of life inimical to it: in the first, old age compels Maràbito to sell his farm for an annuity and to move to an oppressive, over-populated suburb of Agrigento; in the second, speculation turns fertile groves of citrus trees into arid slopes covered with the fumes of the sulphur mines. Although Lars Cleen from his outsider's viewpoint is horrified by the inhuman living con-ditions of the Sicilian farmer, Pirandello's Sicilians are more likely to see the pastoral and idyllic side of country-life: the eccentric Don Filippino Lo Cicero of *Il 'fumo'* is actually represented in aesthetic ecstasy over the verses of the *Georgics* and *Bucolics* which he is shown reading in his refuge on the as yet inviolate hillside.

Like the novels and unlike Pirandello's shorter, anecdotal type novellas, the four stories are teeming with characters, including 'choral' figures such as the delightful *comari* who in *Il vitalizio* surround the long-lived Maràbito with endless solicitude and life-affirming enthusiasm. They foreshadow similar background figures whom we will find with the same function in rural plays such as *Liolà* and *La giara*, and are quite different from their counterparts in the essentially psychological and tragic, middle-class, regional world *à la* Capuana of *Scialle nero*. Related to the choral figures are the many *macchiette* ['characters', in the sense of strange types] that abound in the short stories as in the novels. In *Lontano*, for instance, the old maid, donna Rosolina, is produced by the same matrix which gave shape to signora Popònica in *L'esclusa*: the 'embrace of the empty sleeves' in the novel being paralleled by the eyes that had pleaded for love from don Pietro, 'ma questi, Pietro di nome, pietra di fatto', Pirandello comments with a play on words that is impossible to translate but which means that don Pietro's heart was made of stone. To the choral figures and the *macchiette*, we can add the portraits – such as that of don Mattia Scala in *Il 'fumo'* or of the inseparable friends Bandi and D'Andrea in *Scialle nero* – executed with the same rapid meticulousness and the same accentuation on the inharmonious and distorted that have been remarked in conjunction with *L'esclusa* and *Il turno*.

Like the novels, the four stories are also rich in factual, documentary details worked into the narrative. Passage after passage seems to illus-trate that ability to 'construct' with 'objects' rather than words that

Pirandello recognized in Verga. This is evident in the frequent and characteristic passages dealing with the sulphur trade in *Il 'fumo'* and *Lontano*, repetitions and variations of which can be found in other stories of this same period: in *Il 'no' di Anna* (1895), for instance, which opens with a view of the plain between Agrigento and Porto Empedocle and includes a complete, tight, factual description of the loading of the sulphur on the merchant vessels anchored in the port; or in *La maestrina Boccarmè* (1899) which generalizes the description into the activity of 'un paesello di mare del Mezzogiorno' [a small seaside town of the South] in which the outlines of Porto Empedocle remain, however, clearly discernible. And the same attention to 'objects', the same narrative concreteness is evident in truly exemplary fashion in this passage from *Il vitalizio* in which Maràbito's forty years of farming are concentrated completely in the representation of the activity of his hands: 'E, lavorando, lui non aveva mai pensato a niente: concentrato tutto nelle sue mani e nelle cose ch'esse adoperavano per il lavoro da compiere. Per piú di quarant'anni, in quell'appezzamento comperato col denaro ch'era riuscito a raggruzzolare laggiú, tra lui e l'albero da potare, o la zappa da raffilare, o il fieno da falciare non s'era mai messo nulla di mezzo a frastornarlo, e fuori del filo acciajato e lucente di quella zappa, e il taglio della sua ronca e della sua accetta sul ramo di quell'albero, e il frusciare dell'erba fresca appena stendeva la mano per acciuffarla e l'odore che quel fieno spruzzava reciso dalla sua falce, non aveva né visto né sentito mai altro' (NA, II, 219) [And while working he had never thought of anything else: concentrating completely on the activity of his hands and on the objects his hands used for the work to be done. For over forty years, on that piece of land he had bought with the money he had succeeded in scraping together down there [i.e., in South America], nothing had ever interfered, nothing had ever distracted him from the tree to be pruned, the hoe to be whetted, the hay to be mowed; and except for the shining steel-edged blade of that hoe, and the cutting of his pruning hook and his hatchet on the branch of that tree, and the rustling of the new grass when he stretched out his hand to seize it, and the fragrance that rose from that hay cut off by the scythe, he had never seen or heard anything else].

As in the novels so in the stories – and, incidentally, in the static, lyric world of *I Malavoglia* as well – the span of *erzählte Zeit* (time told, i.e., the chronological limits covered in the story) is considerable, even if we exclude from it flashbacks and antecedent action. In *Il vitalizio*, for instance, Maràbito is in his seventies at the beginning when, unable to continue to cultivate his land, he sells it, and he is 105 at the end when, having outlived two of his 'successors', he is back on it with his 'adopted' grandchildren. One of the traditional devices for synchronizing *erzählte Zeit* with *erzählende Zeit* (the time it takes to *tell* the story) is division into chapters, and it is interesting to note that like the novels these four stories, ranging in length from twenty-eight to forty-two pages, are so divided. (The fact that *Il vitalizio* has no typographically indicated divisions is probably to be attributed to the circumstance that it was not originally included in the collection in which the other two appeared, *Bianche e nere*, 1904, and in which they were 'broken up' in this manner.)

Finally, like the novels these stories start not only *in medias res* but dramatically: *Scialle nero* and *Lontano* with 'spoken action' like *Il turno*; *Il vitalizio* very much like *L'esclusa* with a 'scene'; and even the frankly descriptive opening of *Il 'fumo'* is animated and full of movement not only because it is a description of activities seen in their single and cumulative actions but also because of the intrusion of an occasional spoken comment. In none of these stories do we have a non-dramatic opening paragraph such as that of *La maestrina Boccarmè*, in which in typically narrative fashion the author expresses his view of the story directly, though here through the agency of a metaphor.

Pirandello's prose fiction, both long and short, deserves much greater attention than it can receive in this present introductory study. His place in the history of the modern Italian novel is probably assured, if for no other reason than the inclusion of a 100-page analysis of *Il fu Mattia Pascal* in Giacomo Debenedetti's *Il romanzo del Novecento* (Milan 1971). The situation of his short fiction is different. Short fiction in itself has been a step-child for the literary critic and theoretician. Pirandello's short stories, though greatly admired by some critics who place them even above his plays as successful works of art, have been by and large neglected. The usual approach has been thematic, with special emphasis on the transformation of short story into play within a framing view of the progressive abandoning of narrative for drama in his total *œuvre*. Though not always stated explicitly, there has been an underlying assumption that the stories exist for the plays, that they are a kind of *zibaldone* which provided Pirandello with material when he needed it. In addition, most critics have divided Pirandello's production into novels, short stories, and drama as a matter of convenience for breaking down his vast output for discussion, *not* because they felt that different genres may require different tools for analysis. Renato Barilli is perhaps the only one who effectively abandoned the chronological approach when he made a case for the synchronic study of the short stories in the chapter 'Le novelle di Pirandello' in his *La barriera del naturalismo* (Milan 1964). Of course, there are difficulties involved in thinking of 273 separate works (such is the number of Pirandello's short stories according to the latest, 1969, edition of *Novelle per un anno*) coexisting as one whole which can be subjected to discussion and analysis. This may explain why Jørn Moestrup, whose *The Structural Patterns of Pirandello's Work* (Odense 1972) discusses more single short stories than does any other work on Pirandello, was unable to break loose from the diachronic model and ended up by dividing the stories into chronological units which he then presented together with the other production of any given period. In our own remarks on Pirandello's beginnings as a narrative writer we have tried to suggest that attention to techniques rather than themes may be the most fruitful approach to this area of his work, even beyond the chronological limits of 'beginnings'.

Pirandello's early theatrical works are, like the novels and short stories we have been considering, connected to his Sicilian background. As a matter of fact, it is usual to consider Pirandello's Sicilian period as drawing to an end around 1917 when the success of *Cosí è (se vi pare)*, bourgeois drama turned *grottesco*, inaugurated a new direction in his writing. As all periodization, this too is not completely satisfactory. Not everything Pirandello wrote before this date can be considered Sicilian and he did not lose all interest in things Sicilian after it. But what creates the impression that something radical has taken place is that in the matter of the few years between 1910 and 1917 he had turned from being a predominantly narrative writer to a playwright and that this shift had occurred in close connection with the Sicilian dialect theatre which in the early years of the century enjoyed remarkable success in the urban centres of continental Italy. There was thus a second period for Pirandello – not unrelated to the first, of course, given the continued presence of many of the same persons among his circle of friends in Rome – of close association with Sicilian artists. Just as Pirandello's narrative began under the star of Sicilian regionalism and *verismo*, so his theatre began (excepting some youthful, abortive efforts) with the lessons learned from actors, playwrights, and impresarios who had themselves more often than not learned their trade in acting companies similar to those portrayed in Verga's *Don Candeloro e C.i* or (to use what is probably a more familiar reference though not altogether appropriate in regional terms here)

in Leoncavallo's *Pagliacci*. What is different between the two moments
– and it is no mean difference – is Pirandello's actual use of dialect in
connection with Sicilian subjects in his theatre: what had been the
object of philological studies in his Bonn years thus becomes the
instrument of expression for his *dramatis personae*. Pirandello's protagonists on stage – with the exception of the only-in-retrospect significant performances of 1910–15 (*La morsa, Lumíe di Sicilia, Il dovere
del medico, Se non cosí...*) – begin by speaking dialect.

While Pirandello made only one start as a narrative writer, it might
be said that he made two as a playwright. The first was a false one, the
second the good one. The former is related to the period between 1886
and 1896 and is literary in origin. Of most of the plays that belong to
that period only the title survives: *Gli uccelli dell'alto, Fatti che or son
parole, Gente allegra, Le popolane, Provando la commedia, La signorina,
L'elemosina, Schiavi, La moglie fedele, Armeggiamenti* – titles that invite
conjectures about content and point of view. Only three of that early
crop of plays had a subsequent theatrical history and have come down
to us: *La morsa* (known as *L'epilogo* at the time), *Se non cosí...*, and
Scamandro. As late as 1912, when Pirandello submitted *Il dovere del
medico* to the drama critic Edoardo Boutet, he was still thinking of
drama in literary terms, as a text, that is, which must find actors and a
director to interpret it. His new one-act play, he wrote, is related to
his earlier one (*La morsa*) because both are 'epilogues'. Both 'take the
action by the tail' (as he had put it in *Romanzo, racconto, novella*) and
correspond to Verga's *desideratum* that in a story the point of departure
and the point of arrival should be implicitly present one in the other.
Pirandello explained to Boutet that he thought it unnecessary to
represent the story's 'truce dramma improvviso' [sudden cruel
drama] (the scene in which Tommaso, discovered with Angelica Neri
by her husband, kills him) because 'appar chiaro nell'anima dei personaggi e nella situazione *nuova* che esso determina' [it appears clearly
in the state of mind of the characters and in the new situation that it
determines]. In addition, the situation involves 'un altissimo problema di coscienza' [a deep ethical problem]. Vocabulary and point of
view are those of the literary critic and not of the drama reviewer.

Pirandello's second start as a playwright occurred independently of
the first: for almost two decades after 1896 there is hardly any hint
that he might have been interested in the theatre. It is true that he was
in the audience at the première of D'Annunzio's *Francesca da Rimini* at
the Teatro Costanzi in Rome in 1901 (a performance of which he was
to write later that he had never again 'suffered' as much in a theatre as

at that time). But, in the years bridging the centuries, like the writers interviewed by Ojetti, he expressed nothing but disdain for 'l'arte della scopa'. Giudice tells of the threat of a duel over the rejection of *La morsa* by a theatrical company to whom it had been recommended, and sees this episode as contributing still further to Pirandello's sour view of the theatre. In any case, after his father's mine disaster and his wife's illness his energies were for a number of years concentrated on making an academic reputation for himself and on rounding out his meagre salary with earnings from literary journalism. There was little room for experimentation with a new genre.

Pirandello's major dramatic works all flow from his second start as a playwright. In the light of that development whatever preceded it is only of archaeological interest. The second start was theatrical not literary in origin: stage and actor exist prior to the play and the text comes into being only by virtue of its performance. How different the second start was from the first can be seen from the way in which a play belonging to the early 1886–96 period was reinterpreted by Pirandello himself at the beginning of the second. The play is *Se non così...*, originally probably written in 1899 and later known as *La ragione degli altri*. In 1915 it failed utterly at its première. Two years later Pirandello wrote a preface for it when it was issued in book form. The preface takes the form of a letter written by the author (Pirandello) to the true protagonist of his play, Livia Arciani, the sterile wife of Leonardo (who has had a child by another woman). Fictional and real words mesh in the device of the letter-preface (not to be confused with a straightforward letter-preface such as Verga's in *L'amante di Gramigna*) as they will mesh time and again in the later plays of the trilogy of the theatre-within-the-theatre. In the preface Pirandello (the author) states his intention categorically: Livia is the protagonist because everything that happens in the course of the three acts stems from her, from her particular – distinctive, different, and original – way of thinking and feeling. She is exceptional; those around her conventional. When the play was staged, however, Irma Gramatica, the company's leading actess, had chosen the role of the other woman, Elena, for herself. Thus Gramatica had opted for the conventional interpretation of the figure of mistress as social outcast and consequently (especially when the mistress is also an unwed mother) the focus of audience sympathy. Obviously Gramatica's and Pirandello's views of who is the play's protagonist could not simultaneously occupy the same stage – no more than actors and characters can occupy the same stage in *Sei personaggi* or the bat and the actors

appear on the same stage in the short story *Il pipistrello* (1920). Pirandello attributes Gramatica's erroneous choice of role to Livia's inability to create 'una scena capitale' for herself; her emotion never
overflows into a highly dramatic bravura scene because it is not in her
nature (as character-person) to express herself thus. Elena, on the
other hand, has 'una bella parte facile e di sicuro effetto' [an excellent
role, easy and strikingly effective]. It is not our concern here to determine what the causes for the play's failure actually were. But it is
important to note Pirandello's new-found acquaintance with the
ways of the theatre.

Pirandello's shift from narrative writer to playwright occurred in
close connection with the Sicilian dialect theatre. It will be our purpose now to analyse what effect this connection had, and to justify the
contention that failure to understand his Sicilian plays properly
obscures the most important link – more important even than
L'umorismo – in the history of his development.

'Who are they? Where did they come from? How did they become
such vigorous and original artists?' With these words the drama critic
of the Rome daily *La Tribuna* on 3 December 1902 opened his review
of an unusual theatrical experience that had taken place at the Teatro
Argentina. The occasion was a benefit performance for the flood victims of the town of Modica in southern Sicily. Giovanni Grasso
(1873–1930) and Marinella Bragaglia (1882–1918), members of two
well-known Sicilian families of actors, staged a double bill: *Cavalleria
rusticana* and *I mafiusi*, the latter replaced on the second evening by *La
zolfara*. *I mafiusi* and *La zolfara* have recently become available to the
general public through their inclusion in Alfredo Barbina's anthology, *Teatro verista siciliano* (Bologna 1970). They can help us to
define the kinds of plays in the repertoire of Sicilian acting companies
at the turn of the century. *I mafiusi*, recognized as the earliest work of
Sicilian *verismo* in the theatre, is the work of two itinerant Sicilian
actors, Gaspare Mosca (b.1825) and Giuseppe Rizzotto (1828–95).
Based on the true-life experiences of prison inmates at the Carcere
della Vicaria in Palermo, it was first performed in Palermo in 1863,
and thus belongs to the first generation of the tradition with which we
are dealing. It is an episodic, confusing and difficult-to-follow play
even in the Italian version which was first published in 1885. *La zolfara*, on the other hand, the work of Giuseppe Giusti Sinopoli (1886–
1923), is a conventionally constructed three-act drama concerned
with that recurrent subject of late nineteenth-century Sicilian litera-

ture: conditions of life in the sulphur mines. First performed in Messina in 1895, it is built around the conflict of interests between mine owners and managers on one side and workers – *picconieri* and *carusi* – on the other, and is reminiscent in its sympathies and indignations of other similar works by socially conscious naturalistic writers, such as for example the German dramatist Gerhart Hauptmann (1862–1946). It belongs to the second generation of modern Sicilian dialect drama.

What impressed *La Tribuna*'s reviewer most about the performances of Giovanni Grasso and Marinella Bragaglia were the company's 'human sense for drama' and its 'disdain for theatrical make-believe'; the fact that, in its natural dialect, *Cavalleria rusticana* appeared more 'rapid and concise', with 'flashes of fire that strike the spectator'; and the carefully orchestrated scenic action of *La zolfara*, 'thought out in every movement, in every detail, reproducing the intense thrust of every passion as it reveals itself in different temperaments'. As for the actors, the reviewer commented upon Marinella Bragaglia's Santuzza, 'an unusual Santuzza, devoid of all artifices', and on the 'forcefulness and originality of Grasso', whom he defined 'a dramatic temperament that entrusts itself to nature alone'. Naturalness, passion, authenticity – these traits appear as well in Capuana's remarks, which can be usefully quoted here, apropos two interpretations of the role of Santuzza, one by the great Eleonora Duse, the other by an unidentified Sicilian actress. In the preface to his *Teatro dialettale siciliano* (1911) we read: 'I remember two performances of *Cavalleria rusticana*....In the one Eleonora Duse played the role of Santuzza.... It was in the now distant days when she triumphed by dint of her youth and the power of her art. In the other the role was played by a poor, provincial actress wandering with her company of four or five strolling players (*guitti*) from one inland town to the other....To my Sicilian eyes Santuzza-Duse appeared as a kind of falsification of Verga's passionate figure in her gestures, the expression of her voice, her dress (an unbelievable medley of Lombard and Roman costumes!), in spite of the passionate response which only Duse could elicit. The poor, regional actress, instead, her clothes borrowed from the peasant women of the town she was passing through – shoes, earrings, skirt, the blue cloth cloak – became a real, live "Santuzza", as there may have been one among her audience.'

Two one-act plays, *La morsa* and *Lumíe di Sicilia*, performed on a double-bill, 9 December 1910, mark Pirandello's debut as a dramatist.

La morsa probably goes back to at least 1892, but *Lumíe di Sicilia* was expressly written for the occasion or, more precisely, was adapted for the stage from the short story of the same title (1900). The plays were staged by Nino Martoglio (1870–1921), poet, journalist, dramatist, director, a close friend of Pirandello, co-author with him of '*A vilanza* (*La bilancia*, 1917) and *Cappiddazzu paga tutto* (*Cappellaccio paga tutto*, 1917) and co-author with him and Musco of the enormously success-ful *L'aria del continente* (1915; published under Martoglio's name alone). In the obituary written on his tragic death (SPSV, 2nd ed., 1083–5), Pirandello compared the importance of Martoglio for Sicily to that of Di Giacomo and Russo for Naples, Pascarella and Trilussa for Rome, Fucini for Tuscany, and Selvatico and Barbarani for Venetia, thus, incidentally, providing a capsule survey of the most important regional, dialect writers of the period. But in spite of their being 'Sicilian' in subject matter and their being staged by a Sicilian impresario intent on giving Sicilian regionalism national diffusion and exposure, at their first performance *La morsa* and *Lumíe di Sicilia* were in Italian. As a matter of fact, in an article published in 1909, *Teatro siciliano?*, Pirandello expressed scepticism with regard to the viability of Martoglio's ideals and rejected the contemporary Sicilian dialect theatre as it was being represented by Giovanni Grasso and Mimí Aguglia (b. 1884): 'la terribile, meravigliosa bestialità' of Giovanni Grasso repelled him, and the Sicily that Grasso typified was for him unauthentic and manufactured for 'foreign' consumption.

The Sicilian actor who took credit for breaking through Piran-dello's resistance to the stage and literally 'forced' a play out of him was Angelo Musco (1872–1937), Grasso's almost precise contem-porary. The play was *Pensaci, Giacomino!* (1916), no *novella sceneggiata* (dramatized short story) this time but a work written directly for the stage, written with a specific actor in mind, and written moreover in Sicilian. The year before, in Catania, Musco had acted in a Sicilian version of *Lumíe di Sicilia*, but that play had not been written for him. Born in Catania, cradle of the Sicilian veristic theatre, Musco had begun his career as an actor by being a 'voice', the voice of the *pupi* of the regional marionette theatre. By 1915 he had his own company and was developing a repertoire which included Fausto Maria Martini's *Ridi, pagliaccio!*, Capuana's '*U paraninfu*, Martoglio's *San Giovanni decollato*, Bracco's *Sperduti nel buio*, Giacinto Gallina's *Me figghia*, *L'aria del continente*, and a number of Pirandello's plays. In the strict distribution of parts which typified acting companies such as his, Musco was cast as the *brillante* (Pirandello's 'raisonneur') and not as the *primo attore*.

What kind of performer was Musco? What was it that convinced Pirandello to entrust a number of his works to him, while, according to Giudice, he had at first felt alienated by that insistent, gesticulating, rumbustious individual who had invaded his study? 'He is irresistible', wrote the drama critic, Renato Simoni. 'He possesses the secret, which few have, of causing laughter.... He is all instinct, with his fiery eyes, his sun-burnt face, his devilish mischief, as colourful as an ancient mask.' 'Most of the time he doesn't even have to say a word', wrote another critic, Eugenio Cecchi. 'His legs speak for him...his shoulders ...the folds of his suit...the brim of his hat.' E. Gordon Craig called him simply 'the greatest actor in the world'. André Antoine said that he had never seen on any stage such an overflowing of sheer comic energy. Writing from a wider perspective, Silvio D'Amico, day-to-day reviewer but also drama critic and historian, noted shortcomings as well: 'His fatal insubordination, his congenital infidelity to the text, his physical need to betray it and remake it, improvising evening after evening, never allowed him to become what is called an "interpreter"'. Never allowed him, that is, to subordinate his personality to that of the play's author. In other words, Musco was a great actor in the sense that members of a *commedia dell'arte* troupe are great actors, best suited to working under the conditions of maximum freedom offered by a *scenario* rather than a *script*. He was the character, in a way similar to the Father's being a character when he brings his lived, unwritten story to a company of actors (*Sei personaggi*) or to the actors' wanting *to be* (and not to play) their parts in *Questa sera si recita a soggetto*.

It may seem strange that Pirandello, who became so punctilious, so intransigent about the performances of his plays that he did not rest until he had formed his own company and built his own theatre so that they could be performed as he desired them to be – or, as he might have put it, as they desired themselves to be – should ever have accepted a 'collaborator' as unreliable, as undisciplined and independent as Musco. Many amusing and revealing anecdotes are told about their association. One concerns the dress rehearsal of *Liolà*: Pirandello, outraged that the actors had not yet learned their parts, walked off with the script and called off the performance. Musco ran after him: 'Professore! è inutile che si porti il copione. Stasera lo recitiamo a soggetto' [Professor (the title by which Pirandello was known professionally), it's useless for you to take the script away. Tonight we'll improvise the play]. And after the successful première that night,

Musco explained further that he and his actors were like race horses trained to set off only if they hear the starter's gun: without the sounds of the gathering audience, without the house lights, they are unable to perform. The fact of the matter is that there was compatibility between Pirandello and Musco – a compatibility Pirandello recognized when he *wrote* plays for Musco while he only *adapted* them for Grasso.

The letter which he wrote to Martoglio in 1917 concerning Grasso's objections to *Il berretto a sonagli* bears quoting at some length. Grasso had made some observations about what appeared to him the unmanageable length and involvement of Ciampa's lines and complained about having to 'stand by' while others were reciting *their* lines: 'Le osservazioni di Grasso, se possono aver qualche valore, riguardo al suo temperamento artistico, a cui senza dubbio si confanno più gli atti che le parole, mi pare che non ne abbiano nessuno, riguardo al lavoro stesso, come opera d'arte. Non mi pare affatto che ci siano lungaggini. L'azione e i discorsi degli altri personaggi son tutti necessari, come quelli del protagonista. La commedia, certamente, è scritta per Musco, e capisco che Grasso debba trovarsi a disagio in una parte che invece calza a pennello al Musco. Io l'ho già detto che *non sento* affatto il Grasso: il suo temperamento non m'ispira, è per me troppo primitivo e bestiale; mentre la mia arte è riflessiva. Non potrei perciò adattarmi a scrivere per lui, né adattare la mia commedia alle esigenze del suo temperamento. È inutile dunque che mi rimandi il copione. Se vuol farla, la commedia è così e resterà così. Potrei soltanto far quei tagli o, se mai, quelle modifiche, che tu alle prove con Musco stimassi necessarie e per le quali ti ho dato ampia autorizzazione. Queste sì, perché risulterebbero come volute dall'opera d'arte stessa messa alla prova della sua propria vita; mentre le modifiche e i tagli che vorrebbe il Grasso, sarebbero imposti, non dall'opera d'arte, ma dal suo speciale temperamento, ch'io stimo antitetico alla mia concezione artistica. Per Grasso starà benissimo "La morsa" che ti manderò tra giorni' [While Grasso's observations may have some validity with respect to his own artistic temperament, to which actions are no doubt better suited than words, they have no validity, it seems to me, with respect to the play itself as a work of art. I don't at all think that there are passages that drag. The actions and the lines of the other characters are just as necessary as those of the protagonist. Doubtless, the play was written for Musco, and I can well understand that Grasso should feel ill at ease in a part which instead suits Musco to perfection. I've already said that I don't at all 'feel' Grasso. His temperament doesn't inspire me: it is too primitive and bestial for me, while my art is reflective. Therefore I could not adjust to writing for him, nor adapt my play to the exigencies of his temperament. So it is useless to send back the script. If he wants to do the play, that is how it is and it will remain so. I could only agree to those cuts or, possibly, changes that you and Musco would think necessary when rehearsing the play and for which I have given you full authorization. Those changes yes, for they would be as though willed by the work itself when it is tested by its own coming to life. But the changes and cuts that Grasso wants would be imposed not by the work of art but by his own special temperament, which I judge antithetical to my artistic conception. For Grasso, *La morsa* will do very well, which I shall send you in a few days].

Musco, then, was the first actor with whom Pirandello could identify (Ruggero Ruggeri and Marta Abba will be the later two), and because of this affinity he was granted the privilege of becoming a collaborator, a co-author, at the moment of rehearsal and performance. Years later, in 1935, Pirandello was to write an essay on the historical development of the Italian theatre, *Primato del teatro italiano*, in which traces of his early relationship with Musco are still strongly apparent. He speaks with rare eloquence of those *uomini di teatro* who created the *commedia dell'arte*, men who as *actors* felt the pulse of the public and as *authors* had their own ambitions and personal tastes, and who knew how to combine the different charge of energy that came from each of these roles. It was because they were authors not actors, says Pirandello in an inversion of what is usually thought of as the static, 'learned' roles of the *commedia*, that they were able to 'recitare all'improvviso' [to improvise] (but note how the Italian expression captures the unrehearsed immediacy of the 'suddenly'). And almost as though he were speaking of his own turning from narrative to drama, he added: 'La Commedia dell'arte nasce…da autori che s'accostano tanto al teatro, alla vita del teatro, da divenire attori essi stessi, e cominciano con lo scrivere commedie subito piú teatrali perché non composte nella solitudine d'uno scrittojo di letterato ma già quasi davanti al caldo fiato del pubblico' [The *commedia dell'arte* comes into being…through authors who draw so close to the theatre, to the life of the theatre, as to become actors themselves. And they begin by writing plays that are at once more theatrical because they are not composed in the solitude of a writer's study but almost in front of the warm breath of the audience].

In a total about face from the position of the theatrical reformers of the eighteenth century who denigrated the *commedia dell'arte*, Pirandello has here given new dignity to the actor; the actor who is able to improvise is an author, that is, a creative artist, and not an 'illustratore necessario' [necessary illustrator] as he had called him in the 1908 essay, *Illustratori, attori e traduttori*, or a 'traduttore' as he dubbed him without more ado in *Teatro in dialetto?* Musco, of course, as we have seen, was both actor and author. And Pirandello himself, though not technically an actor, certainly became a consummate *uomo di teatro*, one whose extraordinary interpretational gifts were remarked upon by all those fortunate enough to have been present at his reading of his plays or at rehearsals.

In addition to *Pensaci, Giacomino!*, Pirandello wrote *Liolà* (1916), *'A birritta cu' i ciancianeddi* (1916, *Il berretto a sonagli*), and *'A giarra* (1917, *La giara*) for Musco. He also translated his *La morsa*, *La patente* (1918), and *Tutto per bene* (1920, *Ccu' i 'nguanti gialli*) into Sicilian, but the premières of these plays were not performed by Musco, although they later (with the exception of *La morsa?*) entered his repertoire. We have already mentioned the two Sicilian plays Pirandello wrote for Martoglio. For Martoglio's Compagnia del Teatro Mediterraneo he translated Euripides' *Cyclops* (1919), and he also translated Ercole Luigi Morselli's *Glauco*, a mythological tragedy in verse, which was however never performed in translation. All in all, a quite respectable *œuvre* which would have earned him a not insignificant place in the history of the Sicilian dialect theatre had it not been overshadowed by his work in Italian and had the post-World War I years not seen the progressive dissolution of the dialect companies. Limitations of space preclude our discussing the works that exist only in dialect and those written in collaboration. The one-act plays (*La morsa*, *Lumíe di Sicilia*, *Il dovere del medico*, *La giara*, and *La patente*) would deserve their share of attention, but we shall have to be satisfied with referring to them in passing.

Pensaci, Giacomino!, *Liolà*, and *Il berretto a sonagli* are Pirandello's major Sicilian plays. Their protagonists, the mild-mannered but intransigent Professor Toti, the exuberant Liolà, and the hard pressed Ciampa, bear witness to Musco's versatility as an actor and to his liberating rather than constricting force on Pirandello. Pirandello more than once inveighed against the contemporary habit of writing plays with this or that actor already in mind. In *L'azione parlata* (1899) he criticized dramatists who permitted the virtuosities of actors to influence them. In *Illustratori, attori e traduttori* he repeated the criticism almost verbatim, adding that works that come into being under these circumstances are 'opere schiave e non d'arte; perchè l'arte ha bisogno imprescindibile della sua libertà' [enslaved works, not works of art, for art has an indispensable need of its liberty]. In *Teatro in dialetto?* he compares the dramatist who is asked to keep the peculiarities of his interpreters present while composing a play to a poet forced to compose a sonnet with a pre-set rhyme scheme: 'Non lo scrittore deve adattarsi alle qualità dell'esecutore; ma questi a quelle dello scrittore, o meglio, dell'opera a cui deve dar vita sulla scena' (SPSV, 1166) [It is not the writer who must conform to the qualities of the performer, but the latter must adapt himself to the former, or better still, to the work to which he must give life on stage]. Obviously Pirandello's own relationship to Musco did not fall into the category he was criticizing.

Liolà, set in the countryside near Agrigento, is geographically the most precisely located of Pirandello's Sicilian plays. Related to this exceptional precision in setting ('campagna agrigentina') is Pirandello's choice of the particular dialect in which it was written. Not the generalized Sicilian of the contemporary regional theatre (a parallel to the 'Sicilia d'importazione' which shocked him in the plays performed by Grasso and Aguglia) – 'quell'ibrido linguaggio, tra il dialetto e la lingua, che è il cosí detto *dialetto borghese*' [that hybrid language, something between dialect and Italian, that is spoken by the middle class], as he wrote in the preface to the 1917 bilingual edition of *Liolà* – but the 'pure', 'sweet', 'sound-rich' idiom of the peasants of the countryside of Agrigento. This was not only his native language, his mother tongue, but also the language to which he had devoted his doctoral dissertation in Romance Philology at the University of Bonn. Like all radical innovations this one too was hardly appreciated. The fact that *Liolà* was written in an authentic dialect – that its characters came into being speaking not an artificial language, be it literary Italian or *dialetto borghese*, but their *own* language – resulted in only a half-hearted success at the première. Most of the audience sat uncomprehending and only a few responded with laughter. As a matter of fact, it took many years before *Liolà* finally found its place among Pirandello's masterpieces. When it was first given in Italian, its subject matter was judged offensive. The healthy joyousness of the play – a quality Pirandello recognized while he was working on it and described to his son as 'cosí gioconda che non pare opera mia' [so happy that it doesn't seem a work of mine] – was accepted only later when a new image of Sicily displaced the exclusive accent on the Sicily of *verismo*. The Sicily of *Liolà*, Lucio Lugnani wrote recently, is a Sicily without sulphur fumes, without *carusi*, without hunger, without villages emptied by emigration, a Sicily that does not know suspicion and jealousy, a land in which 'the figures of dreams, of fairy-tales, of ancient comedy move dancing'.

The plot of *Liolà* is based on an episode of *Il fu Mattia Pascal*. Liolà, a light-hearted village Don Giovanni, is already the father of three illegitimate children, whose care is entrusted to his mother, while he earns his living as 'garzone, giornante; mieto, poto, falcio fieno; fo di tutto e non mi confondo mai' [farmboy, day-labourer; I reap, prune hedges, gather hay; do a bit of everything and can take anything in my stride]. (The doubling and tripling here is the stylistic equivalent of Liolà's irrepressible optimism.) The play opens at harvest time as zia Croce is overseeing the work being done for her wealthy cousin, old zio Simone, whose desire for a child to whom to leave his *roba* makes him as vulnerable to trickery and fraud as messer Nicia is in *La mandragola* (a play often compared to *Liolà*). Tuzza, zia Croce's daughter, is Liolà's latest conquest, and she is pregnant. Rather than marry Liolà, however, she plots with her mother to pass her child off as zio Simone's and thus ensure that the latter's wealth will stay in the family. The victim of this scheme will be zio Simone's wife, the gentle, childless Mita. But just as in *La mandragola* the young Callimaco shows the virtuous Lucrezia how to turn her husband's foolishness to her advantage, so Liolà – in the play's wonderful Act II – convinces Mita that if she wants justice done she will have to help herself: like Tuzza, she, too, will have to have a child for zio Simone. Things now happen according to plan: through Liolà's agency there will be an apparently legitimate child to take the place of the illegitimate one in zio Simone's household, while Tuzza's child will become the fourth of Liolà's happy *cardellini* [goldfinches], his term of endearment for his brood of illegitimate children.

The parallel episode in *Il fu Mattia Pascal* is told in chapter IV, 'Fu così' [this is how it happened] (...that Mattia was eventually forced to leave home). It precedes immediately the exordium of chapter V, 'La strega non si sapeva dar pace', already discussed with reference to Pirandello's interest in the occult. We shall recount the episode in some detail because Pirandello's allusive and discontinuous narrative manner – so similar in technique and in effect to Verga's in *I Malavoglia* – leaves many readers confused, and because a comparison between episode and play will help to define more clearly the exceptional aspects of *Liolà* in the Pirandello corpus.

Mattia, whose father had died when his sons were infants, leaving them in the care of their loving but ineffectual mother, is enjoying a free and easy existence while Batta Malagna, who is supposed to look after the brothers' property, is blithely digging away at it. 'La talpa! la talpa!' [the mole, the mole!] Mattia's strong-minded aunt exclaims whenever she thinks of him. Like zio Simone before the opening of the play, Batta Malagna had long been married to a woman who bore him no children. Upon her death he marries again, reluctantly but determined to have an heir to whom to leave his ill-gotten wealth. (Zio Simone is stingy but Batta Malagna, in a darkening of the vision, is downright dishonest.) He chooses Oliva, a young, healthy, attractive girl, as virtuous as Mita, whom Mattia himself (like Liolà, Mita) had been courting. Malagna and Oliva do not have a child, and Malagna begins to mistreat her. So far, novel and play follow an almost identical narrative line. But in the novel a second action is developing which will intersect the first. Mattia's best friend, Pomino (there is no counterpart for this character in *Liolà*, Liolà and zio Simone – except for Liolà's three small sons – being the only male characters in its *dramatis personae*), becomes interested in a girl who is the daughter of a cousin of Malagna and discovers that mother and daughter – the *vedova* Pescatore (= zia Croce) and Romilda (= Tuzza) – are trying to entice the old man into an illicit relationship with Romilda. To protect Oliva and to back up Pomino's suit, Mattia intervenes. But Romilda, instead of falling in love with Pomino, falls in love with Mattia, and their 'game' is turned into an affair. Like Liolà, Mattia is ready to marry the girl he has seduced, and like Liolà, he is rejected because mother and daughter have more profitable plans. What follows in novel and play is identical: Malagna, who is expecting to be made a father by Romilda, discovers that Oliva is pregnant as well. Aware that he has been duped and by whom, and moreover being in a position of power over Mattia (something zio Simone is not over Liolà), Malagna forces him to marry Romilda. The family that thus comes into being is doomed to dissension and unhappiness for the *vedova* Pescatore, now mother-in-law ('strega', *par excellence*), will never be able to forgive Mattia his status of impecunious son-in-law.

Because of the customary compartmentalization imposed on Pirandello's works by critics, the relationship between the *Il fu Mattia Pascal* episode and its reworking in *Liolà* has received only scanty, superficial attention. The most striking contrasts have been remarked: that *Liolà* is set in Sicily while *Il fu Mattia Pascal* begins in Liguria, that *Liolà* is a peasant while Mattia is a bourgeois, that the play is 'homogeneous' while the narrative episode is weighed down by moralizing and 'humorizing' (Gramsci). As far back as 1927 Ferdinando Pasini pointed out that *Il fu Mattia Pascal* is only a partial source for *Liolà*: the character of the protagonist, and indeed his name, deriving from the 1904 story *La mosca*: 'Lavorare e cantare, tutto a regola d'arte. Non per nulla lo chiamavano Liolà, il poeta' [To work and to sing, both done to perfection. It was with good reason that they called him Liolà, the poet]. The fact of the matter is that Liolà has a buoyancy which the 'darker vision' of *Il fu Mattia Pascal* precludes. There is something auroral, something of 'the rich unfolding morn', in *Liolà*, completely lacking in the troubled world of *Il fu Mattia Pascal*: we could imagine Liolà gaily dancing with his shadow; Mattia is overcome with pity at the sight of his. Mattia belongs to the family of the anti-heroes, the 'inetti' (inept) of Italian naturalist and realist fiction from Svevo's *Una vita* to Moravia's *Gli indifferenti*. He cannot, or he can no longer, cope with the difficulties of life except to retreat before them: the first time he runs away from home; the second time he accepts the personality that circumstances have created for him and becomes that paradox, the still-living late Mattia Pascal. Where Mattia is inept, a failure even insofar as the world of work is concerned, Liolà is wonderfully successful. Involved in the same intrigue (as far as the episode we have been considering is concerned), motivated by similar drives and emotions, the one eludes the trap while the other is permanently caught in it. The sun of Sicily, the songs and dances, the music and choreography with which some spectacular modern performances (such as the one at the Temple of Segesta in 1968) have enriched this fundamentally straightforward traditional play, can thus be considered 'objective correlatives' of that most exhilarating of feelings, the feeling of having miraculously escaped.

In *Il berretto a sonagli* Ciampa's 'escape' is won at a different price and finds him not singing at the end but giving vent to his feelings (not unlike papà Camillo in *Capannetta*) in 'un'orribile risata, di rabbia, di selvaggio piacere e di disprezzo a un tempo' [a horrible burst of laughter, rage, savage pleasure, and despair all at once]. The play takes place not in the out-of-doors, in the revived land of Theocritus and the pastoral, but in the claustrophobic milieu of an over-furnished parlour in that typical 'cittadina dell'interno della Sicilia' so harshly described by Signora Ignazia's lines in *Questa sera si recita a soggetto* (MN, I, 266).

The first scene brings together the female characters of the play. In a paroxysm of her habitual jealousy, Signora Beatrice Fior[ca is determined to find out about her husband's suspected infidelity and expose it to public view. Fana, her old servant, counsels age-old wisdom and a measure of resignation. But the junk-dealer La Saracena (a witch-figure similar to the *vedova* Pescatore in *Il fu Mattia Pascal* and Madama Pace in *Sei personaggi*) supports Beatrice in her rebellion against her husband, and has come with a supposedly fool-proof plan for catching Fioríca and his reputed mistress *in flagrante*. The scene, like Pirandello's *exordia* in general, is characterized by the scintillating rapidity of the dialogue: the exposition of the situation takes place within the discussion of that *topos* of folklore and literature, 'What should a wife's attitude be towards an errant husband?' Beatrice's feelings have all the earmarks of those of a woman bent on 'liberating' herself and establishing her rights: 'Mi libero! mi libero! mi libero!' is her thrice repeated cry in answer to Fana's cautious warning that she is ruining herself. Pirandello's own judgment of Beatrice, besides being implicit in the outcome of the play, is already stated in the stage direction at her first appearance: 'sui trent'anni, pallida, isterica, tutta furie e abbattimenti subitanei' [about thirty, pale, hysterical, all sudden fits of activity and depression]. Hysteria in its quasi-medical acceptance, it should be remembered, is a distinguishing feature of almost all his sterile women protagonists, and always of the fragile, self-centred, disruptive ones, such as Beatrice in this case or Silia Gala in *Il giuoco delle parti* (but *not* of Livia in *La ragione degli altri*, to whom the first part but not the second part of the characterization would apply).

Of the three women in Scene 1 only Fana has thought of the possible consequence of Beatrice's determination for Ciampa, signor Fioríca's clerk and husband of his supposed mistress. Only she, like Liolà with respect to Mita, and Mattia with respect to Oliva, has thought of him as a human being rather than as a stumbling block to be temporarily removed. It is the presence of Ciampa – that is, the presence of a fourth involved individual – which turns the situation in *Il berretto a sonagli* from the pattern of the conventional triangle (such as in *La morsa* or *La ragione degli altri*) with its accent on the psychological complications of the private emotion of love, to a relationship in which the public demands of saving face – or of 'honour', to remain within the terminology of the Sicilian milieu in which the action takes place – play a preponderant role. In this respect *Il berretto a sonagli* belongs with *Il dovere del medico* and *'A vilanza* (the play in which the theme of the two couples is developed most directly) rather than with the two plays just mentioned. Ciampa's position as

signor Fioríca's subordinate is an added complication and has led
some critics to emphasize the sociological aspects of the play. Luigi
Ferrante, for instance, feels that Ciampa's 'rebellion', his desire for
social respectability, reaches beyond the circumstances of his wife's
presumed infidelity and rests on the 'ancient humiliation…of the
"poor, old" servant vis-à-vis his "rich, young and handsome" master'
– an insight somewhat weakened by Ferrante's incomplete citing of
self not as *povero e vecchio* but as *brutto, vecchio, povero*, reversing the
self not as *povero e vecchio* but as *brutto, vecchio, pover*, reversing the
order of the adjectives he uses to describe his master, *ricco, giovane,
bello*. On the meaning of that reversal – to which rhetoric and not just
ideology might have contributed – the last word does not seem to
have been spoken.

Be that as it may, a sociological reading of *Il berretto a sonagli*,
especially if pushed to extremes, results in diminishing what Pirandello surely considered Ciampa's dominant characterization, his existential suffering. Ciampa has two entrances in the play. When he first
comes on stage in Act I he already bears the marks of Pirandello's
typically 'disturbed' protagonist: his thick, long hair is dishevelled; he
has a madman's eyes that 'lampeggiano duri, acuti, mobilissimi dietro
i grossi occhiali a staffa' [flash hard, sharp, unsteadily behind his thick
spectacles]. When he reappears in Act II, after La Saracena's plan has
been implemented, the ravages of suffering have increased: 'Ciampa
entra per la comune, cadaverico, con l'abito e la faccia imbrattati di
terra; la fronte ferita; il colletto sbottonato; la cravatta sciolta, e gli
occhiali in mano' [Ciampa enters by the stage door. He is deathly pale.
His suit and face are soiled with earth, his forehead wounded, his
collar unbuttoned, his tie loose. He is carrying his glasses in his hand].

The change that has occurred in Ciampa, his virtual destruction and
its outward signs, is analogous to the change Chiàrchiaro undergoes
in *La patente* (he has only one entrance but the spectator knows in
what way the 'new' man differs from the old); the change 'Enrico IV'
suffers (not only through the fall from his horse but later, too, in the
course of the action on stage); the change in Sampognetta in *Questa
sera si recita a soggetto* (between his initial appearance as *Il vecchio attore
brillante* and his death as Signora Ignazia's husband). In each case
something irreparable has taken place, something that has torn the
mask of convention from the face of an individual who had from the
beginning been conceived as in some respects 'exceptional': Chiàrchiaro because of his reputation as *jettatore* (bearer of the evil eye),
'Enrico IV' because of his 'strangeness' which sets him apart from the

other young men in Matilde's entourage, Sampognetta (the least 'exceptional') because 'distratto, fischia sempre' [absent minded, he is always whistling]. Ciampa's atypicalness, which by itself would show that he is no 'representative' of his class, is that, like Dr Fileno and Anselmo Paleari, he is the inventor of a theory.

The theory is that of the three-keyed 'instrument' that regulates men's actions in their relations with one another: '…abbiamo tutti come tre corde d'orologio in testa. La *seria*, la *civile*, la *pazza*. Sopra-tutto, dovendo vivere in società, ci serve la civile; per cui sta qua, in mezzo alla fronte.…Ma può venire il momento che le acque s'intor-bidano. E allora…allora io cerco, prima, di girare qua la corda seria, per chiarire, rimettere le cose a posto, dare le mie ragioni, dire quattro e quattr'otto, senza tante storie, quello che devo. Che se poi non mi riesce in nessun modo, sferro, signora, la corda pazza, perdo la vista degli occhi e non so più quello che faccio!' (MN, II, 370–1) […we all have something like three keys in our heads. The *thinking* key, the *civil* key, and the *crazy* key. Since we have to live among our fellow-men, we need the civil key above all. That is why it's here, in the middle of the forehead.…But a moment may come when the waters get muddy. And then…then I try first of all to turn the thinking key, to clear things up, get them straightened out, state my point of view, say what I have to say without beating about the bush. But, if I can't manage it somehow, if things get too difficult, why then I turn the crazy key like mad, lose the light of reason, and no longer know what I'm doing!]

Compared to *lanterninosofia* and *filosofia del lontano* Ciampa's 'remedy' deals in more immediate fashion with problems of every-day life. Where *lanterninosofia* attempts to explain the waxing and waning of beliefs on a large cultural scale and *filosofia del lontano* suggests a way whereby anguish can be minimized, the theory of the three-keyed instrument generalizes the basic observation that be-haviour in public and behaviour in private are not necessarily the same, that individuals carry around with them their *personae*. In what Fifí, Beatrice's brother, perceives as a most amusing retelling of the essence of the relationship between his sister and her husband, Ciampa describes the war waged by the *pupo-marito* and the *pupa-moglie* (husband-turned-puppet and wife-turned-puppet) and its temporary pacification outside the privacy of the home: 'Dentro, si strappano i capelli, si vanno con le dita negli occhi; appena fuori però, si mettono a braccetto: *corda civile* lei, *corda civile* lui, *corda civile* tutto il pubblico che, come vi vede passare, chi si scosta di qua, chi si scosta di là, sorrisi,

scappellate, riverenze – e i due pupi godono, tronfi d'orgoglio e di
soddisfazione!' [Inside, they pull each other's hair, they stick their
fingers in each other's eyes; but as soon as they are outside, they walk
arm in arm. She turns her *civil key*, he turns his, and everyone else does
the same. And those that see you passing by – some step aside this way,
some that way, they smile, doff their hats, bow – and the two *pupi*
rejoice, puffed up with pride and satisfaction!]. Indeed, the whole of
Il berretto a sonagli could be seen as an illustration of the three-keys
theory, a demonstration of the correctness of Ciampa's insight and of
the 'model' he has constructed. When, after having tried reasoning
and persuasion, Ciampa 'turns the crazy key like mad', so hard that he
'hypnotizes' Beatrice into giving proof that she is insane so that her
accusations may appear to have been caused not by facts but by the
imaginings of an unbalanced mind, he has on his side the approval of
her family and even of the head of police, Spanò. All these people, the
chorus of the socially well-adjusted, are convinced that Ciampa's is
the only possible way for restoring the order upset by Beatrice's
excess.

But in spite of the conclusion which in the spirit of comedy cele-
brates accommodation, the ending of *Il berretto a sonagli* is not a happy
but a bitter one. Like 'Enrico iv''s, Ciampa's bitterness is corrosive.
How he would love to play the madman: 'Fare il pazzo! Potessi farlo
io, come piacerebbe a me! Sferrare, signora, qua *indica la tempia
sinistra col solito gesto* per davvero tutta la corda pazza, cacciarmi fino
agli orecchi il berretto a sonagli della pazzia e scendere in piazza a
sputare in faccia alla gente la verità' [To play the madman! If I could
do it, as I'd like to do it! To wind here *he points to the left side of his forehead with the usual gesture* the whole key of insanity, to pull down the
fool's cap of the madman to my ears, and get out into the streets to
spit out the truth into people's faces].

Surely it is not without significance that whereas it was possible to
discuss *Liolà* without using quotations, in the case of *Il berretto a sonagli*
Pirandello's language, whether in the descriptive passages (the stage
directions) or in Ciampa's lines, imposes itself to the point of forcing
us to repeat it. This is because the play rests so heavily, so exclusively,
on its protagonist. Even more than the other plays written for Musco,
Il berretto a sonagli shows the impact of that 'star' (*grande attore*) on the
author. It is no doubt its bigger-than-life protagonist, condemned to
live amid the hollow men and women that surround him, that
accounts for a certain lack of balance in the play. The situation of an
'exceptional' individual hounded by the petty persons around him is

f course not unique to *Il berretto a sonagli*, and indeed, in comparison o signor Ponza and signora Frola in *Così è (se vi pare)* or to the mad mperor in *Enrico IV*, Ciampa is not so much hounded as overlooked. But in these other plays a richer cast of characters and more com-plicated and varied stage business fill in the gap left by the absence of n antagonist commensurate to the protagonist. In *Il berretto a sonagli* he scenes in which Ciampa does not appear are slight, much slighter, or instance, than the scenes in *La patente* where Chiàrchiaro is not on tage, for Judge D'Andrea is after all in his way an equal to the dis-traught, hate-filled, self-appointed *jettatore*. The exceptional import-nce of the protagonist sets *Il berretto a sonagli* apart among the corpus f Pirandello's Sicilian plays, a fact underlined by its having had to vait until 1936 for another great dialect actor, Eduardo De Filippo, or performances comparable to those of Musco.

Agostino Toti in *Pensaci, Giacomino!* would by age, position, and manner hardly appear a likely candidate for the role of protagonist nd subverter of accepted values. Pirandello describes him as he first merges from the natural science laboratory in the secondary school vhere he is teaching as a *vecchietto* of over seventy, not too steady on his legs, wearing cloth shoes, a skull cap, and a long green muffler round his neck with the ends dangling down his chest and back. From the room behind him surges the din of a class in uproar: Pro-essor Toti is incapable of keeping discipline because he understands a *ragione degli altri*, in this case the healthy animal spirits of insub-ordination of his young charges. The principal of the school would ike to see him retire, but he is too poor and too lonely to do so. More-over, though he does not have a theory like Ciampa or Dr Fileno, he as a plan: he hopes to get married. Like don Diego Alcozèr in *Il turno*, another spry septuagenarian, he looks forward to spending he remaining years of his life in the company of a cheerful young vife. But there is also a measure of rancour in Toti – missing in don Alcozèr who has had no financial worries. Toti wants to get his evenge for having been an underpaid civil servant all his life: by marrying a young wife he will presumably be forcing the govern-ment to pay her many years of pension as his widow. 'Ma sa che lei è n bel tomo, professore? Mi congratulo! Uomo di spirito!' [Do you ealize that you're quite a character, my dear professor? Congratula-ions! You're a man of ingenuity!], the principal comments, recog-izing Toti's 'exceptionalness', when he hears all this.

But as is usual in Pirandello's fictional universe, Toti encounters lifficulties in trying to bend circumstances to his will. First of all, the

girl he has chosen to be his wife, the school janitor's teenage daughter
already has a lover (Giacomino) and is pregnant. Surprised but undaunted, Toti manages to fit this development into his plan: it simply
means that what he had expected to happen later has already happened. He had never thought that he'd be anything but a 'father' to
Lillina and a 'grandfather' to her children anyway. The second difficulty stems from the inability of the literal-minded people who surround Toti to make that distinction between self and role he is so
eminently capable of making. 'Altro è la professione, altro è l'uomo
[The profession is one thing, the man another] is his explicit statement
to the principal on this point during the very first scene of the play.
But while Toti is 'quite a character', the others are quite conventional.
Thus, instead of being grateful for the solution that marriage offers
for their daughter's predicament, Cinquemani and his wife would
prefer to safeguard her reputation (and incidentally punish her) in the
usual way by keeping the birth of the child a secret. And later when
Toti uses his unexpected inheritance to strengthen the relationship
between Giacomino and Lillina, they can think only of the wrong
done *them* when Giacomino – and not they – is put in charge of
Lillina's financial interests.

The most serious, indeed the only real threat to Toti's plans for Lillina comes from Giacomino's bigoted older sister, Rosaria, and from
Padre Landolina, her spiritual guide. When Toti recognizes the
threat, he acts as Liolà does in defence of the innocent Mita. He acts
not to defend his own small claim to comfort and happiness in old age
but to defend the rights of the wife and mother of the *de facto*, though
not *de jure*, family that already exists. In the magnificently eloquent
final scene Toti tracks his enemy to her home and in the 'salottino
quasi monacale' [almost monastic parlour] of *casa* Delisi convinces
Giacomino that he is committed for life and that he could find no
better wife than Lillina. 'Non posso piú sciogliermi, Rosaria' [I can no
longer free myself, Rosaria], Giacomino tells his sister in the *dénouement* of the action. The story thus ends happily with a 'marriage', as is
suitable in the world of comedy. The *play*, however, ends differently.
Like *La patente*, *Cosí è* (*se vi pare*), and *Sei personaggi*, it has a spectacular
finale that follows the *dénouement*. Immediately after Giacomino's
declaration just quoted, this finale sounds an anti-clerical note so
daring and total that one may speculate that only bravura acting and
the dialect incomprehensible to the majority of the audience in which
the play was originally performed saved it from censorship. Using
Christ's famous admonition to Satan, *Vade, retro!*, Toti bars the way to

Padre Landolina as Giacomino and his small son cross the threshold
and escape from the self-appointed guardians of public morality. Like
Chiàrchiaro's apparently excessive reaction to the death of Judge
D'Andrea's bird in *La patente*, Toti's violent outburst at the end – after
so much diplomacy and forethought – points back to the tremendous
pressure to which he has been subjected but which he has successfully
withstood. Like Liolà and unlike Chiàrchiaro and Ciampa, Toti is
a winner. But the nature-alienated milieu in which his victory takes
place robs it of the joyousness that is *Liolà's*.

Pirandello's Sicilian fictions reflect a social and psychological environment perhaps most inclusively characterized by Nicola Ciarletta, who
has probably written the best essay on Pirandello's *Sicilianità*, when he
speaks of the 'incredible difficulties' of life in it. The economic difficulties are probably the more familiar and more accessible to the
reader. Where Pirandello's work includes them it is closest to Verga's
and also offers a possibility for flight from disturbing and painful
pessimism through the dream of a Utopia to come. But it is the
psychological difficulties that are the more significant for Pirandello.
Here again Ciarletta provides a striking formulation: he describes the
actions of 'Enrico IV' as 'a poor man's revenge', the revenge of 'someone who is accustomed to hiding himself', that is, accustomed to
trying to protect his privacy and dignity in the face of poverty and
want. The attitude, exemplified in Ciampa and Chiàrchiaro for
instance, may be difficult to understand and sympathize with in the
age of expanding welfare states, but it underlines the actions of many
of Pirandello's most important characters. To such an individual, to
what we might call the wounded man, it is almost impossible, as
Judge D'Andrea has understood, 'to do good'. The 'poor man',
everyman (as can be seen in the case of the wealthy and socially pro-
tected 'Enrico IV', which enlarges the meaning of poverty), ends up
by seeing in every other man a potential rival, an enemy. Where
there is no sense of community, men remain isolated, 'each an island
to himself', as Pirandello wrote in the speech on Verga.

Secrecy, reticence, guarded statements, tortuous reasoning, scepticism, the camouflage of irony and paradox, the cultivation of eccen-
tricity become so many strategies of self-protection. The mask almost
becomes the face, the role the man. The margin of freedom that can
be won is minimal: the setting up of an ingenious argument (Liolà's
in convincing Mita that she must become 'dishonest' in order to gain
back her position of respected wife, Ciampa's in showing Beatrice's

family that she must go 'mad' in order to undo the harm she had done by 'being right'); the bending of another's will to one's own (zi' Dima's victory over Don Lolò in *La giara*, Toti's defeat of 'public opinion' in *Pensaci, Giacomino!*); retreat before a *fait accompli* that can no longer be undone (Micuccio's rejection of Sina in *Lumíe di Sicilia*). The 'poor man's revenge' elicits pity and consternation from reader and spectator. Pity is the emotion more easily dealt with: it is both evoked and neutralized by the distance that separates fictional from real life. Consternation is a different matter: it obliterates and denies distance. We are horrified by an action that we recognize as belonging potentially to our own world – and it is such actions that conclude many of Pirandello's plays.

Repression and explosiveness, in Giudice's formulation, are the distinguishing features of the Sicilian personality. At one end a static, rigid society; at the other the one mad moment that will spell permanent disaster. In Pirandello's fictions the solution to a personal predicament can never be simply to walk away from the situation, to start afresh somewhere else. Ciampa feels a different man when he is sent to Palermo on an errand – 'Appena cammino per le strade di una grande città, già non mi pare piú di camminare sulla terra: m'imparadiso!' [As soon as I walk through the streets of a large city, I no longer feel I'm treading the earth: I'm filled with paradise!] – but he must come back to the 'cittadina dell'interno della Sicilia' which is his prison. Mattia Pascal gets away from the *vedova* Pescatore but his bid for self-fulfilment fails and the only freedom he can find at the end is to write the story of his life. Marta Ajala sets off to become independent, to make a life for herself in which she will be person not object, but at the end she is back with the husband who had driven her out. In *L'aria del continente* (not claimed by Pirandello as his work but not repudiated either) the *genius loci* dogs the protagonist's steps to the point of re-establishing for him the typical situation of the *cornuto* [cuckold] with respect to the unprejudiced 'continental' mistress he had picked up in Rome and who turns out to be instead just another Sicilian. Whatever movement, whatever variegated life there is in Pirandello's world, the situations his characters find themselves in must be solved *in situ*, at the still centre of the storm. But the solution of a situation (the *dénouement* in a play) is not necessarily the resolution of the psychological difficulties that have brought it about. As a matter of fact, for the difficulties that lie at the heart of Pirandello's world view there can be no conclusive solutions. There can be no remedies, for such remedies would spell their disappearance and dissolve the tensions that kept the world he knew alive and generated the energy which made it possible for him to give it artistic form. The beginnings of Pirandello's activity as a dramatist are inextricably involved with his meeting with Musco, the 'concretization' as it were of the very tensions that demanded to be expressed. It is significant that this 'concretization' took place in the figure of an individual for this shows how rock-firm Pirandello was in his attachment to the geocentric universe from whose centre man – Western man – in spite of the Copernican revolution had not yet been displaced.

3. 'Teatro nuovo': from *Così è (se vi pare)* to *Enrico IV*

Between 1916 and 1921, between the three Sicilian plays just discussed and the première of *Sei personaggi*, Pirandello wrote and had
performed nine plays in Italian. In 1918 appeared the first volume of
his collected plays, *Maschere nude*, published by Treves of Milan, the
most sought-after publisher at the time for current creative writing.
By 1921 this edition consisted of four volumes containing a total of
ten plays, and a second edition (which was to have 31 volumes by
1935) had already been begun by another publisher, Bemporad of
Florence. Pirandello's success as a playwright was thus established
before the appearance of his most famous work.

The major plays that belong to this period – *Così è (se vi pare)*, *Il
piacere dell'onestà*, *Il giuoco delle parti*, and *Tutto per bene*, among the
Italian ones; *Pensaci, Giacomino!*, *Liolà*, *Il berretto a sonagli*, and *La
patente*, among the Sicilian ones – have received continuous critical
attention, either singly or in various arrangements intended to bring
out particular aspects of Pirandello's thought and art. The period has
nowhere, however, been studied as a whole, nor have the chronological limits been strictly observed in the selection of groups of plays
for scrutiny. This is understandable both because Pirandello's constant re-use of his own material blurs the sense of chronological development and because the facts of literary history and those of
theatrical history do not necessarily coincide. To cite one example,
All'uscita, the play that occupies a particularly important place in
some presentations of Pirandello's development (Leone de Castris,
for instance, refers to it and *Così è* together as *parabole fondatrici*), was
not performed until 1922 although, atypically, it was already in print
in 1916. Its critical assessment will thus vary according to whether the
accent falls, as it does in literary criticism, on the work existing in a
kind of atemporal, ideal space, or if it falls, as it must in theatrical
history, on the concreteness of the interaction of author, actors,
director and drama critics, which determines the production and
reception of the work at a particular time and place.

In now discussing the Italian plays of the period under consideration
two contexts can fruitfully be borne in mind: the emergence of the

Theatre of the Grotesque and the presence of Ruggero Ruggeri, the second actor after Musco to play a significant role in the development of Pirandello as a dramatist. By the time Ruggeri performed in *Enrico IV* (the première took place on 24 February 1922), Pirandello had already reaped fame from the production of *Sei personaggi*, the history of which will be discussed in chapter 4 of this study. After *Sei personaggi* an important aspect of his work will be the continued exploration, as suggested in that play, of the stage as a medium. This will lead him, as we have already indicated and as we shall explore more fully in chapter 5, to found his own acting company and, under the impact of his meeting with the actress Marta Abba, to write a series of plays which can be considered a distinctive unit within his total production. Two of his most powerful plays, however, *Vestire gli ignudi* and *La vita che ti diedi*, both dated 1923, remain excluded from this historical perspective. They belong neither to the group that was inspired by Ruggeri nor to those that are related to Pirandello's activity as a director and producer. They would deserve full discussion, but limitations of space will force us to do no more than refer to them incidentally as the occasion arises.

It is well-known that the term *teatro del grottesco* derives from the genre designation, *grottesco in tre atti* of Chiarelli's play *La maschera e il volto*, first performed at the Teatro Argentina, 31 May 1916, but which had been making the rounds of directors and producers since 1913. Like so many other men of the theatre of his time, Luigi Chiarelli (1880–1947) was not only a dramatist but a journalist, critic, painter and director. In 1918 it was the Compagnia Stabile Romana, directed by him and the much more famous Virgilio Talli (1858–1924), that staged the first Rome productions of *Cosí è (se vi pare)*, the 'parable' considered by some critics as Pirandello's major contribution to the Theatre of the Grotesque. Of course, whether Pirandello can actually be fitted into a group designation or whether by greater power and originality he escapes the constriction of labels altogether – even the label of *pirandellismo* – is open to question, and no completely satisfactory assessment of his relationship to the Theatre of the Grotesque exists. But the day to day contacts of work in the same environment and in pursuit of similar objectives are facts of Pirandello's biography, reflected not only in major dramatic works but also in occasional writings such as the article *Immagine del 'grottesco'* already discussed in connection with the concept of *umorismo*, and reviews of works of his fellow-dramatist Rosso di San Secondo (1887–1956), author of the second best-known work of the Theatre of the Grotesque, *Marionette, che passione!* (1918). It might be useful to consider these two plays here.

All three acts of *La maschera e il volto* are set in the drawing room of Count Paolo Grazia's elegant villa on Lake Como, with a vista on to the terrace and the slope leading down to the water. The group of friends gathered together in Act I represent different ages and different marital situations. The two married couples are the Count and his wife Savina, and the banker Cirillo Zanotti and his wife Elisa. Then there are the lawyer Luciano Spina and his fiancée Marta Setta; the magistrate Marco Miliotti who is a bachelor; Piero Pucci and his little more than a teenager fiancée Wanda Sereni; and the young sculptor Giorgio Alamari who turns out to be Elisa's lover. The setting is thus both realistic and socially emblematic, the familiar microcosm. The initial action strikes the erotic motif, whose 'objective correlative' is music of an exotic nature: the tango being played on the piano by Marta and danced to by Piero and Wanda, and the American song wafting across the lake, a sign that a new adulterous couple has taken the place of the one that the year before had similarly made Como their refuge. Paolo's categorical comment: 'Un marito che si rispetti non si lascia scappare la moglie con un amante' [A self-respecting husband doesn't permit his wife to run away with a lover], and Marta's aggressively challenging question to him: 'Che cosa fareste voi?' [What would *you* do?] at once establishes the problem of the play. Paolo's intransigence, his apparently absolute acceptance of the standard of behaviour will be tested. By the end of Act I he has discovered his wife's adultery (though he doesn't yet know that her lover is Spina), has realized that he lacks the capacity to kill her, has asked her to leave and arranged for her secret departure to Switzerland, and in order to save face has accused himself of having killed her by pushing her into the water. His friend Spina will be his lawyer and will accompany him to the police station the next day.

Acts II and III take place several months later. Because he presumably killed to save his honour, Paolo has been acquitted and is returning home to a festive welcome. He has become a hero ('il Napoleone dei mariti' [the Napoleon of husbands]) and has received hundreds of letters from women admirers, all of whom are ready to become his wife or mistress. Even Marta, now married to Spina, does not hesitate to make advances, thus suggesting the possibility of a swap which in a different kind of play might function as a satisfactory dénouement. But Paolo, who has learned the important distinction that runs between being true to oneself and attempting to live up to the

expectations of others, between face and mask, is repelled by the
ironies piling up around him. The worst of these is the discovery of
an unidentified decomposed body in the lake, at once 'recognized' by
everyone as that of Savina. While his friends are busy in the next room
attending to its disposal, a deeply veiled woman enters. It is Savina,
now living in London under an assumed name, who has come back to
take part privately in the public rejoicing at Paolo's acquittal. He
enjoins her to leave at once, but her departure is delayed until later
that night. In the interval husband and wife are reconciled, and this
might be the end of the play if we were in the world of romance. But
in the 'real' world Savina's reappearance causes legal complications.
While Paolo was found not guilty when he was known to be a
murderer, he is now liable to prosecution for perjury, the crime he
really committed. If Paolo and Savina wish to avoid exposure, they
must leave, running away like common criminals to start life over
again elsewhere. While they passionately embrace, the funeral march
for 'Savina''s burial is heard off stage.

In reviewing the première Adriano Tilgher took his cue from
Chiarelli's own description of the play, and found plot, development,
and characters 'grotesque'. He recognized the two separate com-
plementary aspects of the play, its ridiculing of social prejudice and
its intention to reveal the human face beneath the mask of convention:
'the real face that weeps, suffers, cries out, laughs, and bit by bit
succeeds in peeling off the rigid and deformed mask that covers it, in
order to reappear again in the light of the sun'. And making a distinction familiar to the Pirandello of L'umorismo, Tilgher calls
Chiarelli's attitude to his subject matter 'Pirandellian': he is neither so
detached as to be able to laugh 'ex abundantia cordis', nor so involved
as to turn to satire and moral invective. But Tilgher finds that
Chiarelli has been less successful than Pirandello. Carried away by the
comic possibilities inherent in the basic situation of his plot, Chiarelli
has failed to induce perplexity in the spectator. Thus, though his play
is superior to the usual theatrical fare of the day and though he has an
aptitude for 'this type of ironic and sentimental play that has so far not
had much fortune in our theatre', the laughter of his audience differed
but little from that which normally greeted the more run-of-the-mill
farces and pochades. A far cry, in other words, from the jolt and disorientation felt by Pirandello's audiences.

Later critics, Gigi Livio and Luigi Ferrante for instance, will see the
shortcomings of La maschera e il volto in a different perspective. They
will ask themselves to what degree the play deserves the position of

radical turning point in the history of modern Italian drama that it enjoys, not in terms of theatricality and the development of a genre but in terms of ideological awareness. As for Pirandello, it may well be that he remembered Savina's return in Act III when his own deeply veiled signora Ponza comes on stage at the end of *Cosí è* (*se vi pare*).

Of lesser international fame than *La maschera e il volto* (might Starkie's unequal treatment of the two plays be responsible?), *Marionette, che passione!* appears at once as a different kind of play. It, and not *La maschera*, inspired Pirandello to write a review in which the future theatrical director is foreshadowed a good number of years before he succeeded in founding his own Teatro d'Arte.

Marionette, che passione! begins not with the first scene of a first act but with a long Prelude, a piece of poetic prose which evokes the melancholy Sunday afternoons of a large city when 'gli spostati in tutta la varietà della loro specie' [the displaced in all the variety of their species] suddenly recognize each other in the deserted streets or the empty hall of some public building where they are seeking refuge from the rain. A prefatory note to the actors emphasizes the need for a special kind of recitation. The words that are spoken are not ordinary dialogue but indices of deep, unexpressed feelings that can be communicated only through a learned orchestration of sound and silence: 'Questa è una commedia di pause disperate' [This is a play made up of desperate silences]. The cast of characters is long. It includes many background figures that provide movement in the performance of this essentially static action: 'pura sintesi lirica', Pirandello called it. And there are the anonymous beings that have a role in the plot, individuals defined not by their name, age and social condition, but by some outward appearance or transitory identity: *La signora dalla volpe azzurra, Il signore in grigio, Il signore a lutto, La cantante, Colui che non doveva giungere* [*The Lady wearing the blue fox, The Gentleman in gray, The Gentleman dressed in mourning, The Man who was not supposed to come*].

The first three meet at the Telegraph Office in Milan one rainy Sunday afternoon. None is able to write the telegram he has in mind. *The Lady in the blue fox* has run away from the lover who maltreated her, and wants to go back to him. *The Gentleman in mourning* has been abandoned by his wife and is ready to take her back. *The Gentleman in gray* cannot forget an unhappy love affair in the more distant past and from time to time goes to the Telegraph Office to gain a respite from his unhappiness in the illusion that the affair may start all over again. At the end of Act I *The Gentleman in mourning* has pleaded with

The Lady in the blue fox that they should become lovers so that their new life together might erase the memory of the past, but *The Gentleman in gray* has interrupted them violently to warn them that feelings cannot so easily be controlled: 'Andatevene pure insieme, se vi piace. Vedrete che cosa vi accadrà. Voi credete di poter trattare la vostra anima come si tratta un servo. Ma che servo...' [Go ahead, do go off together, if that's what you want. You'll see what will happen to you. You think you can treat your soul like a servant. Some servant...].

The rest of the action shows the inability of reason to dominate passion, to change the lives of human beings who are like marionettes attached to strings which someone else manipulates. Act III is set in an elegant supper club. In spite of his greater lucidity and disenchant-ment, *The Gentleman in gray* has for the moment joined the other two in their illusion of a new beginning. With macabre humour he pre-pares the stage for the reappearance – or the 'materialization', to use a term more fitting for the sudden appearance of Madama Pace in *Sei personaggi* – of the desired ones who should not be there. Of the three only the lover of *The Lady in the blue fox* actually appears; he takes the woman away with him. *The Gentleman in gray*, who had seemed the most reconciled to his situation, commits suicide. *The Gentleman in mourning*, in his strong attachment to life, turns to *The Singer*. But she, the only 'positive' character in the play up to this point, the only sensible and reasonable one, rejects him and joins the merry-go-round of unrequited love as she seeks refuge in the memory of the other one, *The Gentleman in gray*. The final stage directions and the last line of the play read: '(*pallida, rivedendo invece l'altro nella memoria.*) Peccato! ...Forse avrei potuto amarlo!...' [(pale, seeing the other one in her memory.) Too bad!... Perhaps I could have loved him!...].

It must be obvious at once that *Marionette, che passione!* is in every sense a more interesting work than *La maschera e il volto*. Where the latter, in spite of its suggestive title and an occasional line, is still firmly anchored in the theatrical conventions of the bourgeois drama of the early years of the century, the former is already frankly expressionist. This original aspect of it was recognized by Pirandello in his 1918 review not of a performance of the play but of its published version, its text. In order to find an adequate genre description for it Pirandello reached back to the beginnings of poetic tradition in Greece and Rome: 'Erinni, Dira o Disperata in tre atti avrei voluto che Rosso di San Secondo chiamasse coraggiosamente questa sua opera, che soprattutto è di poesia' [I would have liked Rosso di San Secondo to have called this work of his courageously *Erinni*, *Dira* or *Disperata* in three acts, for it is above all a work of poetry]. The suggestion reminds us that not only was *La maschera e il volto* given the novel genre designation of *grottesco in tre atti* by its author, but that Enrico Cavacchioli called his *L'uccello del paradiso* (1919) a *confessione* and Luigi Antonelli his *L'uomo che incontrò se stesso* (1919) an *avventura fantastica*, not to speak (as we have already seen) of Pirandello's own *parabola in tre atti*, *Così è* (*se vi pare*) (1917), of his *mistero profano*, *All'uscita*, and of Rosso's *notte isolana* [an island (i.e., Sicilian) night], *Per fare l'alba* (1919) – all indications of the radical transformation which the stage was undergoing in those years on its way from naturalism to surrealism.

In addition to Pirandello's observation on genre three other points of his review are worthy of note. The first is the distinction he makes between the text of a play and its theatrical 'translation'. The second is the pervasive recurrence of the *umorismo/grottesco* motif. And the third and most important is his proposal for a possible staging of the play which occurred to him as he was reading the text.

Theatrical 'translation' had already concerned Pirandello in the 1908 essay *Illustratori, attori e traduttori*, where he had analyzed the analogous activities of book illustrators, actors and translators in a perspective of ideas basic in the development of aesthetic theory from neo-classicism to Crocean idealism. The critics most sensitive to Pirandello man of the theatre as opposed to Pirandello man of letters (Sandro D'Amico, for instance) have all remarked on the importance of this early essay. In the Rosso di San Secondo review the ideas that had been expressed there are compressed into one lapidary paragraph in which the work of the author, the text that the reader has before his eyes, is defined as 'espressione unica e immediata' [unique and unmediated], while what the spectators see is 'espressione...varia e necessariamente diversa' [varied and inevitably different], made so by the interpretation(s) of actors and lasting an evening, several evenings, or a season, but fated in the end to disappear. The book, on the contrary, the author's text, remains.

Similarly compressed and concentrated are the echoes from *L'umorismo* perceivable in the review, rapid, allusive touches that show how familiar the dichotomy of *avvertimento* and *sentimento del contrario* had become to Pirandello. Thus he compares the effect of the 'clever game' (*fino giuoco*) of *Marionette* to the apparently only funny *Don Quixote* when read superficially (*a goderselo di fuori*), or the merely amusing *Gulliver's Travels* when read in the same frame of mind.

('Spasso di strampaleria eroica' and 'spasso d'avventurosa strampaleria' are the two epithets, virtually impossible to translate, that
Pirandello uses for these two masterpieces of the comic.) And he
speaks of the three principal characters of *Marionette* as capable of
crying and immediately after laughing, or of laughing and crying
simultaneously, something that Rosso himself had referred to in his
prefatory note when he had said that the play 'non deve dar luogo al
comico, bensí a un sentimento di tragico umorismo' [must not result
in the comic, but in a feeling of tragic humorism]. Indeed there is
much evidence in the plays of the *teatro del grottesco* themselves (even
such a simple line as *The Singer*'s in Act II, Scene 3: 'Non rido, perchè
comprendo' [I'm not laughing, for I understand]) and in the words
of their reviewers (those quoted from Tilgher on *La maschera e il
volto*, for instance) to show how pervasive was the awareness of a
close link between *umorismo* and *grottesco*. Silvio D'Amico probably
put it most incisively when in his *Il teatro dei fantocci* (1920) he dubbed
Il fu Mattia Pascal the first *grottesco*.

 Pirandello wrote his review, we have said, not when he saw the
play but when he read it. As the casual game (*giuoco casuale*) – the
plot, that is, which brings together 'due poveri uomini, una povera
donna...tre grottesche marionette' [two unhappy men, an unhappy
woman...three grotesque marionettes] – progresses from 'giuoco
divertentissimo' [a most amusing game] to 'fino giuoco mortale' [a
clever deadly game], Rosso's poetry, his *erinni*, *dira* or *disperata*,
changes into tones and colours before Pirandello's 'inward eye'. His
words deserve to be quoted here for we seem to be reading one of
those famous *didascalie*, the stage directions of his plays which remind
one of how long his apprenticeship as narrator had been and how total
a control over all aspects of his dramatic work he desired to have:
'...un tono basso, quasi in sordina, intercalato da lunghe pause, e un
color grigio slavato, di cielo piovoso, per il primo atto; un tono
stridulo, tutto scatti e scivoli, e una soffice imbottitura di raso celeste,
da piumino di cipria avvelenata, per il secondo atto; un tono lento,
quasi solenne, un po' declamatorio e una rigidezza di bianco e nero,
bianco di stoviglie da tavola, di tovaglie e di sparati di camicia, nero di
marsine e di cravatte, per il terzo atto; insomma tutta una galanteria
di fino giuoco, che dia sussulti da morirne a ogni improvviso stridore
che minacci di mandare ogni cosa a catafascio da un momento
all'altro, perchè in verità è la galanteria – questa – di un fino giuoco
mortale' (SPSV, 974) [...a low almost muted tone, broken by long
pauses, and a gray, washed out colour, like a rainy sky, for the first act;

a strident tone, all jerky and sliding movements, and a fluffy, sky-blue satin quilting, like a poisoned powder puff, for the second act; a slow, almost solemn, slightly declamatory tone and a black and white severity, the whiteness of china, table-cloths and shirt-fronts, the blackness of tail-coats and ties, for the third act: in short, the elegance of a clever game, which fills one with shivers of fear at every grating sound that from one moment to the next might turn everything upside down, for in truth this is the elegance of a clever, deadly game].

To measure the distance that separates Pirandello's article from an ordinary drama review of the day, it is sufficient to turn for comparison to Silvio D'Amico's comments on the play's Rome première that same year. D'Amico was distressed by what he felt to be the play's lack of clarity, by its author's imperfect realization of its intention: '*Marionette* could have been a work of great poetry, or of exquisite irony, or of tragic passion'. But it is not simply that D'Amico was critical and Pirandello admiring. It is the very concept of the coherence of the work – and by extension of any work for the stage – that is different in Pirandello and D'Amico. 'Art is harmony', writes D'Amico, and because Rosso has failed to achieve harmony in himself his work is imperfect: 'Here exaggeration, confusion, chaos are not only in the characters, but in the author himself, in the act that creates them'. But for Pirandello the play's apparent incoherence is actually its coherence, for its roots are 'nella disperazione, in cui, piangendo o ridendo, si snoda, come a caso' [in the despair in which, laughing or crying, it unwinds itself as though by chance]; it is up to the production to bring this out. D'Amico, although a drama critic, that is a critic who judges plays as they are performed, sees the play in its conception, as the work of its author. Pirandello, although a writer with as yet quite limited experience of the stage, sees it in its 'becoming', as a text that may well be deformed by its 'translation', but that can have no life unless it *is* 'translated'. As empathetic reader of the text, Pirandello prefigures the ideal director who, like the author bending down over his characters to cull their every word and gesture, subordinates his will to the playwright's in order to find the means of making the work's intention perceptible to eye and ear. This second step in the life of a work of dramatic art, comparable to what creative and practical criticism does for a work of literature, will end up by fascinating Pirandello so thoroughly that he will give up the essentially sedentary existence of writer and professor, the rooted existence of the family man, to become a nomad, a tireless wanderer in search of 'two boards and a passion'.

Cosí è (se vi pare) is by virtually unanimous agreement the most important turning-point in Pirandello's career, his abandonment of realism in the theatre. In some respects the play has been worried almost to death. Having become a school text, it has undergone the peculiar flattening-out that overtakes all works subjected to scholastic consumption. Yet it remains one of the most frequently performed of Pirandello's plays and its continued 'relevance' was hailed only a few years ago when on the occasion of a revival a New York Times headline asked in the language of the day: 'Who's This Cat Pirandello?'

Pirandello announced the near completion of the play in a letter to his son, dated 3 April 1917, which declared his satisfaction with it and his confident awareness of its originality: 'È certo d'una originalità, che grida' [It is certainly of striking originality]. A few days later, 8 April 1917, he added: 'È una gran diavoleria, che potrà avere veramente un grandissimo successo' [It is a big piece of devilry, that could really become extremely successful]. Before the play there had been a short story, La signora Frola e il signor Ponza, suo genero, probably written in 1915, but first published as part of the collection E domani, lunedì... in 1917. The story told by the two works is the same, though the manner of telling is of course quite different. Because critics have been attracted over and over again by the relationship between stories and plays in the Pirandello corpus and because this particular instance of transformation of story into play was discussed in Ulrich Leo's seminal article 'Luigi Pirandello zwischen zwei literarischen Gattungen' [Pirandello between Two Literary Genres] (1962), it seems appropriate to make a first approach to the play through the story.

La signora Frola e il signor Ponza, suo genero is a frame-story in which the narrating voice starts out by describing the effect that the arrival of the protagonists, newcomers to the town of Valdana, has had on its inhabitants. Valdana is a 'città disgraziata, calamita di tutti i forestieri eccentrici' [unfortunate city, magnet for all eccentric foreigners], and its current trouble stems from the unsettling mystery that the new family has brought with it. One of the two, signora Frola or signor Ponza, must be crazy, but how are the townspeople going to find out which one? And if they do not find out, and soon, if the 'fantasma' [fantasy, illusion] cannot soon be distinguished from the 'realtà' [reality, truth], irreparable damage will be done to the fabric of the community. For it is not possible that illusion and reality are the same thing and the suspicion that they might be must be nipped in the bud.

Three months, the length of time the Ponzas have been in town, is already too long a time for such a dangerous, disruptive supposition to have been around. This, in essence, is what we are told in the opening frame of the story.

The events that have led up to the situation are now told retrospectively and in order: 'Ma procediamo con ordine' [But let's begin at the beginning,' Eric Bentley translates], are the opening words of the first of the two main sections into which the story proper is divided. When signor Ponza, the prefect's new secretary had arrived in Valdana, he had surprised everyone by renting two apartments: one in a drab, new building on the outskirts of town for himself and his wife, and the other in the centre of town for his mother-in-law. This arrangement was so unusual by common standards that the townspeople assumed that son-in-law and mother-in-law could not get along, and given the greater likeability of signora Ponza – she is a gentle, affable, refined old lady while he is dark and wild looking with intense and gloomy eyes – they concluded that the fault was Ponza's. Matters might have rested there and the anomalous situation become acceptable, had signora Frola not felt impelled to defend her son-in-law, to explain why he was not only keeping her in a separate apartment but actually completely segregated from his wife, her daughter. She says that Ponza is inordinately attached to his wife: some people might indeed think that he is morbidly so, but she, signora Frola, knows that his feeling is neither jealousy nor selfishness but *totalità esclusiva d'amore*. It is because of the absoluteness of his love that he keeps his wife virtually a prisoner, channelling all her contacts with the rest of the world, including her mother, through himself. Having understood him and knowing that her daughter is loved by him, signora Frola is content and has no intention of interfering with a *modus vivendi* that has worked successfully for four years.

In spite of signora Frola's eloquence, the townspeople are not satisfied. They do not share her compassionate understanding of her son-in-law and their indignation against him increases. It is at this point that the ladies of Valdana receive a second visit: signor Ponza, trembling with barely suppressed emotion, more agitated and gloomy looking than ever, asks to be heard. *His* story seeks to justify his behaviour on different grounds. The truth of the matter is, he says, that signora Frola's daughter, his first wife, is dead. She has been dead for four years, but unable to accept this fact signora Frola supposes instead that she is being prevented from seeing her by her son-in-law. Actually the woman whom signora Frola is prevented from seeing is not her daughter but signor Ponza's second wife; and wife and husband, at great cost to themselves, are supporting the old lady's delusion which, paradoxically enough, is her only hold on reality. No, says signor Ponza, it is preposterous to think that he would ever keep a mother from her daughter. The charade he and his wife are engaged in is not a cruel but a kind act, the charity owed to unhappiness.

But no sooner is signor Ponza gone than signora Frola reappears: she is as gentle and reasonable as ever but what she has to say disconcerts the audience even further. She knows what signor Ponza has been telling them, but it is not *she*, it is *he*, who is the crazy one. If she failed to tell them this the first time it was simply to protect his reputation as an efficient and reliable civil servant. For there is nothing wrong with him except this one thing, that he believes his wife is dead and that he goes around saying that signora Frola is crazy because she thinks that her daughter is still alive. Actually, signora Frola continues, what happened is this: Ponza's excessive attentions to his wife had overburdened her to the point that she had had to be sent away to spend some time in a nursing home. Not finding her at home, Ponza thought she had died, and when she finally came back he did not recognize her. As a matter of fact, to re-establish signora Ponza in her home a second marriage ceremony had had to be performed. Signora Frola suspects, she adds, that for some time now Ponza knows what really happened, that he has recovered his sanity, but that he is feigning so that he can keep his wife to himself and avoid her being sent away a second time. What other reason could there be for the kind, affectionate way in which he treats her, signora Frola? Would he be as considerate towards an ex-mother-in-law?

At this point we return to the frame of the story. The question asked at the beginning is repeated: which of the two is the crazy one? Whose is the truth? Whose the illusion? There is one person who might clear up the mystery: the wife. But could she be trusted? Only if she could be questioned in private. But how could that be done? For one thing is sure: signor Ponza is a very jealous husband and does not permit anyone to see his wife. And so suppositions and comments accumulate; to every statement there is a counter statement; all interpretations seem equally plausible. The only fixed point, the only certainty is the visible affection, the consideration signor Ponza and signora Frola have for one another. And the final image of the story is that of signor Ponza and signora Frola contentedly walking down the street together, arm in arm, while the townspeople of Valdana spy on them in angry impotence, chafing that in no way have they beenable to solve the puzzle, to discover – and the formulaic repetition ends the story – which of the two is the crazy one, where the truth lies and where the illusion.

Let us see now how this story, the events and the point of view from which they are told, is transferred to the three-act play. The setting for all three acts is the home of Councillor Agazzi, signor Ponza's immediate superior at the office. Act I takes place in the drawing room, Acts II and III in the study. This slight variation in setting distinguishes between the two halves of the persecution to which signor Ponza and signora Frola are subjected: one concerns their private lives, the other their economic dependence. Signora Frola, it will be remembered, had from the beginning felt that she must protect her son-in-law's reputation, for the family's livelihood depends on it. The drawing-room in which the action of *Così è (se vi pare)* opens is comparable to the parlour in *Il berretto a sonagli* in which another subordinate had fought for the right to live his private life as he saw fit. But the comparison also shows the distance between the two worlds portrayed: *Così è (e vi pare)* has broken out of the regional framework and has left the local colour of the dialect plays behind.

None of the characters who first appear on stage had figured as such in the story. They are the concretization, the personifications as it were, of those generic 'abitanti di Valdana' whose confused and anxious reasoning had been reported by the narrator in the opening frame of the story. Ulrich Leo has defined the story a 'dramatic monologue', a type of literature situated somewhere between narrative and drama. Thus he underlines the centrality of the narrator as the most important of these inhabitants in the economy of the story. The narrator stands out in the play as well: he bears the name of Lamberto Laudisi and is signora Agazzi's brother, the Councillor's brother-in-law. It is he who speaks the first line of the play, obviously continuing a conversation that had been going on for some time. Signora Agazzi and her daughter are indignant: the Ponzas' way of life has upset everyone. In the play the irritant is even stronger than in the story because signora Frola's apartment is next door to the Agazzis' and she has failed to receive mother and daughter when they went to pay their courtesy call on her as a new neighbour. This is the trivial occurrence that has set the action in motion. Signor Agazzi has gone off to the prefect, the town's most important official, to demand that the mystery be solved.

By the end of Act I signora Frola and signor Ponza will both have come to the Agazzis' and their respective retrospective stories will have been told. To the circumstances detailed in the central part of the *novella* and repeated here by mother-in-law and son-in-law, the play adds a crucial item: the public calamity of an earthquake, the immediate cause for the family's moving to the new city. The town they came from has been completely razed and all their relatives are dead. 'Sono sciagure per tutta la vita! Si resta come storditi!' [These are disasters from which you can never recover. You remain in a daze!], signora Frola is forced to explain in an effort to excuse her son-in-law's lack of social poise. But it goes without saying that her audience cannot imagine the magnitude of the blow and that their words of condolence are perfunctory and superficial. The next moment they are all at it again, the Agazzis and the Sirellis and the grotesque signora Cini all hammering away relentlessly in their interrogation. Too insensitive to react with compassionate restraint to the objective catastrophe (*sciagura*) of earthquake and death, how could they be expected to show any understanding for the *sventura* that Ponza speaks of or the *disgrazia* to which signora Frola refers? 'Chi ha una sventura come questa deve starsene appartato' [When a misfortune such as this befalls you, you must withdraw, stay by yourself], Ponza says after he has described how he and his wife live in order to protect signora Frola's tenuous hold on sanity. 'È una disgrazia, signor Consigliere, che con tanti stenti, attraverso tanti dolori, s'è potuta superare; ma cosí, a patto di vivere come viviamo' [It's a tragedy, sir, which we've been able to overcome through many privations and much suffering. But only on condition of living thus, as we've living], signora Frola says after she has described how she and her daughter live in order to protect signor Ponza's delicate mental balance. Three times in as many scenes (1, 4, 5 and 6) Pirandello has created the space within which the 'others' reason' is categorically stated. Structural and linguistic patterns underline the intentional importance of these repetitions. But it may be doubted whether the plea has always been heard. The audience on stage doesn't hear it, and judging from some translations incidentally consulted it would seem that the audience in the theatre could not have always heard it either. Recitation must give proper emphasis if a theatrical text is to be understood, but recitation can do nothing if the meaning has not first been understood.

The play thus 'changes' the setting, the individualized choral figures, and the cause for the family's coming to the foreign town; it also develops the narrator more fully: the *raisonneur*'s voice is now not

merely heard speaking; he also acts. By the end of Act I, when he
bursts into mocking laughter, Laudisi's separation from the rest of the
townspeople has been made perfectly clear and his role of *eiron* (the
man who exposes the hypocrite) to their *alazones* (impostors or
buffoons) – to use Brustein's terminology – has been fully established.
Laudisi is spokesman both for Pirandello and for the Ponza family. He
is entrusted with the function of turning a conventional drawing-
room comedy into a parable, that is, into the illustration of a moral
lesson. The illustration progresses by steps, paralleling the unfolding
of the plot. In Act I, Scene 2 Laudisi uses the Sirellis to give his first
public demonstration that in cases where psychological motivations
and perceptions are involved it is impossible to establish objective
truth. In an amusing by-play which does not interfere with the rapid
give and take of scintillating dialogue, he intervenes in the squabble
between husband and wife to assert that, yes, each single individual is
entitled to believe in what he can see and touch, but that he must also
respect what others see and touch even if it is the very opposite of his
own perception. In Act I, Scene 4 he comes to signora Frola's defence
as she is trying to justify her behaviour toward her daughter. She
thanks him for having succeeded in saying more effectively what she
had wanted to say, thus pointing to his deep understanding, to his
capacity for identification (*immedesimarsi*), to his easy practice of
sentimento del contrario. The importance of Laudisi's role increases in
Acts II and III. These two acts elaborate material which with respect
to the *novella* is new. The introduction of the earthquake into the
antecedent action provides an opportunity for exploring the value of
a factual source of information, different from the psychological
revelations of signor Ponza and signora Frola, but no more reliable.
The direct questioning of signora Ponza as the third witness to the
troubling, controversial events, is the other novelty in the play. It
had already been adumbrated as a possible solution in the story but it
becomes a scene – as a matter of fact the concluding, clinching scene –
only in the play.

Act II includes Laudisi's master scene, an actor's bravura piece
similar to Ciampa's lines about the 'three keys'. It occurs after Agazzi
has learned from the police commissioner that the earthquake had
destroyed absolutely everything, that the municipal archives where
records of marriages and deaths are kept are gone, and that there are
no survivors to be questioned. Undaunted, the Agazzis and the
Sirellis have set the wheels in motion for an apparently accidental
encounter between signor Ponza and signora Frola that will finally

orce the truth into the open. The ladies have gone off to induce
ignora Frola to come to visit them, and Agazzi has run to the Pre-
ecture to have Ponza come too, on a pretext. Left alone on stage,
,audisi engages in a dialogue with his 'shadow', with that *alter ego*
vho looks out at him from the large mirror which in the Agazzis'
raditionally furnished study hangs over the fireplace. Dumbfounded
vitness is the butler, who – like the Secret Councillors in a similar
cene in Act II of *Enrico IV* – is drawn into Laudisi's demonstration of
nother one of his favourite notions: the multiple identities of each
ndividual. The passage is interesting not only in its own right and as a
hallenge to an actor but also for the light it throws on the title of the
hort story, strategically chosen to underline the one incontrovertible
act in this whole business: signor Ponza *is* signora Frola's son-in-law.
The butler has come in to announce the arrival of signora Cini and her
qually grotesque friend signora Nenni. Since there is no one else at
ome, they have asked to see Laudisi: 'Ho risposto che c'era lei', says
he butler [I told them that you were here]. 'Io? No. – Quello che
onoscono loro, se mai!' Laudisi corrects him [I? Oh no. – Maybe,
he man they know!] And aren't the two the same, the butler implies
s he stammers an answer. Until he finally hits on the correct answer:
Hanno detto il fratello della signora...' [They said signora Agazzi's
rother...]. And here Laudisi recognizes himself: 'Caro! Ah... – Eh
i, allora sono io...' [Ah, good for you! – Why yes, in that case it is
...]. As Pirandello does in *Il fu Mattia Pascal*, Laudisi claims ironically
nat the legal identity is the only 'real' one, the only one that makes
ocial, public transactions possible. Or, as he will put it in the very
ext scene while mercilessly making fun of the two foolish old ladies,
iere are some things that can be known: the days of the week, the
nonths of the year, and so on. But *not* the nature of the relationship
etween signor Ponza, signora Frola, and signora Ponza. Of that,
ace Freud, only what they themselves reveal, will ever be known –
nd the philistines will be kept by their literalmindedness from know-
ig even that!

A thorough examination of the structural composition of *Cosí è
se vi pare*), comparable to the one attempted for *Sei personaggi* in the
ext chapter, would isolate other instances of Laudisi's 'lesson'. An
valuation of these blocks of reasoning (hardly nonsense, *filosofia!* as
\gazzi scoffingly refers to them in Act II, Scene 1) would show how
asty most critics have been in reducing the play's message exclusively
o one of two alternatives: either a denial of the existence of truth, or
plea for compassion. De Castris, for instance, writes: 'Truth does

not exist, only its shattering into the relativity of life exists'. To which
Calendoli seems to answer: 'To feel the presence of compassion i
more important than knowing: this is the play's message'. As is to be
expected, Pirandello himself gave a different interpretation when he
wrote to Virgilio Talli (producer as already mentioned of both *Le*
maschera e il volto and *Così è* (*se vi pare*)) that the play's deeper meaning
is contained in its last words: 'parole messe in bocca a una donna da
volto nascosto da un velo impenetrabile: *vivissima* donna, ne
dramma, e pur simbolo di verità' [words spoken by a woman whose
face is hidden by an impenetrable veil: a woman *most alive* in the
drama, and yet the symbol of truth]. A good part of Laudisi's reasoning in Act III immediately after he has hit on what he colloquially
calls 'l'uovo di Colombo' [Columbus's egg], the need for a direct
confrontation with signora Ponza, is devoted to warning his silly
audience that it can hardly be an ordinary woman living on the top
floor of that dreary building on the outskirts of town: 'una donna
qualunque, lassù, non ci può essere' (III, 2). And by the emphasized
word (the italics in both cases above are Pirandello's), Laudis
(Pirandello) surely does not mean that there is a symbol or a ghost
(Pirandello does not pass up the opportunity of playing on the
ambiguity of the word *fantasma* in this very scene) living with Ponza
but a woman invested with *more life*, with a deeper spiritual life than
is usual. The thick veil of signora Ponza hides something quite
different from Savina's veil in *La maschera e il volto*, and the distance
that separates Pirandello from the Theatre of the Grotesque can be
gauged also by the greater density of meaning in the one 'masquerade
as against the other.

In spite of its having been almost from the very beginning a great
success, *Così è* (*se vi pare*) is a difficult play. Slightly less so than *Se*
personaggi, however, inasmuch as its problems are within the possible
range of experience of any man and do not also include the problem
of artistic creation which is after all of concern only to a small and
special group. Because it is both popular and difficult, more use than
necessary has been made, in trying to explain it, of its designation a
a parable. Unable to comprehend the extraordinary existential
demand made of signora Ponza and accepted by her, readers and
spectators have more often than not 'imitated' the Agazzis and
Sirellis in seeking a meaning more consonant with their own limited
capacities of understanding. It would seem that the idea of the denial
or, more accurately, of the transcendence of self – which, according to
a long Western tradition for which Pirandello becomes spokesman

here, is love – is less comprehensible than the idea of the relativity of truth, an intellectual and not an ethical notion. In all superficial assessments of the play this latter notion is offered as *the* lesson of the parable. By thinking of his play as a parable, by giving it an eccentric designation consonant with the style of the 'new theatre', the *grottesco*, Pirandello unwittingly put an extra stumbling block in the way of reader and spectator. Of course, it must be remembered that the word 'parable', so crucially placed in the printed version of the play and therefore so inescapably *there* for the critic, does not figure in the acted version, as indeed it did not figure in the *novella*. One cannot attribute the success of *Cosí è (se vi pare)* to its being a parable or to its belonging (in Bentley's formulation) to the category of 'drama of ideas', any more than one can attribute the success of any work of art to its content separate from its form. Pirandello not only strove for cohesion of form and content in his work; in the best cases he achieved it in exemplary fashion. He had the capacity to *build*. 'Io non so *architettare* per il teatro', Rosso di San Secondo said of himself. 'Pirandello invece che formidabile architetto!' [I am incapable of *building* for the theatre. Pirandello, what a formidable builder he is!]. In its total structure and not in any meaning divorced from that structure, *Cosí è (se vi pare)* is an instance of that capacity.

Leonardo Bragaglia has pointed out that for the plays in which Ruggero Ruggeri was involved – and this included not only *Il piacere dell'onestà* (1917), *Il giuoco delle parti* (1918), and *Tutto per bene* (1920), to which we are about to turn, but also Pirandello's great tragedy *Enrico IV* (1922) – it is not always easy to distinguish what in their success was owed to Pirandello and what to his probably greatest interpreter. As we shall see, the collaboration between author and actor began in many of these cases well before the completion of the script as Pirandello already had the actor in mind while working out the play. Other plays had a more normal genesis and theatrical history and can provide us with a more objective, unimpeded view of Pirandello's affirmation as a playwright. One such play is *Cosí è (se vi pare)*, another *Sei personaggi*. Both are marked in their structure by a multiplicity of important roles, none of which completely overshadows the others. Thus for *Cosí è (se vi pare)* it would be difficult to claim not only that signor Ponza has a more important role than signora Frola but also that his role is overshadowed by Laudisi's. And this latter fact is reflected in the production history of the play which saw the frequent switching of the male roles, the same actor alternately playing the one and the other.

If space permitted, it would be useful to look at some of the minor plays that belong to this period, a period of pivotal importance not only in Pirandello's development as a dramatist but in the emergence and formation of what Renato Simoni referred to with tautological insistence in those years as Italy's 'teatro nuovo...rinnovatore'. It is in transition periods that the 'non-contemporaneity of what is contemporary' (Siegfried Kracauer's expression as used by H.R.Jauss in *Literaturgeschichte als Provokation der Literaturwissenschaft*, 1967) becomes most evident. Thus, for instance, a joint examination of *Ma non è una cosa seria* (1918) and *L'uomo, la bestia e la virtù* (1919) – a procedure justified by the presence in both of the notion of 'the call to duty' (the marital obligation) – would throw into strong relief the reasons for the immediate and continued success of the first play as against the initial rejection and consequent difficult theatrical life of the second. Such an examination would require a historical perspective which could take into simultaneous consideration the double 'horizon of expectations' of the theatre-going public in general and of Pirandello's public in particular. Unfortunately, we can do no more than hint that there is a large untapped area for Pirandello studies here, potentially as rich and rewarding as the study of the relationship between stories and plays has been, with the added attraction of the possibility of combining formalistic analysis with sociological and cultural considerations.

On 25 May 1917, even before the première of *Così è (se vi pare)* which was to take place a few weeks later, Pirandello submitted his second play in Italian, *Il piacere dell'onestà*, to Ruggero Ruggeri in the hope that he would want to produce it. At the time the only Pirandello plays to have been performed were the three one-acters in Italian (*La morsa, Lumìe di Sicilia, Il dovere del medico*); two plays in dialect (*Pensaci, Giacomino!* and *Liolà*); and *Se non così...(La ragione degli altri)*, the only one to have involved him with a major acting company, the 'Compagnia Stabile del Teatro Manzoni di Milano', under the direction of Marco Praga. Novelist, playwright and critic, Praga (1862–1929) was probably the major representative of what had by the early war years become the traditional current in the Italian theatre, 'teatro romantico-verista' Pullini labels it. With the dialect plays, with *Così è (se vi pare)* (first staged by the company directed by Virgilio Talli and with Maria Melato, Annibale Betrone and Ruggero Lupi as leading actors), and with *Il piacere dell'onestà* and *Il giuoco delle parti* (both performed first by the company of Ruggero Ruggeri which had Vera Vergani as the leading actress) Pirandello comes into contact with the contemporary version of the 'compagnie di giro', those nomadic and constantly regrouped troupes of actors under the direction of a *capocomico* [actor-manager], to which the Italian theatre has through so much of its history been entrusted. Characteristic of the history of the drama in the early twentieth century are the changes taking place in all aspects of the life of the theatre. It is not only the repertory that changes, but the shape of the stage, the class from which actors are recruited, and the manner in which productions are financed. Paralleling his affirmation as a playwright will be Pirandello's growing interest in these organizational problems of theatre, which he will come to know first hand, which will find artistic expression in his trilogy of the theatre-within-the-theatre and other plays, and which will impel him to take an active part in the fight for better working conditions for playwrights, actors, and directors.

'Artifex additus artifici' is the sub-title chosen by Leonardo Braglia for the chapter in his book on Ruggeri in which he deals with the encounter between Pirandello, the 'dialettico filosofo' [dialectic philosopher] and Ruggeri the 'lirico dicitore' [lyric elocutionist]. In a period in which the category of *grande attore* still existed, Ruggero Ruggeri (1871–1953) was without doubt the greatest of them. Others who could have competed with him for this designation belonged either to the generation immediately preceding (Ermete Zacconi, for instance, 1857–1948), or to the dialect theatre (Musco, Petrolini). In contrast to the origin of most Italian actors of his time and earlier, Ruggeri did not come from a family of actors (*figli d'arte*, they were called, and among the most famous of these was Eleonora Duse, 1858–1924), but from a well established middle-class family. His father had degrees in law and literature and taught classics in various *licei* in central Italy, including the theatrical centres of Florence and Bologna. Thus Ruggeri came to the theatre as an amateur: the craft (*mestiere*) which other actors learned from birth as they followed their parents onto the boards, he had to acquire through a difficult apprenticeship grafted upon his classical education. 'Ho sempre amato i poeti e le alate musiche delle strofe ispirate e armoniose' [I always loved the poets and the winged music of inspired and harmonious verses], he wrote in his autobiographical notes. His early education, which included singing lessons, contributed to the formation of an exceptionally cultivated and intellectual actor: cerebral (like Pirandello) and *costruito* ('made'), as opposed to 'spontaneous' or 'born', are some of the adjectives that have been applied to him. Ruggeri's repertoire included the popular French plays of the time as well as D'Annunzio and Shakespeare. It had been built up since he was first apprenticed to an itinerant 'compagnia minima' at Montecassino in 1888, then through a succession of short-term contracts with various acting companies in other parts of Italy, and finally through the long association with two major companies, those of Ermete Novelli and Virgilio Talli. In 1906 Ruggero Ruggeri established his own company, with Emma Gramatica as leading actress. It was her sister Irma who failed to share Pirandello's views on the interpretation of *Se non cosí*...and became responsible, because of the practice of 'fixed roles' for the various members of a company, for the failure of that play in 1915.

In the course of his correspondence with Talli after the première of *Cosí è (se vi pare)*, Pirandello was forced at one point to justify himself for having submitted *Il piacere dell'onestà* to Ruggeri without first having offered it to Talli. Under pressure from Pirandello to take on plays he did not consider sure of success (*Se non cosí*...for a rerun, *Marionette, che passione!* and *L'innesto* in particular), Talli had in a letter made a comparison between the 'difficult' *Cosí è* and the 'simple, straight-forward' *Piacere*. Pirandello's answer was immediate and direct: *Il piacere dell'onestà* is not an easy play. On the contrary, it is 'una cosa "formidabilmente" difficile, assai piú "rischiosa" del *Cosí è*' [a formidably difficult play, much more risky than *Cosí è*]. And if he had offered it to Ruggeri, he continued, it was because from beginning to end the play depends entirely on the protagonist, 'che deve avere, a sorreggerla, spalle poderosissime' [who, in order to support it, must be endowed with exceptionally strong shoulders]. As a matter of fact, 'data l'audacia spaventosa dell'argomento' [given the frightening audacity of the subject] Ruggeri was filled with dismay at the première and even at that last moment, so Pirandello reports, had had serious doubts that such a play could be successfully performed. In other words, it was not because of ingratitude that Pirandello bypassed Talli in his search for a producer for *Il piacere dell'onestà*, but because of his conviction that a radically different work required a different medium in order to come to life on stage. Talli, wrote Gramsci in 1918, was perhaps the keenest literary critic then living in Italy. His company excelled at ensemble work: 'Talli cuts up and recreates the plays for his actors. He analyses and seems to destroy them. But a new synthesis is implicit in his analysis, and this is affirmed at the première when the audience that applauds is not even aware of the principal creator, the *maestro* who has gathered the single energies together into one whole and revealed them to themselves.' But in addition to being as creative and intelligent as Talli, Ruggeri was also a 'star', the interpreter needed, Pirandello felt, for *Il piacere dell'onestà*, for that 'mostruosa macchina (a misprint for 'maschera'?) grottesca che improvvisamente al terzo atto si scompone e mostra un volto umano pieno di lagrime' [monstrous, grotesque mechanism (mask?) that suddenly breaks up in the third act and shows a human face covered with tears]. It is interesting to note in connection with this exchange between Pirandello and Talli that only once did Ruggeri play in *Cosí è (se vi pare)* (in 1939 in the role of Laudisi) and that he did so only in order to give his leading actress (again Irma Gramatica) the opportunity to add the role of signora Frola to her repertoire. As far as it has been possible to ascertain, *Il piacere dell'onestà* was never performed under Talli's direction at all.

The text of *Il piacere dell'onestà* includes atypically a page of 'Note per la rappresentazione', which follows the cast of characters and precedes the beginning of Act i. These Notes differ both from the Preface to *Sei personaggi* and the Prelude of *Marionette, che passione!* but like them contain material essential for an understanding of the play. The fact that there is a difference between reading one of Pirandello's plays and seeing it performed runs like a leitmotif through the correspondence with Talli already referred to. 'Your plays cannot be understood at a simple reading', Talli had remarked in the same letter in which he contrasted *Cosí è* and *Piacere*, and Pirandello had enlarged upon that statement when he answered: 'Il pensiero e il sentimento nascosto che guida l'azione e detta le parole, in ogni mio lavoro, si scopre non tanto alla lettura quanto alla rappresentazione, dove l'atto e la parola appaion vivi dell'interna vita racchiusa nel pensiero o nel sentimento nascosto. Perché ogni mia commedia non è costruita esteriormente da fuori, ma da dentro. E questo "dentro" si scopre soltanto alla ribalta' [The thought and the hidden sentiment that guide the action and dictate the words in every work of mine are discovered not so much at its reading as at its performance, when act and word appear alive with that inner life enclosed within the thought or hidden sentiment. For my plays are constructed not externally from the outside, but from the inside. And this 'inside' is discovered only at the foot-lights].

The 'Note per la rappresentazione' are part of the strategy for making the implicit explicit, for supplying performer and reader with indispensable directional signs. Apart from the first two – those

that concern the principals, Baldovino and Agata – they could, however, have just as well appeared in their more normal place as stage
directions inserted at the first appearance of each of the characters in
question. The thumb-nail sketches of the minor characters – signora
Maddalena, marchese Fabio Colli, Maurizio Setti, and Marchetto
Fongi – give no more than the basic physical and psychological
descriptions which fix each in the static mask of his role: mother,
unlucky lover, man of the world, and stockbroker (the latter's lop-
sided, furtive figure unmistakably patterned on the Batta Malagna of
Il fu Mattia Pascal). For Baldovino and Agata the presentation is
different. It is, as it were, 'accumulated', noting not only their initial
appearance but the change that will take place in each during the
course of the play. Obviously, Pirandello felt that the potential for
change in these two characters – the spring of the action – had to be
perceived from the beginning, stated in so many words for the
reader, translated into stance and gesture for the spectator. The
portrayal is no doubt easier in the case of Agata whose alternation
between the extremes of rigidity and despair prefigures the ultimate
break-through of her humanity in the regularization of her situation
with which the play ends. The interpreter of Baldovino, on the other
hand, has an almost impossible task: the 'inside' he must reveal at his
first appearance on stage includes both an 'irregular' past life and a
deeply unconventional attitude ('una strana filosofia piena insieme di
ironia e d'indulgenza' [a strange philosophy composed of both irony
and leniency]). In addition there must be a hint of the double change
to take place: from Act I to Act II and from Act II to Act III, with
Baldovino's situation in Act III returning for a time to that of Act I.
As with Ciampa in *Il berretto a sonagli*, Pirandello has given Baldovino
an 'objective correlative', a pair of spectacles which he holds in his
hands as he enters, puts on as he begins to speak in Act I, but which are
gone in Act II.

As in *Se non cosí…*, *Il berretto a sonagli*, *L'uomo, la bestia e la virtù*, *La
morsa*, and *Il dovere del medico*, the plot in *Il piacere dell'onestà* has its
origin in an act of adultery. Adultery plays a role in *Liolà* and *Pensaci,
Giacomino!* as well – as indeed it will in *Sei personaggi* – but these other
plays do not fall as easily under the rubric of 'i soliti tre: la moglie,
l'amante, il marito' [the usual three: wife, lover, husband], with
which Renato Simoni described Pirandello's next play, *Il giuoco delle
parti*. In *Il piacere dell'onestà* 'i soliti tre' are Fabio Colli (the husband),
the wife from whom he is separated and who does not appear in the
play, and Agata Renni (the lover). The story told, however, is not the

story of these three but the outcome of what their story must have been. Of this earlier story, the antecedent action, spectator and reader learn only what Agata's mother tells in self-exculpation in Act I, Scene I. Watching the years pass for her daughter and seeing her still unmarried, she had in a moment of weakness favoured the affair with a man (Fabio) who had everything to commend him except that he was already married. As she says, she had failed to use 'quel rigore che la prudenza consiglia…dico di piú, che l'onestà comanda!' [the strictness that prudence counsels…I'll say more, that propriety commands], thus giving the word *onestà* its first meaning in this play: sexual virtue or chastity.

The play opens with a crisis for which a remedy must be found. Agata is pregnant and since Fabio cannot marry her a surrogate must take his place. With the appearance of Baldovino a second antecedent story is introduced and in an exchange of parts 'the usual three' become Baldovino (husband), Agata (wife), and Fabio (lover). There is a difference, however, for if Baldovino is surrogate husband he is also legal father, and Agata is now a mother. The story changes from a story of adultery to a story in which Baldovino's presence makes it impossible for adultery to take place, or, as a matter of fact, for any other dishonest act to take place either. Where Fabio had thought that it would be easy to buy Baldovino's name by paying his gambling debts and that when he had served his purpose there would be no difficulty in getting rid of him through a trumped-up charge of misappropriation of funds, it turns out instead that it is Fabio and his friends who must leave the house in which there is no longer any room for them once Baldovino and 'Lady Honesty' had come to dwell in it.

Who *is* Baldovino? The question of identity looms large in Pirandello's work. In the different works it is posed and answered on a variety of levels. In *Il piacere dell' onestà*, beginning with the 'Note per la rappresentazione' reader and spectator learn much about Baldovino. He is presented first by Maurizio Setti, his childhood friend and now the go-between. A portrait results which includes his physical appearance, his social background, his education, his life of dissipation, his philosophical education, his intelligence, intuition, understanding, imagination, the '*superfluo*' in brief, the 'excess' that Fabio begins to fear. Soon he appears himself and his 'sincerità spaventosa', the 'frightening candour' which is another version of *onestà*, his inhabiting (as Maurizio had put it earlier) 'una contrada di sogno, strana, lugubre, misteriosa…ove le cose piú bizzarre, piú inverosimili potevano avvenire e sembrar naturali e consuete' [a strange, lugubrious, mysterious dream landscape…where the most bizarre, most improbable things could happen and seem perfectly natural and normal], is turned into action on stage. Baldovino speaks abundantly, so abundantly, in fact, that if we are to believe Pirandello's correspondence with Ruggeri, part of Act I, Scene 8 had to be moved to Act II, Scene 2 in order to lighten the first impact. He hides nothing; so frank is he, indeed, that by the end of Act I his role in the projected *ménage à trois* has been perfectly delineated. He has told Fabio in so many words that in order to function as 'l'onesto marito d'una signora perbene' [the honest husband of a respectable lady] he will have to become a household tyrant, and that his perfect honesty ('Lady Honesty') will of necessity show up the dishonest actions of the others. With a figure of speech borrowed from the language of finance (which recurs as a leitmotif in this play), he has compared himself to 'uno che venga a mettere in circolazione oro sonante in un paese che non conosca altro che moneta di carta' [someone who puts pure gold into circulation in a country that knows only paper money].

And yet Baldovino continues to be a mystery, a riddle especially to Fabio, the antagonist, to whom he has been most careful to reveal himself. This is so because Fabio is unable to revise his conventional view of what a man who accepts a role such as Baldovino's must be like. He can think only of the stigma generally attached to the situation of husband-in-name-only. As Agata puts it even before Baldovino has entered the house: '…quest'uomo (i.e., Baldovino) che dev'essere vile, vile, se si presta a questo!' (I, 5) [this man must be vile, simply vile, if he lends himself to this]. Thus Fabio fails to perceive the abyss that has been progressively revealed, the unbridgeable distance between his weakness and Baldovino's strength. What does this strength consist of? Critics who have taken their cue from the strategically placed cajolery with which Maurizio seeks to soothe signora Maddalena's apprehension: 'Ora bisogna che il sentimento sia contenuto, si ritragga, per dar posto alla ragione' (I, 1) [Now sentiment must be contained; it must withdraw to make room for reason], have quickly and superficially concluded that the play is a demonstration of the traditional notion of the superiority of reason over feeling. They attribute Baldovino's final conquest of Agata to his great intelligence, his rationalism, his will. 'Superuomini del razionalismo…mostri della logica' [supermen of rationalism… monsters of logic], Leone De Castris has called both Baldovino and Leone Gala (in *Il giuoco delle parti*).

But there is another thread that can be followed equally well. It leads to a different view of what constitutes Baldovino's strength and this view corroborates Pirandello's own 'reading' of the character when he speaks of 'macchina (i.e. maschera) mostruosa grottesca' and 'volto umano', of mask and face, in the letter to Talli which has been quoted. To the first view is connected a passage such as Baldovino's statement, 'Sposerò per finta una donna; ma sul serio, io sposo l'onestà' (i, 8) [I shall be making believe that I'm marrying a woman, but in reality I shall be marrying honesty], where the substitution of an abstraction ('onestà') for a woman of flesh and blood constitutes a precise parallel to Laudisi's comment on the testimony of signora Ponza at the end of Cosí è (se vi pare): 'Ed ecco, o signori, come parla la verità!' [And this, ladies and gentlemen, is how truth speaks]. For the second view, however, Baldovino's final words at the end of Act i are the more important: 'Qui, per me, non c'è colpa, ma solo una sventura' [Here, for me, there is not guilt, but only a misfortune], he says, giving a version of the circumstances that have led to the need for a remedy which excludes the notion of guilt and punishment, something that neither the permissive signora Maddalena nor the involved Fabio nor even the more indifferent Maurizio are able to do. Again there is an echo from Cosí è (se vi pare): 'Qui c'è una sventura, come vedono…' [Here there is a misfortune, as you can see] are signora Ponza's words when she appears deeply veiled at the end, words which in their turn echo the references to sciagura, sventura, and disgrazia in signor Ponza's and signora Frola's lines referred to earlier. Like Laudisi, Baldovino too is characterized on one level in relation to the people surrounding him by the gift for ratiocination, by 'cerebralism', to use the word that has had wide currency for this aspect of Pirandello's work. Like the Ponzas and signora Frola, on the other hand, Baldovino pleads for compassion, for understanding, for the chance to start again afresh. The plea in both cases is directed to the 'others', average men and women from whom the 'exceptional' individual – be it Baldovino, Ciampa, Liolà, professor Toti, Leone Gala, signora Ponza, or the nameless protagonist of Enrico IV – is set apart. There is one person in Baldovino's environment, however, from whom he is not set apart, and it is the presence of Agata, constantly pushed into the background by those – mother and lover – who are trying to live her life for her, that accounts for the anomalous position of Il piacere dell'onestà in the Pirandello corpus.

For Il piacere dell'onestà is anomalous in the Pirandello corpus. And this explains why though frequently performed it has not been the subject of as much critical attention as *Cosí è* (*se vi pare*), *Enrico IV*, or the trilogy, 'Baldovino is one of the very few triumphant and, in their way, victorious characters of Pirandello', writes Leonardo Bragaglia, and he quotes Tilgher on 'Life that has annihilated Form'. Leaving such all-inclusive abstractions aside, we can say more simply that *Il piacere dell'onestà* ends happily, showing us a Pirandello able to accept and impose not only accommodation but even reconciliation in a traditional formula. So far the only other play of which we could say this is *Ma non è una cosa seria*. It too ends with the suggestion that the married pair are well matched and will find happiness with one another. It need hardly be pointed out how rare this solution is and how frequently Pirandello's protagonists are left alone among their fellows. It could be maintained, of course, that in *Se non cosí*...Livia and Leonardo Arciani find their way to one another, that Marta and Rocco do so in *L'esclusa*, Lillina and Giacomino in *Pensaci, Giacomino!*, Mita and zio Simone in *Liolà*, and the Ponzas (whoever they are!) in *Cosí è* (*se vi pare*). But no sooner is the list set up than it becomes apparent how in each case there is something irregular. Is there any one of which it could be said, 'And they lived happily ever after'? But this is the distinct possibility with which we are left at the end of *Il piacere dell'onestà* (and of *Ma non è una cosa seria*). Baldovino has wooed Agata in every scene of self-revelation: in his dialogue with Fabio, which she overhears; in the pre-baptism scene; and in the scene in which he is accused of financial irregularities. At the end he has won her and when her choice is made it is final. This triumph of love is what critics have found the most difficult to come to terms with, so much so that Gigi Livio even disputes Gramsci's report of the reasons for the success of the Turin première which he witnessed, and Roberto Alonge speaks of the failure of Baldovino's polemical stand against the social class to which his antagonists (Fabio and his friends) belong because by winning Agata he is in reality drawn into becoming a member of it.

In discussions of Pirandello's theatre *Il giuoco delle parti* is usually linked with *Il piacere dell'onestà*. Actually the play occupies a place apart among the works of this period. Pirandello chose a scene from it rather than from one of his other plays to be the one rehearsed on the stage to which the Characters of *Sei personaggi* are one morning attracted. Because *Sei personaggi* offers so many other suggestions for critical exploration, this fact has received no more than passing mention, with the result that observations regarding Pirandello's reference at the beginning of *Sei personaggi* to the criticism that he was subjected to have remained unnecessarily generic. In 'Il periodo grottesco del teatro pirandelliano' Gigi Livio has faced this oversight and has based on the very use of *Il giuoco delle parti* in *Sei personaggi* an interpretation of the play which radically modifies the conventional triangle situation by making the wife (Silia) and not the lover (Guido), the husband's antagonist. Livio's is a useful perspective from which to view the play, for Silia is perhaps the first of Pirandello's 'new' women (certainly the first on stage), those mysterious female protagonists who became identified only a few years later with their interpreter Marta Abba. Although Marta Abba eventually played Silia, she did not at the première and it was Ruggeri who left his mark on the première and the first reviews. And though both Pirandello and Ruggeri were enthusiastic about the play ('Ruggeri ne è innamorato, e crede che *Il giuoco delle parti* sia il mio più bel lavoro di teatro', Pirandello wrote to his son [Ruggeri is enamoured of it and thinks it my best work fot the theatre]), the fact that it was performed for only a few evenings showed, as Pirandello put it, that its success had already been compromised by (as we shall see) its ambiguous reception at the première. One may hazard the supposition that had the play's history begun after Marta Abba joined Pirandello's company, *Il giuoco delle parti* might not so long have remained 'la commedia incompresa di Pirandello', as a critic still dubbed it on the occasion of a recent revival.

Pirandello first spoke of the new play in a letter to Ruggeri, dated 22 March 1918. At the time the title was *Quando si è capito il giuoco*, which is the title of the 1913 story on which it is based. There are important differences between play and story, some attributable to the change in medium but others related to the vogue of the *grottesco* in the years following the publication of the story. The most obvious difference, perceivable without reference to the historical context, is the humorous presentation of the protagonist in the story. In *style indirect libre* he is seen through the eyes of the anonymous choral figures (paralleling the inhabitants of Valdana in *La signora Frola e il signor Ponza, suo genero*) who envy his good fortune in having found the remedy of indifference for annoyances great and small. With a name suited to comedy, he is Memmo Viola, 'quel buon Memmone', a parody of the later Leone Gala, the protagonist of the play (as Brancati's Giovanni Percolla is a parody of his prototype Don Juan). The modestly middle-class and regional setting of the story contrasts with the '*casa bene* di una ricca e oziosa borghesia' [the pretentious home of the wealthy and leisured upper classes], which is Roberto Alonge's characterization of the setting of Act I of the play, felicitously arrived at through his pin-pointing the drinks being offered: char-treuse, anisette, cognac. Other differentiations further underline the change in environment and in tone from the story to the play: the names of the wife and the lover (Cristina and Gigi in the story); Memmo's action, twice repeated, of coming to open the door 'in camicia come si trovava e con le brache in mano' [in his shirt, as he was, and holding his trousers in his hand]; the detail of the unexpected inheritance (a parallel stroke of fate occurs in *Pensaci, Giacomino!*) which permits him to give up his job for a life of leisure; and his quarrel with his servant about the three *soldi* (cents) missing from the shopping money, a far cry indeed from the pseudo-philosophical dis-cussions that Leone Gala has with his servant Filippo '*detto* [known as] Socrate'.

The *trovata* of the play and story is the same: while it is the husband's role to come to the defence of his wife's reputation by challenging the offender to a duel, it is the lover's to *fight* the duel. The notion of *richiamo all'obbligo*, which we mentioned apropos *Ma non è una cosa seria* and *L'uomo, la bestia e la virtù*, is here turned inside out in typically Pirandellian fashion. Where in those two plays Barranco and signor Paolino, *tipi buffi* and not antagonists of society, insist on compliance with the letter of the law, Leone Gala and his 'country cousin' Memmo Viola both of whom have 'understood the game' and have thus distanced themselves from society, insist instead on the observation of its spirit. Memmo's equanimity, his good humour never leave him. At the end, watching Gigi go off to take his place in the duel, he is still nonchalant: 'Dall'alto della scala, poi, reggendosi ancora le brache con la mano, gli augurò: – In bocca al lupo, caro, in bocca al lupo!' [From the top of the stairs, still holding his trousers with his hand, he wished him the best: – Good luck, my dear, good luck!]. The finale of the play is, as we shall see, quite different.

Indeed, when Pirandello changed the title of the play to *Il giuoco delle parti* ('Mi sembra piú bello e piú proprio', he wrote to Ruggeri [It seems more attractive and appropriate to me]), introducing the idea of roles which was absent in the first title though not completely in the story, he marked the radical separation between the *trovata* as it is told in the one genre and the other. The expression and the notion of having 'understood the game', of having learned the need for self-protection and discovered how the contrast between being and seeming could be used to that end, go back in Pirandello's fictional world at least to *I vecchi e i giovani* and have a strong naturalistic, not to say Darwinian, flavour. The game in the sense of *fino giuoco mortale*, however, had made its appearance in Pirandello's thinking only more recently. We have seen him explore word and concept in his review of *Marionette, che passione!*, and it is to his visualization there of a staging for that play which would emphasize its formal aspects without forgetting the element of merciless cruelty in its action, that we must connect what may be considered a correct reading of *Il giuoco delle parti*. In other words, in the perspective of the evolution of Pirandello's theatre, it is not sufficient to come up with a facile definition of this play and others contemporaneous to it (including *Enrico IV*!) based on the portrayal of a new class in Pirandello's work. It is true that under the impulse of the success of the *teatro del grottesco* Pirandello appears to have discarded regionalism and the dialect theatre. But if this were the really important change that has occurred, Pirandello would not have expressed himself as he did in his letter of 12 January 1919 to Ruggeri. Writing on the eve of his wife's commitment to a mental institution, he returned once again to the critics' incomprehension of his work in general, to their all-out attacks on the *teatro nuovo* with which he was identified, and, in particular in the case of *Il giuoco delle parti*, to their applying criteria appropriate to the naturalistic theatre to 'un'azione espressamente dichiarata un *giuoco*' [an action expressly declared to be a game; italics Pirandello's]. As we now turn to consider the particular difficulty of *Il giuoco delle parti*, the something in it or the something lacking from it that may have stood in the way of making it *both* difficult *and* popular as are others of Pirandello's plays, we shall have to bear this 'game' in mind.

There are two major difficulties in *Il giuoco delle parti* and they are connected in the figure of the protagonist. Writing in *Il teatro dei fantocci* shortly after the first productions of *Il piacere dell'onestà* and *Il giuoco delle parti*, Silvio D'Amico criticized Pirandello for his technical inexpertise: 'In his passion for schematization Pirandello intentionally ignores the patient details that justify [careful characterization and clear exposition of antecedent action] and which Dumas *fils* in theory and Ibsen in practice thought essential to theatrical art. The result is a dissonance from which even the best of audiences rarely recovers in time.' The jarring effect of Pirandello's plays on the public is well known, though it is not always attributed, as here, to their form rather than to their content. The implication in D'Amico's statement that the many seemingly bizarre events in a play may have a quite different effect when viewed retrospectively than when experienced for the first time in the sequence of their development, is an insight that has guided us more than once. But as far as *Il piacere dell'onestà* and *Il giuoco delle parti* are concerned – the two plays apropos of which D'Amico specifically made the comment – surely a distinction should be made. On the basis of our reading of *Il piacere dell'onestà* there is no lack of 'the patient details that justify', either in the initial presentation of the situation (the exposition) as we have shown or in the successive portraits of Baldovino. The same cannot be said for *Il giuoco delle parti*, however, which begins 'cold' (Leone has been presented only by his antagonist Silia before his appearance on stage) and with a strongly divided focus. The larger number of characters on stage in *Il piacere dell'onestà* prior to Baldovino's entrance do not divert attention from him. But in the first part of *Il giuoco delle parti*, the various touches in the scene between Silia and Guido intended to create suspense (such as the references to a *lui*, to a *quest'uomo*, who is Silia's *incubo* [he, that man, nightmare]), to create that peculiar expectation of the appearance of the protagonist that is a recurrent structural feature of Pirandello's plays, are dampened even as they are being built up, by the presence on stage of one of Pirandello's strongest female characters. And though later Leone is given the opportunity more than once to state his 'reasons', to sketch in the antecedent action – as important for the understanding of this play as for any of Pirandello's plays – what is lost at the beginning is never sufficiently regained. One of the major difficulties of *Il giuoco delle parti* is, then, the insufficient characterization – but I would say more, the insufficient 'identification', the giving identity to – of Leone Gala, a shortcoming that Ruggeri must have helped to redress at the première if, as Pirandello reported to his son, '*Il giuoco delle parti*, accolto ostilmente per incomprensione del pubblico al Iº atto, s'è rialzato al secondo e al terzo, suscitando un'enorme discussione' [received with hostility at the end of the first act because of the audience's failure to understand, (the play) bounced back again in the second and third, sparking off an enormous discussion] (29 November 1918).

The second difficulty has to do with the ending and it is more damaging, giving rise to some of the same ambiguities in audience response that troubled the success of *Se non così*...and of *La vita che ti diedi*. We have already spoken of the ending of the *novella*. The ending of the play takes us one step further in spelling out the dénouement: in the *novella* Memmo sends Gigi off to fight the duel, wishing him good luck; in the play Leone finds out the outcome of the duel. Here are the steps that lead to his (and the audience's) discovery of what has taken place. As Guido runs out, Silia who has just arrived asks Leone for an explanation: Why is he, Leone, still at home? Appalled at the logic (for her, the trickery) that has sent her lover to the death she had planned for her husband, she is about to rush to Guido's side when the doctor hurries in to pick up the surgical instruments he had laid ready. He does not stay to answer Silia's question thrice repeated: 'Non credendo a se stessa: Morto? Gli corre appresso: Morto?... Morto?...' [Not believing her premonition: Is he dead? She runs after him: Dead?...Dead?...]. Leone is left alone on stage, motionless, 'assorto in una cupa gravità' [absorbed in gloomy seriousness]. Filippo comes in with the breakfast dishes and 'nel silenzio tragico' [in the tragic silence] calls him to the table. 'Leone, come se non udisse, non si muove' [as though not hearing, Leone remains motionless].

The ending is elliptical but it is clear. There can be no doubt that this is Leone's moment of truth and that from judge ('Io vi ho puniti!' [I punished you!], he had shouted to Silia but a second before) he has turned if not into the accused then surely into a man who recognizes his responsibility, perhaps even his guilt. But this change in situation, so subtly indicated in the stage directions (assorto in una cupa gravità...nel silenzio tragico...come se non udisse, non si muove) comes too late in the play to gain full audience sympathy for him. In contrast to Baldovino, Leone Gala's humanity shows not an appealing but a fearsome countenance. In contrast to (as we shall see) the progressively more and more eloquent defence and self-defence of the nameless protagonist of Enrico IV, Leone's 'reasons' never become completely convincing, never commensurate to the logic that dictates his course of action. Though it is not Leone's own hand that kills, he ends up to all intents and purposes a killer. The implication is of course that he was forced into his 'game' by a merciless and dangerous opponent who manoeuvred him into a situation where he would have been killed. But while it is relatively easy to accept the sudden and instinctive act of a man ('Enrico IV') who was once crazy and may still be crazy, and who kills his rival and punishes himself by excluding himself henceforth from the society of his fellow-men; it is a different matter to watch a man who is the epitome of lucidity 'plot' to have his rival killed in a crime which is perfect because it is not a crime but a fino giuoco mortale. We have seen earlier how the conventional view that an abandoned mistress is more worthy of sympathy than a wife stood in the way of success for La ragione degli *altri*. The equally conventional view that a young woman in the bloom of life is more worthy of sympathy than a mourning mother was to stand in the way of success for *La vita che ti diedi*. In *Il giuoco delle parti* a similar conventional view muddied the waters from the start: the view that a woman – a wife – is necessarily more gentle and more worthy of sympathy and understanding than a man – a husband.

On 7 December 1919 Pirandello wrote to Ruggeri about a new play he was working on. It is a particularly striking letter for in the course of it, completely in the grip of the situation he is delineating and obviously oblivious that he had told the same story once before (in the *novella Tutto per bene*, 1906), he suddenly breaks into a series of short exclamations which shift his position from narrator to participant. 'Caro Amico', the letter begins. 'Sì, è vero, ho pensato per Lei una commedia in tre atti, che ha per titolo: *Tutto per bene*. Rappresentazione d'un dramma, quand'esso è già da gran tempo finito; il benservito a un uomo, dopo che, a sua insaputa, gli si son fatte rappresentare nel miglior modo possibile e proprio per bene, tutte le parti, d'amico, di marito, di padre, di suocero; e la dimostrazione infine che peggio per lui, se egli non è quel che gli altri lo hanno creduto...' [Dear Friend, Yes, it is true; I have thought of a three-act play for you, by the title of *Tutto per bene*. It is the representation of a drama which has been over and done with for many years; the dismissal of a man who, without his knowing it and in the best and most thorough manner possible, has been made to play all roles – the role of friend, of husband, of father, of widower; and finally comes the proof that so much the worse for him if he is not what others thought him to be]. And at this point the storyteller seems to step back and the comments of the chorus figures take over, of the spectators who are watching this man and would like him to ignore what has happened to him and go back to being the way he was before: 'Oh guarda! E che vorrebbe più fare adesso?... Se ne stia quieto e pensi soltanto a non dar più fastidio a nessuno...' [Just look at him! What does he want to do now?...He should calm down; his only worry should be not to bother anyone any more]. Until finally Pirandello concludes, offering his by now familiar view of things as they are seen from the other side: 'Questa la commedia, veduta dagli altri. Ella se la immagini, Amico mio, veduta e vissuta dalla parte del protagonista, uomo austero, di molta fede, d'alto intelletto, schivo di modi e tutto raccolto in una sua grande pena' [This is the situation as seen by the others. Imagine it, my dear Friend, as seen and lived by the protagonist, a serious, upright, intelligent man, shy in manner and completely absorbed in a great sorrow of his].

The protagonist, Martino Lori, makes his first appearance on stage a little more than a third of the way through Act I. In the list of characters he is identified simply by name and position (he is a high-ranking civil servant). In the course of the first part of Act I we learn that he is a widower and that his daughter Palma has just been married. The play opens as broad comedy with the unabashed entrance into a house where she is not known of La Barbetti [the Barbetti woman], one of Pirandello's grotesque females: 'ha sessantatre anni, ma è tutta tinta e goffamente parata' [she is sixty-three, but with her hair dyed and awkwardly all decked out] – by now we know the characterization well. She is dragging her fully-grown son with her, arguing with him as though he were a naughty child. It turns out that she is Palma's grandmother and that she has come to bring a wedding gift with the intention of re-establishing a relationship that had been broken many years before – indeed, that had never existed. For La Barbetti had left her first husband, the renowned scientist Bernardo Agliani, before her daughter had married Lori and her daughter had never wanted to see her again. Her son, Carlino, is not Agliani's son; he was born out of wedlock and legitimated only later when La Barbetti married her second husband, who is now also dead. The 'prima' – that is, the 'before', the antecedent action – which this initial scene introduces dates back to a distant past, a past buried under other pasts in this play whose different temporal levels approach those of Enrico IV in complexity.

There follows a second introductory scene. The entrance of a new character, signorina Cei ('Bionda, magra, alta, sulla trentina, veste con sobria eleganza' [blonde, thin, tall, thirtyish; she is dressed with sober elegance]), signals a change in tone and provides for background information from another period in the past. La Barbetti has the aura of the provinces about her (the Agliani family lived in Perugia and it is from Perugia that Silvia Agliani had come to Rome); signorina Cei reflects the more sophisticated but also more anonymous city life. We have passed from a 'busy' scene reminiscent of the dialect plays to the refined drawing room environment of the grottesco. Signorina Cei is Palma's companion, something between a friend and a private secretary, not her 'dama di compagnia' [lady in waiting], as La Barbetti's ignorance of precise social distinctions makes her blurt out. We now learn the rest of the antefatto: Silvia's profession as a teacher, her having left home (as Marta Ajala does in

L'esclusa) to pursue her career in Rome, her meeting with and marriage to Lori; and the concurrent and intersecting story of Agliani's disciple, Salvo Manfroni, now a Senator, who had published his professor's posthumous work, gained fame with it, befriended Lori, assisted him in his career, became a second father to Palma and arranged her brilliant marriage to a member of the aristocracy. From a structural point of view the most significant detail that has been revealed is the fact that *La* Barbetti had never even seen her son-in-law and that this creates an opportunity for signorina Cei to speak of him before his entrance. The situation is identical to that in *Il piacere dell'onestà* where Baldovino too is abundantly described by an uninvolved and presumably reliable witness, the go-between Maurizio Setti, and it is different from that in *Il giuoco delle parti* where Leone Gala is first introduced through the potentially less trustworthy report of his estranged wife. The 'before and after' as well as the 'inside' of Lori's existence are stated unequivocally in signorina Cei's lines: 'Ha certi occhi…non so! Vedesse come guarda! come ascolta! Come se le cose, i rumori, le voci stesse a lui piú note, quella della figlia, dell'amico, avessero un aspetto, un suono, ch'egli non riuscisse piú ad avvertire. Come se la vita tutt'intorno, gli si fosse…non so, quasi diradata…Sarà forse per l'abitudine che ha preso…' (MN, I, 1115) [He has such an expression…I can't describe it! You should see how he looks! how he listens! As though the things, the sounds, the voices most familiar to him, his daughter's, his best friend's, had an appearance, a sound that he is no longer able to perceive. As though life all around him had…I don't know how to put it, had thinned out, grown sparse…It may be because of the habit he's gotten into…]. The habit is the daily visit to his wife's grave, which has been going on for sixteen years – a fact so shocking and abnormal by superficial standards that *La* Barbetti (the snooping old woman who in this play has a role analogous to the small town gossips of *Cosí è (se vi pare)*) casts doubt on it by implying that it must be a mistress of flesh and blood that he is visiting. Lori's entrance a few moments later dispels that doubt as the stage directions describe a man prematurely aged, whose facial expression constantly moves from exceptional alertness caused by an intense inner life to a kind of sudden forgetfulness which leaves him defenceless and reveals his 'sad, meek and above all gullible' nature. Pirandello's adjectives *triste, remissivo e sopra tutto credulo* are to be taken not as condemnations of weak mindedness but as invitations to compassion for one of the world's most ordinary individuals, for what the French would call *un homme rangé*.

This obviously 'bruised' individual, who has done nothing to deserve his fate except to be perhaps too trusting, too upright to suspect duplicity in others, will now be tested by a series of trials. The first trial, the first difficult situation to endure, occurs in Act I and is triggered by the presence of La Barbetti in his house, which he considers an insult to the memory of his wife. No one agrees with him. Palma's reception of her long-lost grandmother is lighthearted and jocular, and she is annoyed with Lori for injecting a note of gloom into her wedding-day, for dredging up the past, that 'before' which now with her marriage could well be forgotten. Palma is supported by her entourage: her husband, his friend, and especially by Salvo Manfroni. In their first scene together (there is one in each act) Manfroni expostulates with Lori, shows his irritation, his exasperation with Lori's behaviour: this was not an event to take seriously, he concludes at the end, but 'una farsa. La farsa che quel vecchio pappagallo lí (i.e. La Barbetti) era venuta a offrirci inaspettatamente...' (MN, I, 1124) [the farce that that old parrot there had come to play for us unexpectedly]. (Thus incidentally Pirandello defines the aesthetic function of the beginning of the play within its over-all dramatic economy.) At the end of the act Lori is left alone: in a beautifully orchestrated *decrescendo* all the others have left. No one has wanted to or has been able to listen to his 'reasons' (for wanting La Barbetti out of the house) and he sets off for the cemetery as usual, taking some of the wedding flowers with him to put on Silvia's grave. The first of Lori's trials has not basically changed him nor changed the pattern of his life; his ability to rely on the 'rimedio', the mending patch or the escape valve for his unhappy situation has not been undermined.

There is a time lapse between Acts I and II. We are now in Palma's new home: a new interior marks a total change in social class. In this 'ricco salone' with its glass doors, its beautiful furniture, its vista over the garden, its doors through which one glimpses the dining room and the games room, there is no place for a figure such as La Barbetti, hardly any place for a Lori, and there may not even be a place, as we learn from an exchange between Palma and Manfroni, for as accomplished a 'musino di volpe' [foxy little creature] as signorina Cei has revealed herself to be in the intervening time. The beginning of the act is a lesson in *saper vivere*, in how to juggle appearance and reality in order to keep others from knowing what one knows, in how to bolster their self-image while being actually superior to them. Manfroni's tone is similar to Laudisi's in *Cosí è (se vi pare)* at this point, but instead of a recalcitrant audience to scoff at him, he has Palma and signorina Cei, the first ready to learn the lesson, the second already versed in understanding the 'game'. We are in the social world that Verga recognized as the most difficult to reproduce because of the complicated mechanism of its passions and the smooth formality under which they are hidden (Preface to *I Malavoglia*). Lori's second trial occurs in this setting. He is greeted, as has become usual in Palma's home, with annoyance and impatience and, left alone with Manfroni, he is told by him once again that since conditions have changed he should change too: 'Vieni, ma con un'aria, con un tono piú conveniente, ormai, che renda anche agli altri piú agevole il trattare con te...' (MN, I, 1143) [Continue coming (to Palma's home), but with an attitude, a manner that is more appropriate, that will make it easier for others too to deal with you]. This scene with Manfroni underlines Lori's present condition and shows Manfroni ensconced in the new home while Lori is virtually excluded from it, but it does not dredge up material from the past. That is the function of the next two scenes: a short one between Lori and signorina Cei who has discovered that Lori has for a long time known that Manfroni plagiarized Agliani's work; and a long one, *the* scene in this play, between Lori and Palma, in which the notion of plagiarism, the appropriation of something that belongs to another, is extended to the fundamental relationship that exists between individuals: man and wife, parents and children. We are at the centre of Pirandello's microcosm.

The scene is ushered in by a long pause: Lori has been left alone on stage and has sat down in the arm-chair that Manfroni normally occupies. A servant comes in to turn off the central light. This is a scene to be played by twilight: the focus is on inner life, the revelation will deal with feeling. When Palma comes in she mistakes Lori for Manfroni and approaches him affectionately, calling him 'Father'. The substitution that has been building up over the years is now completely achieved, and it is in the next moments that Lori will learn that it is actually based on a switching of roles that took place years ago. Palma knows that she is Manfroni's child for he has told her so. He has also told her that Lori has known all along. This is Lori's *anagnorisis*, his recognition of his true condition: he has been robbed of his daughter, robbed of his wife, robbed of his self-esteem, for with the word with which Agata had referred to Baldovino before she came to know him ('quest'uomo che dev'essere vile, vile, se si presta a questo' (MN, I, 619) [this man who must be despicable, despicable, if he lends himself to this]), Lori now refers to how he must have

appeared to others: 'Ma che essere vile sono dunque io stato per voi?'
(MN, I, 1152) [But what kind of a despicable being have I been for
you?]. Palma rejects the word *vile*, substituting *ostinato* for it, thus
calling attention to the efforts made in this entourage where the social
niceties are of prime importance, to draw Lori in, to make him give up
his grief, to absorb him into a *modus vivendi* which masks 'the dark
abyss' of feeling with polite formalities. But Lori is now even less able
to respond to this appeal than before. The rest of the act is given over to
the most intense introspection, Lori's part here being surely one of the
most difficult in all of Pirandello's theatre to interpret. In a relentless
crescendo Lori passes from insight to insight (whose lexical clue is the
repetition of the word *see*), from the realization that the deception
had not been in others but in himself for he had misread the signs
('Non m'ha ingannato nessuno! Io, io non ho visto...' [No one
deceived me! It was I, I who did not see]) to the sudden rising up of a
suppressed scene from the past ('Che cosa sto vedendo...' [What am I
seeing]) which was evidence of the adultery had he been able to perceive it, to the complete rupture with which the act ends. 'Nulla tu
per me, nulla io per te, piú nulla' [You are nothing to me, I am
nothing to you, nothing any more], he says to Palma pushing her
from him; and the nothingness, the emptiness, the blank grows to
the harrowing proportions of an all-enveloping and inescapable condition as with lightning rapidity it englobes the past as well: 'E se
sapessi come lo sento adesso, tutt'a un tratto, che sono tanti anni, di
questo nulla!' [And if you only knew how I feel it now, suddenly,
that this nothing has been so for many years]. We are here in the
atmosphere of the highest tragedy: this is a moment comparable to
Oedipus' recognition of his situation or to Christ's anguish on the
Cross, 'Oh, Father, why have you abandoned me?' In Pirandello's
theatre there is only one other comparable moment; it comes, as we
shall see, in *Enrico IV*.

But *Tutto per bene* is *not Enrico IV*. It has affinities with *Il piacere
dell'onestà*, and it is these that have probably influenced the resolution
in Act III, which by contrast to the final total break in the short story
(and in *Enrico IV*) reintegrates Lori into the social environment in
which he lives. The short story ends with Lori setting off for the
cemetery once more: the 'remedy' that had worked for him ever since
Silvia's death continues to do so even after the shattering experience of
the destruction of his past. But his exclusion from the life of his
'daughter', her husband, and his old friend Manfroni (Verona in the
story) is now complete: their *entente* is so perfect ('si erano cosí bene

intesi fra loro' (NA, I, 361) [they were in such perfect agreement with one another]) that there is no longer any room for him among them. Not so in the play. The end of Act II does not mark the conclusion of the action. In an encounter strongly reminiscent of certain scenes in *Enrico IV*, Act III pits Lori first against Manfroni alone, and then against Manfroni and Palma and her husband. With discomposed words and gestures similar to those of the nameless protagonist of *Enrico IV* and the same madman's cunning, Lori unmasks Manfroni (= Belcredi in *Enrico IV*) and play-acts (*fa la commedia*) for him and the others in a scene which at one moment convinces Palma that Manfroni was mistaken in thinking that he is her father and immediately after shows her that he was right. But unlike 'Enrico IV' Lori cannot take refuge in madness: in contrast to 'Enrico''s sense of non being (*'uno che non sono io, che non sono mai stato io'*, MN, I, 1170; emphasis Pirandello's; [someone who is not I, who has never been I]) Lori's is delimited, and his act of aggression is not a sword thrust that kills, but a revelation of the truth that routs his rival.

This solution is possible because there is a truly remarkable woman close to Lori, something that 'Enrico' is deprived of. 'Una donna *qualunque*, lassù, non ci può essere' [There can be no ordinary woman up there], we quoted Laudisi apropos signora Ponza. Palma is almost, though not quite, another signora Ponza. The word that Pirandello had failed to use in *Così è* (*se vi pare*) appears in *Tutto per bene* as he names the sentiment that is the spring of Palma's (and signora Ponza's) action: *caritas*. As Lori tries for a last time to ward off his humanization, his becoming as others are, Pirandello writes in the stage directions: *'per tentare ancora una difesa contro questa carità di lei, che lo investe, lo frastorna, e quasi lo fa mancare a se stesso'* (MN, I, 1174) [to try one more defence against this charity of hers that overwhelms, confounds, and almost stuns him]. The moment is identical to the one in which Baldovino breaks down and accepts the words that Agata speaks to him as a man and no longer as a 'maschera di padre' (MN, I, 667) [a father's *persona*]. But because in *Il piacere dell'onestà* the conciliation, the accommodation, the *exodos* of comedy occurs for a traditionally conceived couple (husband and wife standing for the even more traditional 'girl and boy') and in *Tutto per bene* the 'triumphant' couple is a daughter and a man who is not even her real father, the parallel in the two plays has not generally been recognized.

Instead, the critics have almost always spoken of the 'bitter irony' of the ending, giving the last words uttered by Lori, 'tutto per bene', the meaning of 'all as it should be' (and as it is not), thus reading the play

as an exposé of duplicity in social life in line with the canonical interpretation of that other *grottesco*, *La maschera e il volto*. But Lori's final
comment can also mean 'all done properly' (decently, with good
intentions), done in the acceptable, conventional way which is capable of restoring order out of chaos. This second interpretation supports our awareness of Pirandello's feeling of compassion for Lori, a
point well perceived by Silvio D'Amico in *Il teatro dei fantocci* when
he speaks of Pirandello accompanying Lori in his despair ('si mette ad
accompagnare la disperazione del suo Martino'), a despair that leaves
Lori shattered and weak, all his energies spent, barely able as he is led
away by Palma to wave a friendly greeting to the exorcized, no
longer threatening Manfroni.

On 12 October 1920 Pirandello assured Ruggeri that there would
doubtless be a new play written expressly for him: 'La [la commedia]
penserò e la scriverò, tenendo Lei sempre presente, come ho fatto per
Baldovino, per Leone Gala, per Martino Lori, che mi vivono sempre
davanti con la sua persona, la sua voce, col suo gesto e coi suoi silenzi'
[I shall think it (the play) up and write it keeping you in mind, as I did
for Baldovino, Leone Gala, Martino Lori, who continue to live before
me in your person, with your voice, your gestures, your silences].
Before he turned to the new play, however, another year was to pass,
the year that saw the premières of *Come prima, meglio di prima*, *Cecè*,
La signora Morli, una e due, and most important of all, *Sei personaggi*. In
the letter to Ruggeri of 21 September 1921 which presents *Enrico IV*
in the same manner in which *Tutto per bene* had been presented two
years earlier, Pirandello refers to his disappointment at having had to
entrust the role of the Father in *Sei personaggi* to another actor while
'm'ero figurato *Lei* e non Gigetto Almirante nella personificazione
della parte del *Padre*' [I had imagined *you* and not Gigetto Almirante
in the personification of the role of the Father]. To be noted in
particular is the underscoring of 'Lei' and what might be considered
the redundant use of 'personificazione' were it not that the word so
strongly and economically expresses that union of character and
actor on which is based Pirandello's view of drama as externalized in
performance, and also, as we can see here, as conditioning the very
genesis of the work.

In the second (Bemporad) edition of *Maschere nude*, the only one to
make use of genre designations, Pirandello reserved the term
'tragedy' for only three of his plays: *Enrico IV*, *La vita che ti diedi*, and
Diana e la Tuda. If form is, according to Kenneth Burke, 'the arousing

of the expectation in an audience and the gratifying of that expectation', then genre is the arousing and gratification of a specific expectation. The aspect of tragedy in *Enrico IV* has been variously dealt with by critics, many of whom were not even aware that Pirandello had at one time actually called the play a tragedy. In *Storia di Pirandello*, for instance, Leone De Castris describes the nameless protagonist as 'the most desperate, the most tragic of Pirandello's characters', the one in whom 'passion and consciousness, illusion and reality' coexist inextricably from the beginning, making him 'a figure of superhuman greatness, the symbol of human despair'. In his review of the first Rome performance in October 1922, Tilgher defined the play as 'the tragedy of Life that was kept from living, strangled by a Form through which it should have passed and that instead swallowed it'. Benjamin Crémieux, in his 1928 dissertation *Henri IV et la dramaturgie de Luigi Pirandello*, mindful of the Greek concept of tragedy, differentiates 'Henry IV' from his predecessors in Pirandello's theatre because he is completely innocent: 'Fate alone is responsible, and this innocence of the hero raises the tragedy of *Henry IV* to a kind of absolute, makes it a kind of "pure tragedy"'. Implicit in these statements is the belief, obviously shared by Pirandello, that a distinct literary form continues to give expression to the concept of the tragic, a concept whose definition ranges from 'the representation of personal suffering and heroism' (George Steiner) to 'the literary obsession with extremity, with the exceptional' (Murray Krieger), 'the vision of life which in its comprehension of complexity, incongruity, and paradox, is the antithesis of the popular vision' (Herbert J. Muller), and 'the summit or end stage, always concerned with problems of value, human life seen in an ultimate perspective' (R. J. Dorius). More recently, reflecting a diffused awareness of the historical 'death of tragedy' in an age sometimes characterized as under the domination of 'the bourgeois ideology [which] does not admit that its own claim to totality... be questioned by the challenging and negating function of the tragic' (Bárberi Squarotti) and sometimes as an age that has lost the sense of the sacred, *Enrico IV* has been denied the designation of tragedy altogether or else the noun has been qualified by modifiers that profoundly change its original meaning of an absolute. Thus Eric Bentley has called *Enrico IV* 'not tragedy, a heroic genre, but post-Dostoevsky psychological drama showing the decline and fall of a man through mental sickness to crime'; Karl S. Guthke cites it (and *Sei personaggi*) as the best of the tragicomedies of the *teatro del grottesco*; Roberto Alonge gives it an 'absurdist' reading and coins the expression 'tragedia astratta' (i.e., not socio-historical) for it; and Bárberi Squarotti continues the degradation of Pirandello's representation of existential suffering by calling it 'tragedia carnevalesca' (insanity being only one form of the masks or masquerades of man).

Federico Doglio, not a literary scholar but a student and practitioner of 'theatre arts', in his review of documents which can help in understanding – in 'taking hold of', as he puts it – *Enrico IV*, recalls Ruggeri's extremely successful performances of *Hamlet* beginning in 1915, and quotes from Silvio D'Amico's review of one of them. The passage (in which D'Amico is actually critical of Ruggeri's interpretation) is of the greatest interest for the light it throws on the possible influence of *Hamlet* on *Enrico IV*, not generically by way of tragedy in the abstract but specifically by way of Ruggeri. Faced with the problem of turning the essentially static culmination of tragedy into action (a problem exacerbated in the case of *Hamlet* because its theme is precisely the inability to act), Ruggeri 'modernized' the Danish prince, according to D'Amico, by 'making him move about agitatedly, running, raising his arms, expressing his despair physically. ... The somewhat noisy and garish, and yet methodical, insanity that Ruggeri feigns in the presence of others and that gives way to introspectiveness when he is alone, is not Hamlet's glacial insanity...' – but, we might add, it is remarkably close to 'Henry' 's. Ruggeri's representation of Hamlet's madness, then, may have been an important factor in Pirandello's 'idea' for the new play he was readying for him, a play for which, atypically, there is no precedent in the narrative works (although Alonge suggests such a precedent in *La tragedia di un personaggio*), and which by contrast with the other plays written for Ruggeri – not to speak of the earlier ones written for Musco – draws 'le sue note di significazione universale' not in a setting of 'povere piccole creature miserevoli' (D'Amico's words in his review of the Rome première) but among 'i grandi del potere', among the makers of history (Bárberi Squarotti's words), in the setting, that is, usual to tragedy.

A second important feature differentiates this play from the others first performed by Ruggeri, though not from those *written* for him if we remember that the role of the Father in *Sei personaggi* was also intended for him and that he indeed played it later and even produced and directed the play. It is the conscious and explicit exploitation of the theatrical – understood here in the concrete sense of the space where theatre is made – which Pirandello had just explored in many of its aspects, as we shall see, in *Sei personaggi*.

In a number of Pirandello's plays – *Sei personaggi*, *Ciascuno a suo modo*, *All'uscita*, *I giganti della montagna* – the Cast of Characters is divided into two groups, the typographical arrangement highlighting the distinction in function and essence between the two. This strategy is not used in *Enrico IV* although it might have helped to clarify, as it does in the instances used, the complicated double story experienced as an initial stumbling block by spectators, readers, reviewers and critics alike. Bentley calls the exposition in Act I 'heavy and overcrowded' and finds that 'confusion here is presented confusingly'. The criticism, often repeated, bears examination, for part of the 'confusion' arises from the identity of the historical Henry IV at issue, and we know that the question of identity in general looms large in Pirandello's work. The Henry IV of the play is *not* the better known Henri IV of France, the sixteenth-century restorer of French unity whose 'Paris vaut bien une messe' was long a European household expression, but the eleventh-century German emperor whose struggles with Pope Gregory VII over the right of investiture led to his humbling at Canossa (in Tuscany) where he was forced to wait two days in the snow before being admitted to present his submission to the pope. That there was never any question in Pirandello's mind which Henry the play dealt with nor any doubt that his Italian audience would find no difficulty in making the correct identification readily is borne out by the absence of any reference to the historical facts of Henry's life in his 21 September 1921 letter to Ruggeri. That letter deals, instead, with the facts of the life of the nameless protagonist of the play, whose masquerade as Henry IV had lasted about twenty years when the tragedy on stage begins. Yet a good part of Act I *is* devoted to the exposition of the historical facts, for without a fresh and selective, a pointed, rehearsing of them, it would be impossible for them to be acted out and it would be impossible for the impersonators to judge one another and for the audience to judge the impersonators. Like a troupe of actors, the habitual entourage of 'Enrico IV' and the visitors who come to see him on this particular day must be assigned their parts and directed in their performance. But since, unlike *Sei personaggi*, *Enrico IV* is not a play-within-a-play and presents the audience with only one stage – the traditional space where theatrical illusion is created, and not that additional space where it is unmasked – the play's references to itself as a play remain implicit and the play-acting is so much part of the action itself that the characters, whether they wear costume or not, remain themselves, caught up in one of those 'real' situations in Pirandello's theatre in which an 'exceptional' individual fights for his *Lebensraum*. The Cast of Characters gives only one slight hint of a difference in essence between the various characters: *i quattro finti Consiglieri Segreti* [the four make-believe Secret Councillors] are listed with their historical names first and their real names in parentheses (*not* their nicknames, as Edward Storer has it in the English version, for though some of the names are nicknames, they are not nicknames of the historical names). All the other characters are listed with their real names (no indication of the roles they are to play is given, inasmuch as some of these roles are interchangeable). The protagonist himself is nameless, a sequence of ellipsis points followed by the name of his role in parentheses. He is referred to as 'Henry IV' in the present writing.

Who *is* 'Enrico IV'? We asked the same question apropos Baldovino in *Il piacere dell'onestà*, and saw how there and in the two subsequent plays Pirandello delayed the entrance of the principal character so that he could be properly 'introduced'. In contrast to Verga's rejection of *mise en scène* for his characters, whom he preferred to have step forth at once and reveal themselves dramatically through action rather than through commentary, Pirandello feels the need for careful narrative building-up of the character, his original distrust of the theatre – 'Il teatro è l'arte della scopa', we quoted him earlier – coming to the fore again in the fear (all too often justified!) of having his work misunderstood. What we, spectators and readers, first learn of 'Henry IV' is the role he has chosen for himself: the form whose content is missing, Landolfo puts it, the most interesting of the minor characters, whose similarity in function to Laudisi has gone completely unnoted. It is 'Henry''s role which made necessary the hiring of a new servant to replace the one who before his death had represented the Bishop Adalbert in 'Henry''s delusion; and it is because Fino (or Bertoldo, as he is known in the fiction) must be briefed that we learn of the circumstances of the historical Henry's life and are reminded of the people who surrounded him: Gregory VII, Peter Damiani, the Empress Bertha, her mother the Duchess Adelaide, the Countess (Pirandello gives her the title of Marchesa) Matilda, the Abbot of Cluny, etc. In his role, 'Henry' is a persecuted man, fearful, suspicious and wilful, at the mercy of his enemies, an imperilled if not a fallen king. But to learn about current living arrangements in this 'solitary villa in Umbria, today' (except for what can be gathered visually from the stage set and incidentally from some remarks during Fino's briefing), we must wait until later in the act, when the majordomo

Giovanni, anachronistically dressed in tails, enters to announce the arrival of visitors. It is then that the second story begins to unfold alongside the first, the content not of Henry's life but of 'Henry''s.

A link between the first and subsequent scenes of Act I are the two portraits which 'thrust forth' (*avventano*) from the back wall: the supreme anachronism of the setting, 'una bella stonatura' [quite a discord] as even the stolid Bertoldo perceives them. They represent a modern-day lady and gentleman dressed up as Matilda of Tuscany and the Emperor Henry IV, and they have already been commented upon in Landolfo's 'mirror speech', a pendant in the minor key to Laudisi's exuberant words. Among the visitors is Marchesa Matilde Spina, the original of the portrait, and her daughter who is engaged to Di Nolli, 'Enrico''s young nephew, the man who hired Fino in the first place. There is also a doctor with them, one of many, we are given to understand by Landolfo, who over the years have come to examine 'Henry'. And there is a fifth person, Matilde's lover Belcredi, an ambiguous individual 'with a curious bird-like head', in whom great alertness and somnolent Oriental laziness clash: a redoubtable swordsman (like Miglioriti, Leone's intended opponent in *Il giuoco delle parti*), who speaks with an unexpected nasal drawl, as Pirandello takes the trouble to describe him in the stage directions. They have come ostensibly on a mission of mercy, to fulfil Di Nolli's deathbed promise to his mother that he would look after his uncle, who she felt was close to recovery. Through the verbal skirmishes of Matilde and Belcredi, and through the Doctor's questions, both of which have Matilde's portrait as focus, we learn of the circumstances of the accident that years earlier had led to 'Henry''s fixation. The reconstruction places the following facts in evidence: in his youth 'Henry' belonged to a group of wealthy aristocrats whose amusements included carnival revelries; from an illustrated weekly Belcredi took the idea of an historical cavalcade for which each of the participants would choose a figure to impersonate; influenced by her name, Matilde chose the Countess Matilda of Tuscany; to this 'Henry' countered that then he would be at her feet, as Henry at Canossa; during the cavalcade he fell from the horse and fainted; when he came to again and rejoined the party he seemed at first perfectly recovered, unscathed; but when he drew his sword against the pranksters who were needling him, it became obvious that he was playing his part in earnest, his mask no longer a coarse and freakish one but the terrible mask of madness, Madness personified, as Matilde recalls with a renewed shudder of almost awe-filled horror. It is one of the high

points of Act I, the past made present in a moment of suspension of
time.

These are the external events, the story that can be retold in sequence. Underlying it, is a predisposition – 'Henry''s being different,
more intense, more talented and unpredictable, extreme in his elation
and in his watchful lucidity, a man to fear, capable of impressing, if
only briefly, even a vain, superficial, immature girl like Matilde at
the time – a predisposition for suffering, for self-inflicted punishment.
All this is already present, implicit in that first scene with the visitors,
in which the model of victim and chorus group from *Cosí è (se vi pare)*
is repeated, but with the added complication of a triangle situation.
'Enrico IV' is not only alone, where the Ponzas and signora Frola form
a mutually supporting unit, he is also vulnerable in the particular way
that an unrequited lover is.

This initial insight, this first exposition of *sentimento del contrario*,
is cut short by a return to farce, by a demonstration of the subterfuges
to which the insane condemn the sane. Bertoldo rushes in, unable to
abide by the terms of his employment any longer, and he throws
everything into confusion. Off-stage, 'Henry' is in a rage. To calm
him Landolfo suggests that the 'visit' take place at once. Roles (and
costumes) are distributed, for though it would be enough for the
Doctor to see 'Henry', neither Matilde nor Belcredi, egged on by
sinister curiosity, want to miss the opportunity. The flurry dies down
as one of the Councillors throws open the door and solemnly
announces the entrance of the Emperor.

The figure that steps on stage has precedents in Pirandello's theatre.
Like Ciampa and Chiàrchiaro, Baldovino and Lori, he bears the
visible marks of the mental anguish he has suffered. Like Madama
Pace and the old woman in *L'umorismo*, his garishly dyed hair renders
him grotesque. But nowhere else has Pirandello created a figure
equally frightening and pitiful, so totally arresting as the visual
emblem of a disturbance, a spiritual cataclysm that is all-engulfing.
Not to look beyond the surface here, to snicker rather than to be
struck dumb, to see in 'Henry' the fortunate child of wealth, coddled
in the princely prison that money can buy, or to see in him (as the
Doctor does) a guinea pig for a cure that is no more than a silly
stratagem, is to be indeed innerly dead, incapable of grasping the
meaning of insanity for its victim and for the society which must
segregate it as a potential contamination. And indeed, 'Henry''s
appearance precludes, cuts short and makes impossible, any reaction
such as that of the Agazzis and Sirellis, punctuated by the expectant,

excited repetition of 'pazzo lui o pazzo lei'.

In terms of the double story which is being developed, and which is now, already, rushing to its resolution, the figure that steps on stage is both Henry and 'Henry', and it is at the same time neither. His regal garb is covered by the penitent's habit, as at Canossa. He is in his fifties, deathly pale, his hair at the back gray. But in the front and along the temples he is blonde, the hair awkwardly dyed. And amidst the tragic pallor his cheeks too are painted, doll-like. The suggestion of the puppet-world is unmistakable, but there are no echoes of childish voices or scraping chairs to recall that old and popular form of entertainment. Instead, there is the expression of his eyes, 'una fissità spasimosa, che fa spavento' [a convulsive fixedness, which is frightening]. And there is his bearing, half humble repentance, half suppressed rebellion against undeserved humiliation. From this point on, the main line of tension, the suspense in every scene in which 'Henry' appears, will be the constant interchange of parts; the questions whether, when, and how he is insane never conclusively answered. This is the case in the hastily concerted scene in Act I in which Donna Matilde is sure that he has recognized her in spite of her disguise as Henry's mother-in-law, the Duchess Adelaide, and in which he 'unmasks' Belcredi, insisting that he is Henry's bitterest enemy Peter Damiani while the Councillors reassure him repeatedly that it is only a poor monk in the Abbot's entourage. It is also the case in the brief leave-taking scene in Act II when 'Henry' reveals his secret love for the Countess Matilda to Donna Matilde (as Adelaide) and confides in the Doctor that he is the victim of hallucinations: 'tante immagini scompigliate, che ridono, smontate da cavallo' [so many distorted images that laugh, just dismounted from their horses], an all too-transparent reference to that moment of 'Henry''s life of which Henry could have no knowledge. And it is again the case in the first scene of Act II, in which 'Henry' does not appear but in which his case is diagnosed. This scene lacks the dramatic intensity of the rest of the play, but is not for all that less important. After the tumultuous succession of extraordinary events in Act I, almost as though there had been no intermission, Pirandello provides the audience with a breathing spell. The different assessments of 'Henry''s condition, the inferences to be drawn from his behaviour, the details of his proposed cure, as *all* the outsiders are on stage together – not only Donna Matilde, the Doctor and Belcredi, but also Di Nolli and Frida and finally Landolfo representing the Councillors – offer different interpretations and rationalizations which must be weighed by the audience before reaching its own conclusions, before that act of judgement which is required of it here as it is in all of Pirandello's theatre.

The last part of Act II consists of a scene which is unique in the play, but which points beyond the ending of the play itself to what 'Henry''s life will be afterwards. It begins with a break, an instant and abrupt change that no preceding action has prepared us for. Left alone by the departing 'visitors', surrounded only by his Councillors, not in the public throne room but in a more intimate living room or study, 'il grande Mascherato', as Pirandello calls him in what is perhaps the absolute high point of the play as *written* text, reveals himself to be sane. He recognizes his power for what it is, his companions for what they are, and he brands the visitors who have just left with his utter moral contempt: 'una è una baldracca, l'altro un sudicio libertino, l'altro un impostore' [one is a whore, the other a filthy libertine, the third an impostor]. But his disgust and clairvoyance go even further, enveloping life itself with its dead weight of tradition and custom, of stale, repeated words which yet have the power to stigmatize and destroy: 'Credete di vivere? Rimasticate la vita dei morti!' [You think you're living? You're only rechewing the life of the dead!], he barks out, rejecting everything that men live by, and stating in his own words what Pirandello will repeat only moments later in the stage directions. For what is being acted out in this remote Umbrian villa is but a metaphorical transposition of the essence of all living: 'una spaventosa miseria che non è di lui solo, ma di tutti' [an appalling misery which is not only 'Henry''s but every man's]. Antidote, cure for this insight – as 'filosofia del lontano' and 'lanterninosofia' are in a lighter vein for others of Pirandello's characters at different junctures in his work – is 'il piacere della storia', the certainty of knowing that what has happened in history cannot change, that 'every effect will obediently follow its cause…every event unfold precisely and coherently in its every particular'. And the act ends as 'Henry', disappointing the expectation of his Councillors that now that he is sane everything in his life will change (but not Landolfo's, the only one to have 'understood'), opens the door to Giovanni, 'who is coming as he does every evening to play the monk', and sitting down in the dusk, by the flickering light of an ancient lamp, in a scene of incomparable peacefulness, takes up again the dictation of his memoirs.

'Henry''s reasons, which have been told in metaphysical terms in the final scene of Act II, will now be retold differently, as befits a different audience, in Act III. 'Henry' will be addressing not the privileged audience that shares his life, but the ordinary audience, the improvised visitors who for whatever motives have come to spy on him, the enemy audience, one of whose members – as in the best detective novels – has actually been the cause of his exclusion, the instrument of what turns out to be not Fate but a vile practical joke. An important change has occurred in the throne room as 'Henry', finished with the evening's dictation, now crosses it wearily. The two portraits have been removed and Frida, dressed as Matilda of Tuscany, and Di Nolli, as the young Henry IV, stand in their place. Like Melisande and the troubadour Rudel, the figures in the tapestry of Heine's ballad referred to in Pirandello's 1899 essay *L'azione parlata*, Frida 'comes alive', leans out of her niche, and calls to 'Henry'. He is not startled but terrorized, 'come colpito a tradimento da una rasojata alla schiena' [as though hit traitorously in the back by a razor slash] – the Sicilian peasant act of violence evoked here pointing back with lightning rapidity to the very subsoil of Pirandello's art. As he thinks that he is indeed mad and as Frida cries out in fear, the others rush in, including Donna Matilde (who is also dressed as Matilda of Tuscany), and the eerie lighting of the electric bulbs hidden in the ceiling suddenly floods the scene.

We now learn the rest of the story: 'Henry''s recovery twelve years after the accident and his realization then that there was nowhere for him to go, that the time that had not passed for him had passed for others, and that there would be nothing left for him at the 'banquet feast' of life; and from the more distant past, that the horse from which he fell on that fatal Carnival day had been pricked from behind by Belcredi and that that was the reason why it reared. The scene demonstrates, acts out, what has been referred to earlier: 'Henry''s 'difference' from the young aristocrats whose pastimes he shared in youth, and his rejection of the alternative course of action he could have chosen when he discovered that he was well again, that of re-joining the crowd and taking up his life once more where it had been interrupted. With cutting sarcasm and pent-up disgust, he asks the intruders – the professionally deformed Doctor, the evil Belcredi, and the vacillating Donna Matilde – whether they are now expecting him to take off his costume and don that other one, 'marsina e cravatta bianca' [tails and white tie], in which to accompany Belcredi to the Club or to Donna Matilde's. It is important to make a distinction here: just as Mattia Pascal's quotation from a novel whose principal characters are a count and a countess is not to be taken as Pirandello's criticism of literature dealing with the upper classes, so reference to evening clothes here is not a rejection of a way of life defined in class-conscious terms. Nor is it a rejection of life *tout court*. 'Henry' does not choose suicide, as Ersilia Drei is forced to do in *Vestire gli ignudi*. Only a little later in the play he refers again to the costume he wears, this time to say that the four young men who are his Councillors must be forgiven for their stupid assumption that now that they have revealed to the others that he is sane, they could still all five continue play-acting together: what they have not understood, as he has, is that 'l'abito, il loro abito' is 'la loro stessa persona'. But again a distinction is to be made: the statement does not say that 'clothes make the man' in a sociological or psychological sense (there would be no difficulty in understanding that), but that without clothes there would be no man, without form there is no content. The difference between the two groups surrounding 'Henry', neither of which has 'understood', is that the one is evil while the other is benign. And that is why the last two scenes balance one another so perfectly: the first (last scene of Act II) ending in the tranquillity of routine, the second (all of Act III) in murder. For, with a madman's cunning, as though completing an action that had remained in suspense for twenty years and whose urgency is now redoubled by Belcredi's renewed taunting and unfeeling references to insanity as a joke, a disguise playfully put on and as lightly taken off, 'Henry' lunges for the real sword that hangs by Landolfo's side as part of his make-believe get-up, and kills his rival.

As in *Il giuoco delle parti* so in *Enrico IV* the violent end, the sword thrust that kills, could not be avoided. To the squeamish the 'punishment' meted out may seem excessive. But we must think of the magnitude of the 'crime'. The 'fino giuoco mortale' of *Il giuoco delle parti*, which leads to Silia's 'setting up' her husband to be killed by 'one of the best swordsmen in town' because she cannot tolerate her feeling of inferiority to him, has its debased counterpart in Belcredi's practical joke in *Enrico IV*. It is one of those stupid, thoughtless acts of aggression laughingly condoned in the respectable circles of the well-adjusted, of those who in self-protection against feelings of sympathy and compassion remain firmly attached to the lower level of *avvertimento del contrario*. Leone's revenge is by proxy, 'Henry''s, direct, Both succeed in eliminating their rivals but, 'having understood the game', can take little joy in the victory. In the Christian universe, moreover, whose moral laws are based on the sacredness of human life because it is God-given, the ultimate crime must be followed by the ultimate punishment. 'Henry''s act of murder has taken place before the eyes of the audience; so will his assumption of punishment. Drawing his Councillors around him, 'as though to shield himself', he murmurs horror-stricken: 'Ora sí...per forza...qua insieme...e per sempre!' [Now, yes...perforce...together here...for always]. To interpret this conclusion, as has been done, as a cold-blooded decision on 'Henry''s part to continue to feign insanity in order to escape conviction for murder is to be numb to the cumulative effect of all that has preceded it and to be guilty of one of those intolerable trivializations that abound in Pirandello criticism.

As is so often the case for works of art, *Enrico IV* and the figure of its nameless protagonist gain in depth when viewed against the background of the specific period of activity that saw their conception. From *Così è (se vi pare)* to *Enrico IV* Pirandello lived through a period of exceptional creative productivity, buoyed by the pervasive conviction that a turning point had been reached in the history of Italian theatre and by the fortunate encounter with a fellow artist in whose sympathetic understanding and interpretive capacity he had full confidence. On 14 July 1922, before a ten-year break in his published correspondence with him, Pirandello again wrote to Ruggeri that he was thinking of a new play for him: he had two possibilities in mind, but he was conscious of how difficult it would be to equal 'l'altezza vertiginosa da Lei raggiunta con l'interpretazione dell'*Enrico IV*' [the intoxicating height reached by you in the interpretation of *Enrico IV*].

4. *Sei personaggi in cerca d'autore*

Sei personaggi was first performed in Rome, 10 May 1921. Pirandello was in his fifties. He had behind him, as we have seen, considerable literary activity. To his early poems and essays, the 1904 success of the novel *Il fu Mattia Pascal*, and the publication of fifteen volumes of short stories, had been added since 1917 the more and more frequent composition and production of plays. 'Il mio è stato un teatro di guerra', he was to write in retrospect. 'La guerra ha rivelato a me stesso il teatro: quando le passioni si scatenarono, quelle passioni io feci soffrire alle mie creature sui palcoscenici' (in *Quadrivio*, 18 nov. 1934). [Mine was a war theatre. The War revealed the theatre to me. When passions were let loose, I had my characters suffer those passions on stage].

In 1921 Europe was still recovering from the effects of war and revolution. The relatively stable political and social world of the late nineteenth and early twentieth centuries had been shattered, the map of Central Europe redrawn, Russian exiles had fled to the West bringing with them their characteristic artistic talent, Slavic intenseness, and experience of theatre. In Italy there was deep internal turmoil soon to be calmed and controlled by the Fascist rise to power. Many in the audience at that première of *Sei personaggi* no doubt shared with Pirandello the disorienting experience of rapidly changing times which he, born in a Sicilian backwater in 1867, epitomized in the image of succeeding lights: 'Perchè quattro generazioni di lumi', a minor character in *Quaderni di Serafino Gubbio (Si gira…)* says, 'quattro, olio, petrolio, gas e luce elettrica, nel giro di sessant'anni, son troppe, sa? e ci si guasta la vista, e anche la testa; anche la testa un poco' (TR, II, 609) [Because four generations of lamps, oil, paraffin, gas, and electric light, in the course of sixty years, that's too much, you know. It ruins one's eyesight, and one's mind too. One's mind too, a little].

The early productions of *Sei personaggi* made theatrical history. As the play moved from Rome to Milan, to London, New York, Paris, Vienna, and Berlin, with stops in many other cities along the way, its meaning became progressively clarified in the interpretations of

directors, actors, and critics. Among a host of others, there were Dario
Niccodemi (the first director), Lamberto Picasso (who directed the
play later and also played the role of the Father), G.B. Shaw (who
insisted on its being performed in London in spite of the strictures of
the censor), Stark Young (who reviewed it for the Ametican public),
Benjamin Crémieux (who translated it into French), Georges Pitoëff
(who introduced a spectacular innovation in his 1923 Paris production), Adriano Tilgher (whose 1922–3 articles on Pirandello are said
to have revealed Pirandello to himself), and Max Reinhardt (whose
German productions of Pirandello did more than any others to bring
out the typically theatrical in his art).

In 1925, at the end of this period, Pirandello had ready a significantly
revised edition of the play, introduced by a preface originally published with the title 'Come e perchè ho scritto *Sei personaggi in cerca
d'autore*' ('How and Why I Wrote *Six Characters*'). Today the Preface
must be considered an integral part of the work, even though it is of
course not 'performed' with the play itself. Its existence and its
strategic placement legitimate the inclusion in any discussion of the
play of a consideration of the author's intention. It discloses this
intention and from a formal point of view it reveals something of
Pirandello's habitually complex and on the surface ambiguous tactics
of communication in which the techniques of aggression and suggestion are welded. By virtue of the Preface the play, while remaining
a play, takes on features of narrative, foreshadowing a sub-genre of
the novel which was to become popular later, the *romanzo-saggio*
(essay-like novel) with its strong emphasis on the presentation of the
author's personal point of view. Indeed, *Sei personaggi* is equally well
suited to being read or viewed. In the history of critical reaction to it,
its dual nature of work of literature and work for the stage has
repeatedly made it subject to the dichotomies in judgment and
evaluation that such a distinction suggests.

'Every performance of a play, even by the same actors represents a
different realization of its possibilities, and no single performance can
fully realize all its possibilities'. Thus in *Elements of Drama* (1971)
Scholes and Klaus formulate the principle which justifies a critic's
interest in what happens to a play after it is written, in its *Fortleben*. No
less important as documents for a fuller understanding of a work are
its pre-history, genesis, and early evolution, a study of which represents the more familiar approach in literary studies. In the case of *Sei
personaggi*, designated by Pirandello himself *commedia da farsi* [a play
to be composed], the two approaches can be usefully joined. They

are reciprocally illuminating, not simply in terms of one another (the play's *Fortleben* reflects back on its genesis and forces the author to clarify his ideas and to make his intentions more manifest), but for what they contribute to the elucidation of the text itself, mastery of which in its details must precede all attempts at interpretation and evaluation.

Sei personaggi was first mentioned in a letter by Pirandello to his son, at the time a prisoner of war in Austria, which was written on 23 July 1917: 'Ma ho già la testa piena di cose nuove! Tante novelle...E una stranezza cosí triste, cosí triste: *Sei personaggi in cerca d'autore*: romanzo da fare. Forse tu intendi. Sei personaggi, presi in un dramma terribile, che mi vengono appresso, per esser composti in un romanzo, un'ossessione, e io che non voglio saperne, e io che dico che è inutile e che non m'importa di loro e che non m'importa più di nulla, e loro che mi mostrano tutte le loro piaghe e io che li caccio via... – e cosí alla fine il romanzo da fare verrà fuori fatto' (*Almanacco letterario Bompiani*, 1938) [But my head is already full of so many new things! So many short stories....And a strange thing, so sad, so very sad: *Six Characters in Search of an Author*: a novel to be composed. Maybe you understand. Six characters, caught in a terrible drama, who come to me to be formed into a novel, an obsession (of theirs), and I want to have nothing to do with it, and I tell them it's useless, that I don't care about them and that I don't care about anything any more, and they show me all their sores, and I chase them away....And so, in the end, the novel to be composed will turn out composed].

The passage is of the greatest interest. It shows that some of the basic elements of the work are already well in place: the paradox of characters coming to importune an author, the number of the characters involved, the 'terrible' nature of their predicament, Pirandello's own reaction to it, his annoyance at their insistence enveloped in the feeling of sadness released by their story and probably also by his own helpless and at the same time essential relationship to them. What is not yet fixed is the work's form: the *persona* of the author has not yet divided itself into the characters of Manager and Members of a company of actors, nor has the setting become a stage, nor – to push the projection one step further – has the stage itself been declared to be a metaphor, the concretization of the space in the mind where the creative act takes place. It is in this second area – in what the 1917 letter does not include – that the development of the work down to 1925 takes place. The other features (the inner story of the Characters' lives and their desire for it to be shaped and immortalized by art) had by 1917 an already long and varied history in a number of Pirandello's other works. *Sei personaggi*, which is reported to have been written in the feverish activity of three days and which would be 'rewritten' in the successive four years, was not only to remain but had already been 'in the making' for some time.

How far back we place the origin of the idea for the play depends on how comprehensive is the view we have in general of the genesis of a work, to what distant recesses of infancy and childhood experience we wish or are able to trace it, and on how well we can or care to disentangle the various strands that go to make up Pirandello's copious production. In Pirandello's creative universe *tout se tient* and there are no occasional pieces that are not also attached to the centre. Even the literary journalism of his student years, his book reviews, and his introductions to the works of friends, contain expressions and remarks that are echoed elsewhere in the major works and can serve to add depth to our understanding.

Commonly cited as precedents of *Sei personaggi* are two short stories, *La tragedia di un personaggio* (1911) and *Colloqui coi personaggi* (1915). In both the first-person narrator is a writer who speaks of his habit of granting regularly scheduled interviews to the characters of his future stories. *La tragedia di un personaggio*, endowed as it is with a fully fictional character, Dr Fileno the eccentric discoverer of 'the philosophy of remoteness', has become one of Pirandello's best known stories. But *Colloqui coi personaggi* is only rarely related to the play inasmuch as its strong autobiographical slant has stood in the way of critical success: its 'author', watching the gathering of nascent characters ('shadows in the shadow') in a corner of his room on the 'long sultry summer afternoons' of 1915 shortly after Italy's entry into the War is none other than Pirandello himself. Even closer to *Sei personaggi* than these stories are two entries in Pirandello's notebooks, tentatively and perhaps incorrectly dated 1910 or 1912. The first is a narrative passage describing the feelings of a man of fifty (not yet the play's Father, however) on his way to a certain signora Pace's establishment. The second is a variation on and an expansion of the passage from the letter to Pirandello's son quoted earlier: the characters – the girl, the mother, the son, the other children – have left their author and have begun to act out the scenes of their novel before him, the unhappy and complicated relationships hinted at being already those which we shall come to know better in the play later.

If we wish to cast our net wider and at the same time begin to distinguish between the bodies of material which we shall shortly describe as the three basic structural elements in the play, there are a host of other sources or, perhaps better, analogues to which we can turn. The Father struggling to bend the chaotic and fluid stuff of life to his reason has one of many antecedents in the irascible lawyer Ciro Coppa who in *Il turno* dies of a stroke while trying a case. In his insight into the often woeful consequences of a man's desire to do good, he echoes the sad and gentle Judge D'Andrea in *La patente*. In his single-minded drive to plead his case, he is reminiscent of the wronged husband Ciampa in *Il berretto a sonagli*, of Don Lolò, the stubborn plaintiff in all possible lawsuits in *La giara*, of signor Ponza, the harried small-town functionary in *Così è (se vi pare)* – indeed, of all the *raisonneurs* that Pirandello defended with a sensitive play on words in the afterword to *Il fu Mattia Pascal*, added in the very year of *Sei personaggi*: 'Mai l'uomo tanto appassionatamente ragiona (o sragiona, che è lo stesso) come quando soffre' (TR, I, 581) [never do men reason as much (or are as irrational, which comes to the same thing) as when they are unhappy]. There is almost no end to the parallels that per-ceptive ingenuity can find between the characters in different works of Pirandello. The same holds true for recurrent patterns in the selection of subject-matter. In this context, the relationships within a family unit are certainly the most basic. And depending on the degree to which we accept or are willing to work with Freudian concepts an almost limitless number of possibilities present themselves. The tri-angle which forms the basis of the plot in *La morsa*, the consequences of a triangle which provide the reason for the clash of interests and wills in *La ragione degli altri*, the withdrawal of Leone Gala from the life of his wife in *Il giuoco delle parti* (the play not without reason being rehearsed when the six Characters appear on stage), the two men who vie for the affection of Agata Renni in *Il piacere dell'onestà* – all these complicated and abnormal deviations from the ideal of nine-teenth-century family life – provide a depth of reflecting mirrors from which can be viewed the real-life situation of the six Characters within the shaping imagination of Pirandello.

There are other links between *Sei personaggi* and Pirandello's earlier as well as later works. They are significant for other aspects of the play: the materialization of characters as *realtà create* [created realities] rather than as the specific figures of the Six; and the dialectic tension between narrative and drama, one facet of the discussions of stage-craft that occur in the play. Illuminating for the first are *La tragedia di un personaggio* and *Colloqui coi personaggi* already men-tioned. But more can be made of the exploration of the nature of characters as distinct from persons, a point that the Father in the course of his encounter with Manager and Actors cannot let go of, so important is it for a statement of his existential anguish (as distinct from his need to justify his actions as a man). All those works in which Pirandello deals with the supernatural or the occult can be considered as precedents here. From his ghost story *La casa del Granella* (and even further back from his close friend and fellow-writer Capuana's fascination with similar manifestations) to the séances in *Il fu Mattia Pascal* and the apparitions of *All'uscita* – there is a line of thought that culminates, as it were, in the comic representation of the 'materialization' of a character (Bertoldo) in Act I of *Enrico IV* and in the impassioned defence of the creative imagination by the magician Crotone in *I giganti della montagna*. As far as the tension between narrative and drama is concerned, the inevitable triumph of drama is already foreshadowed in the 1899 essay *L'azione parlata* in which, to signify the transition in ancient Greek literature from epic narrative to tragedy, Pirandello quotes Heine's famous ballad on the troubadour Geoffrey Rudel and his lady Melisande: 'Nel castello di Blaye tutte le notti si sente un tremolío, uno scric-chiolío, un sussurro: le figure degli arazzi cominciano a un tratto a muoversi. Il trovadore e la dama scuotono le addormentate membra di fantasmi, scendono dal muro e passeggiano su e giù per la sala' (SPSV, 981) [Every night in the castle of Blay one can hear strange noises, quivering, creaking, rustling: suddenly the figures in the tapestries begin to move. The ghostly troubadour and his lady flex their sleeping muscles, leap from the wall, and walk through the halls].

What has been suggested so far is the usefulness, for a work as complex and difficult as *Sei personaggi*, of an approach that goes at least provisionally outside the text itself. But the question that remains to be asked is whether *Sei personaggi* is actually a difficult work? Whether it has deserved the half-century of exegesis which it has by now behind it? And whether it continues to deserve and can indeed withstand the close attention to which it is inevitably subjected when chosen as a world classic and studied in schools?

As is well known, the play caused a scandal at its première. The Rome audience did not understand it, affronted at finding the empty work-a-day stage displayed to full public view when they entered, at being asked to witness the preparatory comings and goings of actors, manager, property man, and prompter; annoyed at Piran-

lello's intentionally provocative references to himself right at the
beginning, as an author who leaves actors, critics, and audience for-
ver dissatisfied with plays that no one can understand and that are
n insult to everyone concerned. Nor were matters helped when the
Characters appeared, ushered in by the doorkeeper from the stage
loor: '...Una strana tenuissima luce, appena percettibile, si sarà fatta
ttorno a loro, come irradiata da essi: lieve respiro della loro realtà
antastica' (SP, 12) [a strange, tenuous, hardly perceptible light will
ave formed around them, almost as if irradiated from them: the
aint breath of their imagined reality], Pirandello had written in the
tage directions. Given the stormy reception of every subsequent
ction on stage (even after the performance an angry crowd sur-
ounded Pirandello as he was leaving the theatre, continuing the
hythmic chanting of 'Buf – fo – ne.... Ma – ni – co – mio' [Clown....
To the madhouse] that had begun earlier), it may be doubted whether
his subtle touch, reminiscent of the techniques of suggestion of the
Symbolist theatre, had the desired effect. The audience which had
ome to abandon itself to the conventional creation of illusion on
tage (a tradition to which Pirandello's plays had adhered hitherto)
elt rebuffed by his attack on their expectations, by his aggressive
demystification' of the stage. Thus what had been no more than a
abitually guarded reaction of public and critics to Pirandello's dis-
urbing *themes* was fanned into open and vociferous rejection by this
articular theatrical aspect of *Sei personaggi*.

A comparison with what happened at the première of *Cosí è (se vi
are)* should bring this point home. The earlier play, first performed
n Milan on 17 June 1917, was according to all reports a success. But
n his review of it the drama critic Renato Simoni astutely noted that
he public's warm reception went not to the ideas expressed by
Pirandello but to his extraordinary dramatic ability. 'The artist',
Simoni wrote, 'won the battle that the philosopher would have surely
ost in the face of a crowd whom you could never convince, as
Professor Bergeret [protagonist of Anatole France's *Histoire con-
emporaine*] used to say, that Being does not involve substance but
nly expresses a relationship.' *Sei personaggi* repeats Pirandello's dis-
oncerting ideas, those ideas later summarized in the frequently
quoted paragraph from the Preface: 'Senza volerlo, senza saperlo,
ella ressa dell'animo esagitato, ciascun d'essi, per difendersi dalle
ccuse dell'altro, esprime come sua viva passione e suo tormento
quelli che per tanti anni sono stati i travagli del mio spirito: l'inganno
della comprensione reciproca fondato irrimediabilmente sulla vuota

astrazione delle parole; la molteplice personalità d'ognuno secondo
tutte le possibilità d'essere che si trovano in ciascuno di noi; e infine il
tragico conflitto immanente tra la vita che di continuo si muove e
cambia e la forma che la fissa, immutabile' (MN, I, 60) [Without
wanting to, without being aware of it, in the struggle of their tor-
mented souls, each one of them (of the Characters) to defend himself
against the accusations of the others, expresses as his own living
passion and torment the pangs of spirit that for so many years were
mine: the deception of mutual understanding founded on the empty
abstraction of words, the multiple personality of everyone corresponding to the possibilities of being to be found in each of us, and
finally the inherent tragic conflict between life which is continually
moving and changing and form which fixes it, immutable]. In addition, by the alienating effect produced by the use of the device of the
play-within-the play *Sei personaggi* undercuts the identification of the
spectator with the imitation of life taking place on stage. And finally,
that imitation itself fails to reach a completed shape, the play-within-
the-play breaks off, the six Characters being in the end forced off the
stage, authorless as they had come.

The difficulties of *Sei personaggi*, like those of Joyce's *Ulysses* (the
two works are exactly contemporary), are such that they cannot be
dispelled at one sitting. The education of the public to innovations of
magnitude takes time. Arnaldo Frateili, who was present at the
première, wrote as recently as 1961 on the occasion of the International Congress of Pirandello Studies: 'Today everything that
happens in *Sei personaggi* appears to be obvious, clear, so normal that
any insignificant little director feels called upon to stage the play
*except that it then turns out that he hasn't understood it at all and has
misrepresented even those parts explicitly described in the stage directions*
(italics the present writer's). Of course, much of the effect of the play,
its inner dynamics, rests on its ambiguities. But it is important to be
able to make a distinction between the ambiguities that Pirandello
wanted in the play and those that through successive glosses he did
his best to remove.

In contrast to the première, the second performance, given by the
same company in Milan, on 27 September 1921, ran smoothly. As
Pirandello's recent biographer, Gaspare Giudice, suggests, this may
well have been because the text of the play had meanwhile been
published, thus giving public and critics – especially the critics – the
opportunity to become better acquainted with it. What reading a
play of Pirandello, as opposed to viewing it, can add to one's under

standing of it is revealed clearly in the passage from the stage directions describing the Characters' first entrance quoted earlier. Like
Shaw's Pirandello's stage directions go far beyond the usual bare
instructions concerning actions, positions, entrances and exits, and
touch upon matters that may be difficult if not impossible to translate
into the visual language of the stage. In the instance just referred to,
they state something of crucial importance to the play's basic situation, that is, the fundamental distinction in essence between Characters (with a capital 'C') and persons. The Father's later *verbal* explanation of this distinction is prepared for in this passage, but it is a
preparation that the audience at the première had to do without.

That audience had to do without a number of other aids that are
available to readers today: I refer not to critical studies of the play and
its author, but to documents such as reviews (which provide the most
direct testimony to a play's initial reception and hence its inherent
strengths and weaknesses), and more important still the recollections
of critics, directors, actors and friends who were close to Pirandello
when the play was originally written and performed. Such, for instance, is the journalist Orio Vergani's article, published at the time
of Pirandello's death, in which he remembers having been present in
Pirandello's study when the latter was at work on the second act of
Sei personaggi. Of similar interest, for the vividness with which it
records the impressions created by Pirandello's first reading of the
play to a group of friends in Rome, is Frateili's introduction to a
recent reprinting of the review which he had published in the Rome
daily *L'idea nazionale* the morning after the première. And Dario
Niccodemi, director of that performance, wrote of the rehearsals
that led up to it and of Pirandello's untiring patience with actors who
had in his view been completely corrupted by their reliance on the
prompter (an inveterate custom on the Italian stage in his day).

For our purpose the value of these documents lies not in their
incidental contributions to Pirandello's biography but in the light
they throw on the interpretation of the play. Variously emphasized
are the depth and intensity of Pirandello's involvement with his
characters (on an anecdotal level this distinctive psychological trait
appears in the 1919 story *Il pipistrello*), the eminently 'spoken' style
of his dramatic language, and the urgency that he constantly felt to
explain the nature and polemical intention of his play. Frateili reports
that those who heard Pirandello read *Sei personaggi* at a gathering at
Frateili's home in the early Spring of 1921 were overwhelmed, 'not
only because of its aggressive originality but also because of the

passion he put into the reading, a different passion and a different voice for each character'. Niccodemi shows him listening intently to the recitation of the actors, his lips silently forming each word as it was spoken, his face reflecting the expression of each of the actors in turn: 'Each muscle is in movement. His mouth, running the gamut of all possibilities of expression, becomes countless mouths. His face reminds one of a crowd of faces in action'. And the letter that Pirandello himself wrote to Ruggero Ruggeri in 1936, when the great actor was about to play the role of the Father in a new production, shows how little he was satisfied even after fifteen years of successful performances that his play had actually been understood: 'Vorrei che questa nuova edizione attuasse interamente, o almeno nel miglior modo possibile, la visione che ho avuto del lavoro, quando l'ho scritto. Bisognerà evitare *l'errore che si è sempre commesso*, di far apparire i personaggi come ombre e fantasmi, anzichè come entità superiori e più potenti, perchè "realtà create", forme d'arte fissate per sempre e immutabili, quasi statue, di fronte alla mobile naturalità mutevole e quasi fluida degli attori' [I would want this production to carry out completely, or at least as far as possible, the vision I had of the work when I wrote it. One must avoid *the error that has always been made* of making the Characters appear as shadows and phantasms, instead of as superior and more powerful entities by virtue of their being 'created realities', art forms fixed forever and immutable, almost statues, in face of the mobile and almost fluid naturalness of the actors (italics the present writer's)].

Multifacetedness (*poliedricità*), wrote Lampedusa, is the distinguishing characteristic of works of absolute first rank. Because *Sei personaggi* possesses this quality and presents different aspects of itself to different viewers, I judge it a work difficult enough to require exegesis and rich enough to withstand it. Of the three bodies of material that for purposes of analysis can be seen as constituting distinct structural elements in the play – (1) the story of the Characters' lives, (2) the attempt on the part of Manager and Actors to turn this story into a play, and (3) Pirandello's own telling of the story within his representation of the Company's attempt to give it shape – it is the first that in early productions attracted the greatest share of attention and that continues to awaken a good deal of perplexity even today. An inveterate habit of mind demands an answer to the question. 'What exactly did happen?' and conceives of the question as referring to Father, Mother, and their offspring, rather than to that odd group of beings who one day appeared on a stage set for a rehearsal. Only after a satisfactory answer has been given can the reader or viewer go on to consider and appreciate other aspects of the work before him.

The story of the Characters as it unfolds on stage begins in good epic fashion *in medias res* or, if more properly dramatic terminology is preferred, close to its *dénouement*. The Father is in his fifties; the Son is twenty-two. This is the first chronological fact given: it is spelled out in the stage directions and made visually apparent in performance through make-up and the assignment of parts. Chronology appears again when twice in rapid succession the Stepdaughter says that she has been an orphan for two months and that for that length of time she, the Mother, and her siblings have been wearing mourning for her father. The Stepdaughter's father is not *the* Father, whose only child is the Son. The blood relationship of the Six, by normal standards confusing, could not be more explicitly stated than it is in the very first few minutes of the play. But Manager and Actors, already disconcerted by the Father's initial presentation of himself as a character (while they see him as a person), are further bewildered by this intricate family relationship. Their questions, quips, and remarks, however, serve to elicit a full clarification of the facts.

These facts must be fully established to satisfy the natural curiosity of the audience in the hall and of the other audience, Manager and Actors, on stage. They are moreover the facts that explain the particular intensity of the feelings of Father, Stepdaughter, and Mother (the only three of the Six who speak at first), an intensity which keeps the Characters more tightly enclosed within their relationship than the Members of the company are united by their community of shared work and professional pride.

The emotions displayed by the Characters have been building up over a long period of time. They are emotions typical of the long, intimate, and ambivalent association that characterizes family life. Their intensity can also be measured by the fact that Stepdaughter and Father, in different degrees and for different reasons, have lost their sense of shame and reserve. Secrets normally shielded by the bourgeois family are here pulled into full public view. The Stepdaughter especially is driven by a ferocious fury to unmask the Father's motives in taking the family back home with him; and in her vindictive grudge against him, however justified, she does not hesitate to reveal her own degradation at the hands of Madama Pace, the brothel keeper. It is significant that the scene she cannot wait to act is judged damaging to her reputation by both the Mother and the Manager, the two guardians of propriety in the play. As for the Father, the life-time of isolation he has behind him has obliterated his sense of self-awareness to the point that he permits himself to be dragged into performing the very scene (his meeting with the Step-daughter at Madama Pace's) he should have every reason to want to keep hidden. His need to justify his actions, especially his original decision about the Mother, has been pent up so long that it now sweeps all restraints before it. The Son's contempt both for the Father's empty phrases and the Stepdaughter's vilification, his refusal to have anything to do with the others (so that he even rejects his Mother), his complete withdrawal – a reaction to hurt just like the Stepdaughter's aggressive pushing forward – all these are the results of long pent-up resentments.

To know what the Characters' relationship is and for how long their association has lasted is not however sufficient to form a judg-ment. That a judgment is being asked for is obvious: the Father, not the Stepdaughter, finds himself in a symbolic court of law and it is he who presents the evidence for his defence. The evidence forms the retrospective exposition of the story. The Manager sits down to listen to it and the Father begins it in the imperfect, the *de rigueur* tense for background information in historical narrative: 'C'era con me un pover'uomo...' (MN, I, 88) [There was a poor devil of a man working for me...].

The Father, who was married to a woman of humble background, mother of a child that for its health had been sent to a wet nurse in the country, noticed the mutual sympathy that developed between his employee (the *pover'uomo*) and his wife, the support they sought in one another for putting up with his irascibility. Finding the situation intolerable – not because of jealousy, he says, but because the drawing together of the two implied a tacit criticism of his very being – the Father fired the man. The Mother remained at home, a lost soul, 'come una di quelle bestie senza padrone, che si raccolgono per carità' [like an animal without a master that one takes pity on and carries home]. Not out of cruelty, the Father says, (just as it had not been out of cruelty that he sent the Son away) 'quanto per la pena – una pena angosciosa – che provavo per lei' [as because of the pain – a veritable anguish – that I felt on her account]) he sent the Mother to join the other man, better suited than he was to live in harmonious unity with her. But, as such stories go, what had been intended to correct circumstances actually complicated them. Upon his return home, the Son felt estranged and no bond developed between him and his father. As for the Father, he describes himself too as wandering through the empty rooms 'come una mosca senza capo' [like a fly without a head].

It is thus that the Father in his loneliness began to take an interest in the Mother's new family, particularly the Stepdaughter, who had reached school age and whom he could watch on her way to and from school. Of the other children the Boy was still too young to go to school and the Little Girl (who is four to the Stepdaughter's eighteen when they appear on stage) had not yet been born. Some time after the Father had become interested in the Mother's new family, they moved away and remained away for a number of years. Then, upon the other man's death, they came back to the city and it was at that time that the encounter at Madama Pace's took place. Horrified to see what poverty had done to his wife and her children, the Father took them back into his home. The Son resented the intrusion of the strangers, his mother's bastard children, and though he had no affection for his father, was antagonized by the Stepdaughter's insulting behaviour towards him. The Mother, rejected by her Son, could think of nothing but of winning back his love. The Boy, like his own father 'umile' [humble] (as the Father repeats), was completely lost in the new environment, and indeed ended up by committing suicide. Before that happened, however, the Little Girl, neglected by the Mother in the same way as the Boy was, drowned in the garden fountain. As a result of this accumulation of tragedies the Step-daughter left home.

These facts, which constitute the entire story (as distinct from specific episodes) of the six Characters' lives, all emerge in the course of Act I though not in this order and not as schematically summarized. They are surrounded and engulfed by the emotional reactions of all concerned and their motivations are variously played out, interpreted by those who were affected. But the *dénouement*, the finale of the drama to be made, is already clearly hinted at by the Stepdaughter in her initial appeal to Manager and Actors. 'Senta, per favore', she pleads with the Manager, 'ce lo faccia rappresentar subito, questo dramma, perchè vedrà che a un certo punto, io – quando quest'a-morino qua [the Little Girl] – vede com'è bellina? cara! cara! ebbene, quando quest'amorino qua, Dio la toglierà d'improvviso a quella povera madre: e quest'imbecillino qua [the Boy] farà la più grossa delle corbellerie, proprio da quello stupido che è – allora vedrà che io prenderò il volo! Sissignore! prenderò il volo! il volo!' (MN, I,

82–3) [Just listen: let us play it for you right now, this drama, for at a certain point you'll see that I – when this little darling – look how sweet she is! Sweetie! Sweetie! – well, when God will suddenly take this darling away from that poor mother of hers, and that little idiot there will do the stupidest of things, like the nitwit he is – then you will see me getting out! Yes sir! Getting out! Out!].

Reproduced without the accompanying stage directions and read without being able to see the gestures and actions, the Stepdaughter's words with their broken syntax, the interruptions and resumptions, reflect in miniature the process by which the facts of the story are revealed. These facts are repeated, with the exception of the Step-daughter's flight, at the end of the act when in answer to the Manager's comment that children are a nuisance on stage the Father reassures him: 'Oh, ma lui [the Boy] glielo leva subito, 'l'impaccio, sa! E anche quella bambina, che è anzi la prima ad andarsene…' (MN, I, 97) [But he won't be a nuisance for long. Nor will the little girl, no, for she's the first to go…].

Obviously Pirandello was convinced that the facts of the story as recounted in Act I of the definitive version of the play (the text we have been following in our own reconstruction) were sufficiently explicit for the spectator to grasp. This explains why he felt that he could excise from the original version the part of the Father's long speech that followed the sentence just quoted. In those lines the Father had given an interpretation of the *dénouement*: the very interpretation which forms the basis of Eric Bentley's 'Father's Day' (from a Freudian point of view one of the best pieces written *not* on Pirandello's play but on the inner story which it tells). Through the ending, says the Father, the original family is reconstituted, Father, Mother, and Son 'resi, dalla scomparsa di quella famiglia estranea, estranei anche noi l'uno all'altro, in una desolazione mortale, che è la vendetta …del Demone dell'Esperimento che è in me…' (SP, 53) [ourselves alienated from each other by the disappearance of that alien family, alienated and utterly desolated – the revenge of the Demon of Experiment that I carry inside me].

The second recurrent structural element in *Sei personaggi* consists of the repeated efforts of Manager and Actors to create the illusion of reality on stage with the 'real' reality which the Characters bring them. In contrast to the Six, who are tragic if for no other reason than because they feel their predicament, Manager and Actors are comic. Like characters of comedy in general they may be described as believing in what they can touch, see, and understand and eager to preserve their sense of dignity. They may be seen as working out their problems on the level of action rather than abstract thought, as being strictly empirical. Whenever attention shifts to them there is a resultant change in tone. The audience identifies with them in their patronizing humouring and more often intolerant rebuffing of the Characters, in what Hobbes calls the 'sudden glory' of abruptly perceiving one's superiority to others. But because of the play's dynamic movement the identification does not hold. The language of the Characters, especially that of the Father, the furthest removed in its specious (the word is Pirandello's) ratiocination, is again and again the more powerful one and repeatedly engulfs and drowns out the more trivial language of the Actors.

This situation is similar to that in *Cosí è* (*se vi pare*), Manager and Actors taking the place of the small town gossips who in that play are the uncomprehending spectators of the anguished, harrowed family in their midst. The parallel, however, does not of course imply identity. Signora Frola and the Ponzas are persons not characters; the Agazzis, Sirellis, and the others are ordinary citizens not actors. The setting is a middle-class apartment not a stage. Laudisi, though like the Father the spokesman for typically Pirandellian ideas that recur in all the writer's works, is not the Father. Yet the pattern of the one play fits into that of the other, and the audience that identifies at first with the outer group ends up, if the lesson of the parable has been successfully imparted, discovering its oneness with the inner. The epithet *pazzo* [mad] used by the Manager to brand the Father and his family when they appear on stage is also the pivot for the action of *Cosí è* (*se vi pare*). 'Comedy justifies, defends, or elevates us in relation to the oddity, the alien, the scapegoat. It enables us to surmount our doubts about those that are different by laughing them out of existence' (R.J.Dorius). This is the mechanism that tries to function in *Cosí è* (*se vi pare*) but which Laudisi interferes with and the inner group itself succeeds in deactivating. It is also the mechanism that Manager and Actors instinctively have recourse to every time the Father soars too high in asserting his uniqueness.

We shall see when we turn to the third recurrent structural element in *Sei personaggi* that as potential characters Father and Stepdaughter are thoroughly acquainted with the experience of literary creation. As non-authors, Manager and Actors have no first-hand knowledge of that experience and as non-characters, they are ignorant of the particular anguish of a transitional state of existence between non-being and being that Father and Stepdaughter experience and express. But as members of a theatrical company they are well versed in the techniques of stage-craft, and their long association with the life of the theatre has acquainted them at least superficially with most of the theoretical notions that have had currency in the history of drama. (Pirandello's own equally empirically derived knowledge in this area constitutes the core of his Introduction to Silvio D'Amico's 1936 edition of *Storia del teatro italiano*, an expanded version of an article that had appeared the previous year in the review *Scenario*). The stage business constantly interrupts the Characters' efforts at telling, or rather, portraying their story, thus providing a commentary perceived immediately as comic by the audience. In their totality the incidental observations that accompany it lay down the 'rules' that the inner episodic, unfinished play, which remains a fragment, should have followed.

The play begins with an unset stage: the directions, calling for a raised curtain, no wings or scenery, and a stage almost completely dark and empty, have remained unchanged in successive editions of the play. The Company's very first action shows the audience the expertise of its technical staff, from stage manager (a character added in the 1925 edition) to stage crew. Immediately following but still prior to the entrance of the Characters, Manager and Actors prepare themselves for the rehearsal of a play. It happens to be a play by Pirandello, the same author who is responsible for having gathered together the audience in the theatre, and this fact provides a particularly lively and pointed context within which some stage conventions can be quickly sketched. The introductory scene can thus be seen as a frame for the whole play, underlining its specific genre of play-within-a-play.

Reflecting Pirandello's characteristic use of repetition and complication by way of repetition, the first part of Act II, up to the appearance of Madama Pace, reproduces with a greater abundance of details the business of setting up a play already gone through in Act I. But whereas in that instance there already was a text of the play and the Manager's task was therefore limited (he explained the author's intentions and because of the particular play being rehearsed tried to overcome his Company's resistance to the 'incomprehensible' Pirandello), in Act II more is at stake. Here there is no written play and consequently everything, including the assignment of parts, the selection of props, the application of make-up, as well as the meaning of the author, remains to be settled and thus becomes the subject of prolonged and heated argument between the Characters, and the Manager and Actors. By Act III some of the friction has gone, some of the stage conventions have been accepted. As a result, the curtain rises on at least part of the shadow setting (*simulacro di scena* are Pirandello's words) already in place: a small garden fountain is seen where previously Madama Pace's famous parlour had been erected piece by piece before the eyes of the audience. Other props are added in the course of the first part of the act, in another repetition, this time on a reduced scale, of what had occurred in Acts I and II.

We can now ask what kind of play Manager and Actors have in mind as the vehicle for the raw material of the Characters' lives. It comes as no surprise that in terms of both dramaturgy and stage practice, Manager and Actors are traditionalists. Like the audience in the theatre they feel that art must give a recognizable structure to reality, that it must reduce chaos to order.

A first distinction is made by the Manager when he enunciates the basic characteristic of drama: on stage there is action, event, not narration. 'Ma tutto questo è racconto, signori miei!' (MN, I, 91) [But all this is story telling, my friends!], he exclaims interrupting the Stepdaughter's recollection of the Father waiting for her at school when she was a child. A little earlier the Stepdaughter, shouting down the Father, had raised the same objection: 'Qui non si narra! Qui non si narra!' (MN, I, 87) [This is no place for story telling!]. (For Pirandello speaking in his own voice on this point, see *L'azione parlata*: 'Ogni sostegno descrittivo o narrativo dovrebbe essere abolito su la scena' (SPSV, 981) [All descriptive and narrative props should be banished from the stage].) At the end of Act I the Actors, who up to that point have been little else than spectators vis-à-vis the entanglements of Characters and Manager, in a brief excited choral scene give its technical name to the kind of play that seems to be in the making: *commedia dell'arte*, the improvised drama gone out of fashion two centuries before and to which *they* would not deign to stoop. Thus the act that had begun with the reading of stage directions from a script ends symmetrically with the reiteration that, on the stage of *Sei personaggi*, written – that is, fully structured – plays are performed, not plays for which only a rudimentary sketch exists.

As far as dramaturgy is concerned, the most important point made regarding the kind of play the Company is accustomed to performing and the audience to viewing is the Manager's enunciation of the rule of unity of action or coherence. 'Ma io voglio rappresentare il mio dramma! il mio!' (MN, I, 119) [But I want to play *my* drama. Mine!], the Stepdaughter cries passionately in Act II in the course of her tug-of-war with the Father. The Manager's answer runs the whole gamut from annoyance to persuasion to conciliation. There is not only the Stepdaughter's drama, he says, but the drama of the others as well. One character cannot simply take over the stage for himself and crowd out the others: 'Bisogna contener tutti in un quadro armonico e rappresentar quel che è rappresentabile!' (MN, I, 119) [Everyone must be placed within the frame of one harmonious whole. Only what is performable can be performed]. And after all, he concludes, it will be in the Stepdaughter's own interest to play down her drama at this particular juncture in the story if she wishes to win greater audience sympathy.

Beyond these theoretical desiderata – a play is action not narrative; it must be written down not improvised; it must have unity – there is the whole area of dramatic practice. Unity, for instance, may be achieved through unity of place but it can equally well be achieved by starting the action with an event already far along in the development of the situation. The problem of unity of place appears in Act III apropos the Stepdaughter's observation that not all of the second act of the proposed drama can be set in the garden because the events that concern the Son and the Boy actually took place in the house. The problem of the relationship between preceding action (*antefatto*) and dramatic action appears in Act I when the Father agrees that the narrative part of the Characters' lives will not be represented but only referred to. And in fact the three acts of the drama to be composed focus on three scenes that took place at the end of the story to be told: the Father meets the Stepdaughter when she is a fully grown young lady and not when she is a child; the children will play the scene of their death and not moments of their life with their own father; Mother and Son will come together at the moment of their reunion and not at their separation ten years earlier. As we have already pointed out in connection with the story of the six Characters, the action on stage is the epilogue of a situation created much earlier. In this respect *Sei personaggi* repeats the pattern of Pirandello's earliest extant play, *La morsa* (1892), whose original title was *L'epilogo*.

Problems of acting or interpretation are furthest removed from the area of theory and are most central to practice. In *Sei personaggi* they are dealt with directly in Act II and their presence there contributes to making that act the busiest, most animated, varied and colourful of the play. Friction between the Characters and the Actors starts early in the act when the Manager assigns their roles to the Members of the

Company. It is significant that he should find no difficulty in doing so, while the Father and the Stepdaughter find it impossible to recognize themselves in the Actors that will play them. Even with the best make-up, the Father observes, the Leading Man will hardly resemble him, and as for playing him as he really 'is' that is obviously an impossibility. The Stepdaughter, for her part, simply laughs in the Leading Lady's face. Yet a little later, immediately after the scene with Madama Pace and the meeting between Father and Stepdaughter, Leading Lady and Leading Man take the initiative and propose to rehearse the scene just 'played' by the two Characters. Within the world of *Sei personaggi* this becomes a rehearsal of a rehearsal, in its turn even further distanced from the audience when the Manager gets up on stage to show his actors how it should be played.

Pirandello's stage directions at this point (they are already in the original edition) call for a scene that is not a parody of the one just performed but one that might be described as a clean, corrected copy of it, the artful imitation of reality. The Manager demands ease, *souplesse*, in the acting. But the performances delivered are wooden, exaggerated, conventional. For the Characters they are a torture to watch (though the Stepdaughter's sense of alienation is expressed paradoxically in frenzied peals of laughter). For the audience in the hall they are irresistibly funny, caricatures. But for the Manager and Actors they are exactly what they expect them to be, not yet perfectly timed, still capable of being improved, but essentially correct. The Leading Man is playing 'un vecchio, che viene in una casa equivoca… con l'aria spigliata, sbarazzina d'un vecchio galante' (MN, I, 114) [an old man who enters a house of ill repute… with the self-possessed roguish air of an elder Don Juan]. The Leading Lady plays a world-weary prostitute 'socchiudendo penosamente, come per disgusto, gli occhi' (MN, I, 116) [closing her eyes painfully as though in disgust]. What in the original 'performance' of Father and Stepdaughter were words and gestures indissolubly united in genuine psychological reactions, in the Actors' interpretation become so many discrete and separate samples of emotions, for each one of which there is a set and predetermined tone, a studied and practised posture. Obviously, in the eyes of Manager and Actors, the Characters are types not persons, interchangeable with the cast of stock characters the Company excels at playing. This fact provides an ironic retrospective comment on the Manager's boast in Act I that his Company has given life to immortal works 'qua, su queste tavole' (MN, I, 79) [here, on these boards], and earlier in Act II that his actors have given 'corpo e figura, voce e gesto' (MN, I, 104) [body and face, voice and gesture], that is expression, to much loftier subject-matter than the paltry story that the Characters have brought him. The scene almost seems to have been written to illustrate the reasons for Pirandello's well-known reservations about the theatre as an art form (an excellent comprehensive statement, particularly relevant to this aspect of *Sei personaggi*, is the 1908 essay *Illustratori, attori, e traduttori*), or to support the Stepdaughter's conjecture in Act III that their author had rejected the Characters because of his discouragement with the theatre as it was usually made available to the public at that time.

We could perhaps step back for a moment and try to cast the action of the inner story of *Sei personaggi*, the story that tells the content of the Characters' lives, into the mould of the traditional three-act play. The differences between the first and definitive versions of the play indicate that Pirandello must have done something like that at some point, must have passed, that is, from what the ancient theories of rhetoric called *inventio* to *dispositio*, or from what Alfieri called *ideare* to *stendere*, from the 'thinking up' of the subject to its arrangement into scenes. We have already noted that there are three scenes into which what would otherwise be the narration of the Characters' story is to be absorbed: the meeting between Stepdaughter and Father, the death of the children, and the Mother's pleading of her case with the Son. Of these only the first one, the encounter at Madama Pace's, is set off in the text, explicitly labelled 'The Scene', and played through in its entirety. The second one is set up by the Manager, but though its *dénouement* (the revolver shot with which the Boy kills himself) takes place, it is not actually played. The reason for this is that it intersects what should have become the third scene, which to suit modern stage conventions is first transferred from inside the house (where it reputedly took place) to the garden and is then violently rejected by the Son who claims that it never took place because he walked out on his Mother – in a play on words – 'Proprio per non fare una scena!' (MN, I, 136) [precisely in order not to make a scene]. Under normal circumstances these three scenes could have turned into the necessary three acts. As it is, they are out of phase from the beginning, 'The Scene' being played in Act II, the second act of the play-to-be-made being announced at the beginning of Act III (why the whole adventure in the theatre which *Sei personaggi* describes should have begun with the rehearsal of Act II of another play now becomes apparent in retrospect), and the third act never being even begun. That something like this outline must at some time have occurred to Pirandello can be deduced from the displacement of the second scene from the beginning of Act II (where it was in the original version) to Act III. The only scholar who has so far compared the different editions of the play, Jørn Moestrup, attributes the displacement to Pirandello's desire to maintain suspense by avoiding foreknowledge. This explanation, if not perhaps actually incorrect, is certainly insufficient. We have already shown how the story of the six Characters is revealed in its entirety in Act I. It would seem more likely therefore that the second scene was moved to Act III not only because it is the conventional tragic climax but also because there was no place for it in Act II, the act reserved for 'The Scene'.

We come now to the third body of material that can be isolated as a distinct structural element in the play: the discussions of the peculiar state of being of a character and, subsidiary to that, the consequences for the author that result from it. In those parts of *Sei personaggi* that dramatize the problematic interplay of characters and actors, it is the character's strong personal traits, his unique individuality, the fact that he is *someone* ('Perchè un personaggio ha veramente una vita sua, segnata di caratteri suoi, per cui è sempre "qualcuno". Mentre un uomo...un uomo così in genere, può non esser "nessuno"' (MN, I, 126) [Because a character really has a life of his own, marked with his special characteristics; for which reason he is always 'somebody'. But a man...a man in general, may very well be 'nobody'], says the Father in Act III), that may stand in the way of his being adequately represented by an actor professionally trained but incapable of 'that supreme renunciation of self', that 'spiritual creative activity of the rarest kind', which Pirandello speaks of as the mark of the great actor in his essay on Eleonora Duse (*The Century Magazine*, June 1924). In the other parts, those that deal with the relationship of characters and author, it is the character's need for untrammelled development that may find itself in conflict with the shaping imagination of the author. And indeed in speaking of the creative moment elsewhere in his work Pirandello returns over and over again to his basic claim that no worthwhile work of art can be produced, no living and breathing character be given life unless the author 'si sia veramente immedesimato con la sua creatura fino a sentirla com'essa si sente, a volerla com'essa si vuole' [has really become identified with his creature to the point of feeling it as it feels itself, of wanting it to be as it wants itself to be] (*L'azione parlata*, SPSV, 982).

It was pointed out earlier that the paradoxical situation of charac-

ters coming to importune an author was fixed from the beginning of
Pirandello's conception of the work. This paradox gives the play its
title and is its most striking invention as well as its structural keystone.
It calls for attention. Obviously, characters are not persons. It is true
that in familiar discourse the word 'character' may be used as a
synonym for 'person', specifically, 'a person who is peculiar and
eccentric'. But when the word occurs in conjunction with the concept
of authorship, it is removed from the every-day world to the world
of fiction. In that context characters are distinguished from persons,
the former being creations of authors, the latter products of pro-
creation and environment. A character should not normally be
thought of as having a life outside the work of which he is a part, nor
of existing prior to the creative act of his author.

Yet Pirandello felt, as we have seen in the 1917 letter to his son and
in the two short stories mentioned earlier, that he was 'visited' by his
characters – by some more insistently than others – *before* they had a
place in the man-made world of art. Being 'visited' by a character, a
figment of the imagination, means that a particularly close relationship exists between the author and the character, not necessarily in the
sense of an autobiographical identification but in the sense of the
'archaic image' as described by Jung: 'the image...presents itself more
or less suddenly to the consciousness as the latter's product, similarly
to a vision or a hallucination, but without the pathological character
of these'. Other writers besides Pirandello have described the phenomenon, but none, as far as I know, has made as much of it as he.
Chekhov, for instance, is reported to have remarked: 'There is a
regular army of people in my brain begging to be summoned forth,
and only waiting for the word to be given'. Ibsen wrote: 'Often my
characters astonish me by doing or saying things I had not expected –
yes, they can sometimes turn my original scheme upside down, the
devils!' Dickens confessed: 'My notion is always that, when I have
made the people to play out the play, it is, as it were, their business to
do it and not mine'. That many writers felt the characters in their
works to be more alive than the persons of flesh and blood that
surrounded them in their daily lives is borne out by Balzac's feeling
that through his novels he was contributing to the citizenry of France.
But if we examine these instances in the light of Pirandello's more
complex statements, we note that it is not so much the autonomy of
the character that astonishes Pirandello as the demand the character
makes on him and that he must answer with an act of love. The
rejected character, the character without an author, is the one that has

been denied this kind of love. Pirandello's *immedesimarsi*, the author's identification with his creature 'to the point of feeling it as it feels itself, of wanting it to be as it wants itself to be', is quite different from the identity of sensations felt by Mme Bovary and Flaubert when, as is reported, he had the taste of arsenic in *his* mouth as he was describing *her* death. As for Flaubert's frequently quoted remark, 'Mme Bovary c'est moi', I would interpret it as meaning that he understood Emma through himself, that he lent her something of himself, in contrast to Pirandello's understanding his characters by listening to their 'reasons', by foregoing some of his own ego for their sakes.

The basic situation of *Sei personaggi*, then, is a variation on a theme familiar to Pirandello and not unknown to other writers. The variation means that contrary to what is the case for Dr Fileno, for instance, the Six in the play encounter not an author but the Manager and his Company of actors. If the invention of having characters act as though they were persons, with the spontaneity of the undetermined, is paradoxical, then when these characters-turned-persons are forced to become actors (even if only in a rehearsal), something fundamental happens in the history of the theatre. Actors and characters as different entities cannot simultaneously occupy the same stage. Characters are essences; actors are roles. The creation of illusion on stage demands that the actors become the characters for the duration of the performance. In Pirandello's play the Characters are in the end forced off the stage. There is no room for them in that particular space which is the space reserved for actors, that is, for persons who have studied and learned the parts they are to play. The Characters have 'lived' their parts, each one his own part, each one in his own incommunicable experience of it. The parts have not been orchestrated; they make little sense as a whole. Instead of a story there will be fragments of a story. Instead of a resolution there will be the empty stage at the end. The audience that in accordance with a well-established custom has come to abandon itself to the conventional creation of illusion will go home unsatisfied, its expectations frustrated. Catharsis has not taken place, and the experience of the play is replaced by heated discussions, not as in normal after-theatre conversations of its performance, but of its very meaning. (For Pirandello's own dramatically detailed reconstruction of audience reaction to his works, see the First Choral Interlude of *Ciascuno a suo modo* and especially the lines spoken by One of the Author's Champions.)

In the Preface to *Sei personaggi* Pirandello wrote what is surely one of the most lucid and comprehensive analyses of the play. One passage summarizes what happened once he, in the *persona* of the author, decided to let loose on stage the Characters, who had so to speak served their acting apprenticeship in trying to get him to write their story: 'è avvenuto naturalmente quel che doveva avvenire: un misto di tragico e di comico, di fantastico e di realistico, in una situazione umoristica affatto nuova e quanto mai complessa; un dramma che da sé per mezzo dei suoi personaggi, spiranti parlanti semoventi, che lo portano e lo soffrono in loro stessi, vuole a ogni costo trovare il modo d'esser rappresentato; e la commedia del vano tentativo di questa realizzazione scenica improvvisa' (MN, I, 60) [what had to happen happened, and the result was a mixture of tragic and comic, of fantastic and realistic, in a completely new and extremely complex humoristic situation: a drama that seeks at all costs to represent itself by means of its characters, breathing, speaking, self-propelling, who carry it within them and suffer it; and the comedy of the vain attempt, at this sudden theatrical realization]. It should come as no surprise that Pirandello's answer to 'what happened' once he set the play-within-the-play, or better the drama-within-a-comedy, in motion refers not to the first of the linked terms but to the second, not to the substance or plot of the inner story but to the shaping of the work, the artifact created by the outer story. In choosing as the genre designation for his play the expression *commedia da fare* [comedy to be composed], which we read on the title page of the 1921 edition and which fits perfectly into the mould *romanzo da fare* used to refer to the work initially, Pirandello underlined his awareness of the comparative importance of its two indissolubly joined halves.

We have had occasion more than once to point to *La tragedia di un personaggio* as in many ways indispensable for a proper and satisfying understanding of *Sei personaggi*. But the strong analogies between the two works do not, of course, obliterate the differences. Thus, while Dr Fileno and the Father are both in search of an author, Dr Fileno is already a character while the Father is seeking to become one. If as a character in *La tragedia di un personaggio* Dr Fileno is at least twice removed from being a person, the Father's status is as yet problematic. He finds himself in a no man's land, in transition to a place for which he longs – a kind of Paradise of Essence – and which he may never reach. Indeed, *is* he a character or is he only one of *the* Characters? The difference in the meaning of the word brought about by its capitalization deserves attention. For the Father (as are the other five, but not Madama Pace) is nameless, just as the protagonist of *Enrico IV* is nameless, his identity in the void of the ellipsis points which appear in that play's *dramatis personae*:...(Enrico IV).

In order to acquire a name the Father would have to convince an author that he should be given one. But the only author the Father has met so far is the one who, as we have seen, left some fragments of a projected novel, in which the gentleman on his way to signora Pace's cannot actually yet be said to be the Father. As for the author of the Preface, *he* did not encourage the fictional realization of the Six; he blocked it. 'Siamo qua in cerca d'autore' (MN, I, 77) [We are here looking for an author], the Father says as he leads his little band up to the stage. But on the stage of *Sei personaggi* there are no authors, and the Father will have to plead his case before what are at best humble craftsmen. In *La tragedia di un personaggio* Dr Fileno, already in the privileged state of being really a character, had been luckier.

The fact that it is craftsmen and not an author that the Father will be addressing makes all the difference. The variation on the theme – the lucky find made by the author of the Preface to rid himself of the characters he didn't want to coddle, didn't want to give fictional life to – has far-reaching formal results. The encounter becomes a sequence of misunderstandings. Between Dr Fileno and his author there were no misunderstandings. The author knew what was wanted of him; he knew how much of himself he would have had to give to satisfy the character; by an act of judgment he refused to become involved. Not so the Manager and his Company of actors. They are seduced, willing to help. They listen and watch. They comment and analyze. They imitate. They question. But they are unable to help. Potential creators with the unfashioned raw material which the Characters bring them of what the magician (i.e., a kind of author) in *I giganti della montagna* calls 'fictitious reality' (MN, II, 1362), they cannot rise to the challenge, imprisoned as they are in material reality.

Three times, once in each act, the Father comes forward to try to explain what the nature of the Characters is. Each time the explanation is interrupted. The Characters and the Actors do not speak the same language. The Actors cannot understand the Father. When in Act I he asks, 'Non è loro ufficio dar vita sulla scena a personaggi fantasticati?' (MN, I, 78) [Isn't it your job to give life to creatures of fantasy on stage?], the Manager interprets the question as a slur on the actor's profession. 'Ma io la prego di credere che la professione del comico, caro signore, è una nobilissima professione!' (MN, I, 74) [But I beg of you! The actor's profession is a very noble one], he counters indignantly.

When in Act II Madama Pace miraculously appears at the very

moment she is needed, the Father is radiant but the Manager is again indignant, 'Ma che trucchi son questi?' [What kind of tricks are these?], and the Actors echo him: 'Ma dove siamo insomma?' [What goes on around here?], 'Di dove è comparsa quella lì?' [Where on earth did *she* come from?], 'Questo è il giuoco dei bussolotti!' (MN, I, 107–108) [Hocus pocus!]. The Father's exhortation ('Ma scusino! Perchè vogliono guastare, in nome d'una verità volgare, di fatto, questo prodigio di una realtà che nasce, evocata, attratta, formata dalla stessa scena, e che ha più diritto di viver qui, che loro; perchè assai più vera di loro?' (MN, I, 108) [But pardon me! Why would you want to destroy in the name of a vulgar, factual truth, this miracle of a reality which is born, called forth, attracted and formed by the stage itself and which indeed has more right to live here than you because it is much truer than you?]), would fall on completely deaf ears if the scene between the Stepdaughter and Madama Pace which has immediately come to life were not so compelling – so 'natural' – that Manager and Actors are momentarily rapt in it (incidentally, an illustration of the aptness of Simoni's distinction between the success of the artist and the failure of the philosopher, referred to earlier). But the truce, in spite of this magnificent demonstration of both what a character is and what literary creation is, is short-lived. From the realm of art, Manager and Actors quickly fall back into the shop-talk of their trade.

Act III contains the Father's longest and most complex gloss on the condition of being a character. It begins with the Manager's taunt, 'E dica per giunta che lei, con codesta commedia che viene a rappresentarmi qua, è più vero e reale di me!' (MN, I, 126) [And you'll be saying next that you, with this comedy of yours that you brought here to act, are more true and more real than I am!]. And it continues as the Father, following the lead shown by Dr Fileno and repeating parts of his defence *verbatim*, calls upon the experience of literary creation to explain his point. In underlining the close link between author and character – a link made even closer by his addressing an author already singled out as potentially receptive to his plea – Dr Fileno had begun his defence with the words: 'Nessuno può sapere meglio di lei, che noi siamo esseri…' (NA, I, 717) [No one can know better than you that we are beings…]. Between Father and Company of actors, on the other hand, there is no common ground of experience and so the Father's speech begins: 'Non l'ha mai visto, signore [i.e., he has never seen a character getting out of his part and philosophizing about himself], perchè gli autori nascondono di solito il travaglio della loro creazione' (MN, I, 127) [You have never seen such a case, sir, because authors, as a rule, hide the labour of their creation]. There follows a recapitulation of the genetic moment in a character's life, until the Father's abstract, verbal presentation is replaced by the scene which the Stepdaughter, stepping forward in a dreamlike trance, plays out. She enacts, in other words, the temptation scene barely hinted at in the second fragment of the novel mentioned earlier ('Soprattutto lei, la ragazza. La vedo entrare...' (SPSV, 1217) [She especially, the girl. I see her coming in...]), described with greater pathos and wonder in *Colloqui coi personaggi* ('Nell'ombra che veniva lenta e stanca...' (NA, II, 1131) [In the darkness that gathered slow and tired...]), and related specifically, in the Preface, to Pirandello's decision to turn novel into play.

The Father's three passages stand out within the overall structure of the play and form one thematic unit within its strategy. When the theme re-emerges in the last act, the Manager's mocking lines contain the same two adjectives, *vero* and *reale*, that the Father had used in Act I. Actors, he had said, give life to 'esseri vivi, più vivi di quelli che respirano e vestono panni! Meno reali, forse; ma più veri!' (MN, I, 79) [living beings more alive than those who breathe and wear clothes: beings less real perhaps, but more true!]. In the linking and at the same time separation of *vero* and *reale* there lie, quite incidentally and curiously embedded, echoes of the history of the development of a literary concept – realism, naturalism, or what in Italy was known as *verismo* – by the 1920s completely surpassed in the work of Pirandello. The importance of *Sei personaggi* in the literature of the twentieth century derives also from the statement of the non-mimetic function of art so insistently repeated in its exploration of the relationship between character and author.

In analyzing the dramatization of the inner story of the Characters' lives and the interplay of characters and actors on stage, we spoke briefly of some of the changes that took place in the text between the original and definitive versions. These changes consist of excisions, additions, and transpositions, and concern all three aspects of the play. In addition to the Father's speech toward the end of Act I, Pirandello dropped the important lines of the Son in Act II in which the latter rebelled against the Father's forcing upon his children a recognition of their parents' needs as man and woman (SP, 64); an exchange between Father and Manager at the beginning of Act III in which the Father reiterates Pirandello's conviction that men reason because they

suffer (SP, 121–3); and by transposing the beginning of Act II to
Act III, the attempt at a scene between Mother and Son. But of con-
siderably greater significance are the additions which radically change
the beginning and the ending of the play. Instead of the Manager's
lines with which the play originally ended: 'Finzione! Realtà! Andate
al diavolo tutti quanti! Non mi è mai capitato una cosa simile! E mi
hanno fatto perdere una giornata!' (SP, 141) [Pretence? Reality?
To hell with it all! Never in my life has such a thing happened to me.
I've lost a whole day over these people, a whole day!], there is now a
pantomime which changes the resolution of the story – the recon-
stitution of the original family and the departure of the Stepdaughter
– into visual terms and emphasizes for the last time the radical,
essential, metaphysical distinction between the Characters and the
Actors. The beginning of the play is correspondingly more elaborate:
the 'frame' has been expanded. The addition of the Stage Manager
with his liaison function serves to break up into its components the
realistic rendition of theatrical life on stage and thus to spell it out in
its particulars. No doubt reflecting Pirandello's increased familiarity
with the practices in the theatre, the stage directions in the later version
also pay greater attention to lighting effects.

But the most important innovations are the two stairways, left and
right respectively, that connect the stage with the auditorium. The
stairways did not exist in the original version, which was written for a
typical proscenium stage, like the one of the Teatro Valle at the time
with a framed playing area strictly separated from the audience. Thus
while the Actors continue to enter from the back of the stage, the
Manager now uses one of the two stairways. He is dressed in street
clothes, and his progress from the auditorium door down the aisle and
up the stairway is watched by the Actors. As a matter of fact, in order
to attract attention to the unusualness of the proceedings, the Actors
are made to interrupt the dance they had just begun.

The entrance of the Characters who in the original version had
used the door on stage now repeats and amplifies that of the Manager.
Like him they come up from the auditorium, preceded by the Stage-
Door Man, but Manager and Actors will become aware of their
presence only at the end of their walk down the aisle. When the
Father says the words, 'Siamo qua in cerca d'un autore', with which
the action proper begins, he is standing at the foot of one of the stairways. He will be preceded by the Stepdaughter who in her first
demonstration of aggressiveness and insubordination pushes him
aside as he has just barely begun to speak. The Father then follows the

Stepdaughter up the steps; the Mother, the Little Girl and the Boy remaining on the lowest level, the Son hanging back, still on the auditorium floor. This tableau is held as the dialogue between Father and Manager engages the emotional reactions of the Actors in an initial skirmish. With the Father's lines: 'Mi dispiace che ridano cosí, perchè portiamo in noi, ripeto un dramma doloroso, come lor signori possono argomentare da questa donna vestita di nero' [I'm sorry to hear you laugh, because, I repeat, we carry a painful drama within us, as you all might deduce from the sight of that lady there, veiled in black] identical words in the two editions, with the exception of the addition of *doloroso* in the later one), attention shifts to the Characters again. The Father helps the Mother up the remaining steps, and a new tableau – the Mother, the Little Girl and the Boy close together, the Son standing to one side at the back, the Stepdaughter also standing apart from the others, downstage, leaning against the proscenium arch – is formed on one side of the stage. This action, in which there is no dialogue, is accompanied by a play of lights which serves to divide the stage in two, creating the same kind of distance between Characters and Actors that already exists by virtue of the stage itself between spectators and performance. At the end of the action the Actors applaud, thus underlining the theatrical nature of what has just occurred: among other things the Father is an accomplished director whose gifts are recognized by the professionals before whom they have been displayed.

The stairway will not be used by the Characters again until the very end of the play when the Stepdaughter runs down it for her spectacular exit. In Act II its role is that of simple passageway from stage to auditorium floor, used by the Manager (as he had already used it in Act I) in his frequent moves from and to the stage as he observes the effectiveness of 'The Scene' being enacted. The difference in essence between Madama Pace and the Characters is stressed by the fact that she does not use the stairway but enters from the back of the stage as she had done in the original version. Her sudden appearance, however, greeted in the original version by no more than deep amazement and indignation on the part of Manager and Actors, sets off a lively by-play in the definitive version as they rush off the stage with a yell of terror, running down the stairs and starting up the aisle as though fleeing. In Act III the stairs are twice on the verge of being used by the Characters. The first time is when the Son tries to walk out on the scene with the Mother but is held back within the acting space on stage: his trance-like walk from stairway to stairway is watched with fascinated awe by the Actors. The second time is during the violent flare-up between father and son as the Father grabs the Son and shakes him only to be grabbed in turn. Then in an escalation of hatred and rebellion – in the definitive version as against the earlier one – the Son throws the Father to the ground next to the stairway. Again attention is directed to this architectural feature which in the strategy of communication of *Sei personaggi* acts at once as link and barrier.

Of the changes we have been reviewing, the excisions (whose main function is to add to the *antefatto* which it is up to spectator or reader to reconstruct) and the transposition of material from Act II to III (which results in a better articulation of the compositional elements of the plot) stem from 'literary' rather than 'theatrical' considerations. They could conceivably have occurred even if *Sei personaggi* had never been performed and if in the years between 1921 and 1925 Pirandello had not increased his personal involvement in the production of his plays to the point of desiring and planning his own company and theatre, the Teatro d'Arte, which opened its doors in Rome at the beginning of April 1925.

The new conception of acting space, however, and the suggested use of masks – the other major innovation in the definitive version – are no doubt to be attributed to Pirandello's contacts with milieus in which discussions of theatre architecture were the order of the day and with productions of *Sei personaggi* whose actors and director had not been briefed and rehearsed directly by him. One of the most famous new theatres of the time was the Berlin *Komödie*, built by Oskar Kaufmann for Max Reinhardt in 1924, with loges opening directly on to the stage to facilitate that union of audience and performers already called for in the 1915 *Manifesto del teatro futurista sintetico*. Virgilio Marchi, the architect who rebuilt the theatre of the Palazzo Odescalchi for Pirandello's company, was himself a Futurist and he, too (as demonstrated by the setting and staging of *Sagra del Signore della nave*, the one-act play with which the theatre was inaugurated), was concerned with breaking down the traditional separation of auditorium and stage. As far as Pirandello's experience of *Sei personaggi* in the interpretation of other directors is concerned, the most important was that afforded by his first trip to Paris in April 1923. At the *Comédie des Champs Elysées* he witnessed the entrance of the Six Characters not from the door on stage as his directions called for but, as 'invented' by Georges Pitoëff, lowered from above by means of an old freight elevator with which that stage happened to be equipped. Alarmed by this departure from his conception when he had first heard of it in correspondence with Pitoëff, Pirandello was so taken by it when he saw it enacted that he adopted it, according to one report, for a later performance under his own direction (see, Jean Hort, *La Vie héroique des Pitoëff*, Geneva 1966, p.178). Of similar significance, though Pirandello was not present at any of its performances, was the Max Reinhardt production of *Sei personaggi* which ran at the *Komödie* from 30 December 1924 till 8 March 1925. Max Reinhardt's Characters made their entrance neither from the stage door, nor from the auditorium door, nor from above, but were on stage from the beginning, hidden from the audience until a violet light made them appear out of the darkness like 'apparitions' or ghosts.

It is probably impossible fifty years after the event to go back and pinpoint the exact cue from which Pirandello derived the double means (stair and masks) by which to underline in truly spectacular and theatrical fashion the play's fundamental *donnée*: the difference in essence between characters and persons, and the accompanying superiority of art (not artifice) to life. This aspect of the play, which constitutes its uniqueness in Pirandello's dramatic corpus, was obscured when in 1933 he joined *Sei personaggi* to *Ciascuno a suo modo* and *Questa sera si recita a soggetto* to form the first volume of his collected plays. Seen as one of the trilogy of the theatre-within-the-theatre, *Sei personaggi* does indeed illustrate one fact of the interaction of characters, actors, author, manager or director, drama critics, and spectators which should result in the creation of the illusion of life on the stage. In the Preface, however, which 'completes' the play, and was indeed written well before *Questa sera si recita a soggetto* (though not before *Ciascuno a suo modo*), the emphasis was elsewhere.

As portrayed in the Preface, *Sei personaggi* is not primarily (as it appears in the Premise to the trilogy) the representation of the conflict between characters and actors and manager taking place in the theatre but the representation of the author's creative act which takes place in the mind and is externalized (or concretized and 'personified') through the medium of the stage. Such is the meaning, Pirandello says explicitly, of the sudden appearance of a seventh Character, Madama Pace, who does not arrive in the theatre with the others but 'materializes' when the action calls for her presence: 'È avvenuta una spezzatura, un improvviso mutamento del piano di realtà della scena, perché un personaggio può nascere a quel modo soltanto nella fantasia del poeta, non certo sulle tavole d'un palcoscenico. Senza che nessuno se ne sia accorto, ho cambiato di colpo la scena: la ho riaccolta in quel momento nella mia fantasia pur non togliendola di sotto gli occhi agli spettatori; ho cioè mostrato ad essi, in luogo del palcoscenico, la mia fantasia in atto di creare, sotto specie di quel palcoscenico stesso' (MN, I, 66) [A break occurred, a sudden change in the level of reality of the scene, for a character can be born in this way only in the poet's imagination, not on a stage. Without anyone having noticed it, I all of a sudden changed the scene: I gathered it up again into my own imagination without, however, removing it from before the eyes of the spectators. That is, I showed them, instead of the stage, my imagination in the act of creating – my imagination in the form of this same stage].

The full implications of this important passage so necessary to a total understanding of the play are easily overlooked in the thematic richness of the Preface which recapitulates the history of the genesis of the play and offers a probing analysis of its constituent elements. But the dominant chord is actually sounded at once with the introduction at the beginning of the Preface of yet another 'character', Pirandello's unconventional little servant maid, Fantasia, the fleshed-out image of the writer's creative faculty. In his fictionalized retelling of the historical facts which we have used in this chapter to throw light on the making of the 'comedy to be composed', Pirandello is concerned with what in *I giganti della montagna* Cotrone refers to as 'the real miracle': 'E il miracolo vero non sarà mai la rappresentazione, creda, sarà sempre la fantasia del poeta in cui quei personaggi son nati, vivi…' (MN, II, 1362) [And the real miracle will never be the representation itself, but always the fantasy of the poet in which those characters were born living…]. In Pirandello's conception fantasy, or better, imagination, is a life-giving force similar to nature in its overwhelming drive to creation. Metaphors of birth, gestation, survival, and death recur time and again in his remarks on the psychology of literary invention. Indeed, nowhere has the organic metaphor, so deeply embedded in the aesthetics of Romanticism, been developed as fully as in the work of Pirandello. In the midst of a totally pessimistic view of life which cannot remove its gaze from the inevitability of death, Pirandello has triumphantly affirmed the immortality of the work of art: 'Tutto ciò che vive, per il fatto che vive, ha forma, e per ciò stesso deve morire: tranne l'opera d'arte, che appunto vive sempre, in quanto è forma' (MN, I, 66) [All that lives, by the fact itself that it lives, has form, and for that very reason must die; except the work of art, which lives forever precisely because it is form].

Because of the importance of this aspect of Pirandello's thought and because the text of *Sei personaggi* and its becoming are a full illustration of it, my discussion of the play has assumed its present form.

5. The Later Pirandello

The years 1922–3 mark the zenith of Pirandello's career. As a result of the London and New York performances of *Sei personaggi* and the Paris performance of *Il piacere dell'onestà*, he is invited abroad. From this time on his theatrical experiences outside Italy, the most important of which are in Germany, will become more and more frequent, and amid mounting difficulties of all kinds he will often feel not only misunderstood but actually rejected in his own country. The last twelve years of his life, from *Ciascuno a suo modo* to *I giganti della montagna*, see the addition of nineteen plays to his collected works, almost half of his entire output. Together with the three one-act plays performed in 1922–3 (*All'uscita, L'imbecille, L'uomo dal fiore in bocca*) and *Vestire gli ignudi* and *La vita che ti diedi* already referred to, these plays would merit full discussion. All the more so for having been so thoroughly overshadowed by the major works, the works that first established his reputation as one of the great theatrical innovators of the twentieth century and which subsequently and consequently entered the canon of masterpieces handed down from one generation of students to the next.

Mindful of the audience for which the present study is intended, it too has emphasized the major works, addressing itself to recurrent problems in their explication and evaluation, re-examining familiar material and bringing fresh material to the task. Similar documentation – letters, reviews, reminiscences of participants, internal cross-references within Pirandello's works, comprehensive and selective critical studies – exists for the later Pirandello as well, inviting a continuation of the critical method exemplified so far. In the pages that follow, however, it will be possible only to focus on problems and indicate lines of research still to be pursued in order to round out that knowledge of Pirandello's work, which in spite of a vast bibliography remains fragmentary, incomplete, and slanted.

Of particular importance at this juncture is the thorny question of the relationship between Pirandello and Adriano Tilgher (1887–1941), the philosopher-critic who has been variously referred to as his tutelary spirit, his evil genius, or, with regard to the Renaissance theorist and critic, his Castelvetro. Like the majority of the early critics of Pirandello as a playwright (Simoni, D'Amico, Gobetti, Gramsci), Tilgher was a day-to-day drama reviewer and he had written about Pirandello as far back as *Pensaci, Giacomino!* But his most important contributions date from the success of *Sei personaggi* and thus belong to the period of 'Pirandellism', that loose term used to describe both what has been perceived by some as Pirandello's involution, his conscious imitation of himself, and what Gigi Livio considers an entire movement involving the whole of the theatrical avant-garde in Italy immediately after the vogue of *teatro del grottesco*.

How and how much Tilgher contributed to 'Pirandellism', whether he derived his famous explanation of Pirandello's work as embodying the antithetical pull of Life and Form from Pirandello himself or whether he imposed it on him as a strait-jacket – these are questions that have been debated ever since Pirandello's and Tilgher's original mutual admiration for one another degenerated into personal attacks and bitter polemics. It is not so much the merits of the case that need to be re-examined as the repercussions: Tilgher's critical formula, made more and more facile through repetition, made a fresh and immediate response to the new works as they appeared impossible. In writing of Pirandello's success in France, Vittorio del Litto summarized pithily the rapid transformation of the initial enthusiasm into satiation and rejection when it was discovered that Pirandello's plays were closely related to one another, that 'his message, often repeated in very similar forms, was the same or almost the same in all his works'. Tilgher's comprehensive critical formulation – his 1922 essay in *Studi sul teatro contemporaneo* was the first to treat Pirandello's work in its entirety, identifying its principal themes in relation to the major cultural currents of the time – no doubt contributed to this feeling of *déjà vu*. It provided an intellectually-rooted exegetical tool that could be used to replace the reader's or viewer's personal effort. Like the flattened-out, reductive reading of *L'umorismo* referred to earlier, Tilgher's formulation emphasizes Pirandello's 'philosophy' abstracted from the fictional setting in which it finds expression. On this crucial point Pirandello himself was to state categorically: 'Senza dubbio la mia opera d'arte non è mai un concetto che cerchi d'esprimersi per mezzo d'immagini; è, al contrario, un'immagine, spesso vivissima immagine di vita, che, nutrendosi dei travagli del mio spirito, assume da sè, per sola e legittima coerenza d'arte, un valore universale' (*Almanacco letterario Mondadori*, 1927) [There can be no doubt that my work of art is never a concept that seeks to express itself through images, but on the contrary it is an image, often a most vivid image of life, that, nourished by the pangs of my spirit, takes on by itself and through the legitimate coherence of art alone a universal value].

But in spite of this disavowal of Tilgher's interpretation in its totality, there are traces in Pirandello's work of his encounter with the critic: one very important one (if we are to follow Moestrup) in the reworking of *Sei personaggi*, others in the Preface to *Sei personaggi* and the Postscript to *Il fu Mattia Pascal*, and the one most frequently worried-over in the very conception of *Diana e la Tuda* (1926), a play to which we shall have occasion to return.

The second question that should be touched upon at this point concerns Pirandello's relationship to Futurism, the only Italian movement in Modernism to have reached international recognition. In very recent years, in the wake of a more positive evaluation of Italy's avant-garde movements than had been the case in the 'classical' (i.e., Croce-dominated) part of the century, a perhaps inordinate amount of interest has been shown in Pirandello's rather fugitive contacts with Futurist milieus. In 1926 Pirandello staged Marinetti's *Vulcani* with his Compagnia del Teatro d'Arte; in 1928 he wrote the scenario *La salamandra* (related to the later one-act play *Sogno* [*ma forse no*], 1929), which was performed with music by Massimo Bontempelli (1878–1960) as part of a Futurist evening devoted to pantomime at Enrico Prampolini's (1894–1956) Teatro della Pantomima Futurista.

In a 1967 article (*Sipario*, December) regularly referred to, Giovanni Calendoli has summarized the apparent influence of Futurism on Pirandello as (1) the rejection of consistent, well-developed characterization (a contention at least partially to be modified in view of some of the analyses contained in the present study), (2) a conception of theatrical time and space as 'created' or 'invented', and (3) audience participation in the performance. Marinetti himself claimed that Pirandello clearly owed his 'alogical, unexpected scenes, such as Madama Pace's entrance in *Sei personaggi*' (*Almanacco letterario Bompiani* 1938) to Futurism. But unless we are ready to use the term Futurism as a kind of short-hand notation for early twentieth-century experimentalism in all avant-garde movements, it would be better to broaden the context here by remembering that from its beginnings Pirandello's theatre had contacts outside the *teatri stabili* and the main acting companies.

The premières of *La morsa* and *Lumíe di Sicilia* (1910), of *Il dovere del medico* (1913) and *La patente* (1919), took place thanks to 'little' theatres, and if Musco were not so much of a 'grande attore' we could add all of Pirandello's dialect production as falling outside the main line of Italian theatrical life at the time. In 1922–3 there was the premiere of *L'uomo dal fiore in bocca* at the Teatro degli Indipendenti, directed by Anton Giulio Bragaglia (1890–1960) pithily described as 'by temperament unconventional'. There was also a performance of *All'uscita*, presented as part of a 'tri-synthesis' together with Marinetti's *Bianca e Rosso* and the pantomime *Malagueña* interpreted by Jia Ruskaja (a Russian dancer and choreographer who became a naturalized Italian). This brings us practically to the eve of the foundation of the Teatro d'Arte and its opening performance of yet another experimental one-act play *Sagra del Signore della nave* (1925, on the same programme with Alfred Lord Dunsany's *The Mountain Gods*).

This rapid review of Pirandello's contacts with experimental theatre establishes the potential importance of the one-act plays as a key to his entire production. The one-act plays not only span his entire career as a playwright but, synchronically considered, they form an exceptionally interesting unit, whose various implications have however been completely overlooked. The situation stems both from the lack of critical attention accorded this minor genre in general – a step-child even more than the short story has been – and from the predominantly thematic approach which has prevailed in Pirandello studies. Moreover, information about the one-act plays is less readily available than for the three-act ones, except perhaps for *L'uomo dal fiore in bocca* which is often ranked with the masterpieces. One of the difficulties arises at the moment of production itself and casts its shadow over the subsequent history of reception and assessment. A one-act play alone does not constitute an evening at the theatre. It must always be given together with some other performance, as has been indicated in passing in the instances cited in the preceding paragraph. The play(s), dance(s), song(s) accompanying it no doubt interfere with sustained and focused attention. Yet, at the same time, they provide a new and unusual context within which to situate the work, a context which is not limited to textual material. In Pirandello studies these contexts have rarely been stated and never explored. And yet, with the exception of the trilogy of the theatre-within-the-theatre, the one-act plays offer an almost text-book illustration of Pirandello's interest in transcending the limitations of a given medium, be it written narrative or traditional drama. From the short stories turned plays as 'novelle sceneggiate' [dramatized short stories] (this is how the first version of the play *La patente* was designated) a direct line leads to the much later public readings of Pirandello stories, the musical versions of some of the plays, and the adaptations of both narrative and drama for the screen, the radio, and after his death television.

But there can be no doubt that the most important aspect of Pirandello's later years was his encounter with Marta Abba (born 1900), the third 'actor' to have had a determining role in the conception and fashioning of his theatre. Once again works would come into being in which the 'character' did not exist prior to the actor who was to impersonate him, where a 'part' did not exist prior to the assignment of that part, where there was a minimum in break of continuity between the play as it was in the author's mind and as it would be on stage. And since this time the spark that set the creative process in motion came from an actress, we shall have an opportunity to concentrate on Pirandello's female characters more directly than we have up to now.

The relationship between Pirandello and Marta Abba was of course quite different from that with the other two 'grandi attori' who preceded her. Musco and Ruggeri were Pirandello's contemporaries, and when Musco persuaded Pirandello to write a play for him and Ruggeri agreed to take on a play that had been written for him, they were both well-established in their respective specialties, actors of great drawing power, with distinct personalities capable of both reflecting and influencing Pirandello's conception of his male protagonists. But when Pirandello met Abba she had but shortly completed her training at the Accademia dei Filodrammatici in Milan and her first two seasons with the Compagnia del Teatro del Popolo in that same city. Though she had had rave reviews for her interpretation of Nina in Chekhov's *The Seagull* under the direction of Virgilio Talli, she was virtually unknown when in 1925 she joined the Company of Pirandello's newly founded Teatro d'Arte as its leading lady. 'She showed herself born for the stage and immediately ready to test herself in a major role', Marco Praga had written of the Milan performance, 'and that is why I call her to the attention of producers and directors who are looking for a leading lady free of spurious blandishments and theatrical conventionalism, and equally free of ornate or loutish traditionalisms'.

Abba made her debut in Rome on 22 April 1925 in the Pirandellian play *Nostra Dea* – whose protagonist changes personality with every change in dress – written by Massimo Bontempelli (1878–1960), one of the co-founders of the Teatro d'Arte and leading Italian modernist. A week later she acted in Eugenio Giovannetti's (b. 1883) *Paulette*, another of the representative new works the Teatro d'Arte had pledged itself to produce. Vincenzo Cardarelli, at the time drama critic for *Il Tevere*, praised her interpretation of an unusual, unideal-ized Paolina Borghese (Napoleon's sister immortalized by Canova): 'the fire of youth and the warmth of her recitation succeeded in over-coming the difficulties of a somewhat ticklish role'. By mid-June she had played in *Enrico IV* and *Sei personaggi*. Bontempelli writes that this performance (the first directed by Pirandello himself) was 'a completely new interpretation of that masterpiece' – referring, no doubt, to the specially prepared final, revised version of the play dis-cussed in the previous chapter – and that Abba brought to the role of the Stepdaughter 'the restlessness, the mysterious self-flagellation that constitute the very personal, unique foundation of her artistic person-ality'. It was not until 1927, however, that she was to act in a play written expressly for her by Pirandello: *Diana e la Tuda* and *L'amica delle mogli*. By that time she had added or was about to add to her repertoire the roles of Signora Frola in *Cosí è (se vi pare)*, Ersilia in *Vestire gli ignudi*, Evelina in *La signora Morli, una e due*, Agata in *Il piacere dell'onestà*, Silia in *Il giuoco delle parti*, and Fulvia in *Come prima, meglio di prima*. (She had played Gasparina in *Ma non è una cosa seria* earlier, even before being called to Rome.) The London *Times* critic who reviewed the 1925 performances of Pirandello's Company on tour was struck by Abba's versatility: she 'showed herself as clever at representing dowagers [Signora Frola] as the young heroines [the Stepdaughter and Ersilia] for which hitherto she had been cast'. Of her interpretation of Dea, Silvio D'Amico had written: 'We came to know in turn a roughish, passive, tender, dreamy, treacherous, com-posed and suppliant Abba'. More than anyone else she succeeded in achieving Pirandello's wished for, complete identification between actor and role ('immedesimarsi' or 'calarsi nel personaggio'), to the point that she is reported to have been in the habit of tacking up on her dressing room door not her own name but the name of the character she was playing.

Much – perhaps too much – has been written about Pirandello's male characters. *The* Pirandellian character, suffering *raisonneur* or character in search of an author, is always understood to be a male character. But if instead of starting with the premise of a certain predetermined development in Pirandello's work and fitting Mattia Pascal and Ciampa, Baldovino, and Chiàrchiaro, Serafino Gubbio

and Signor Ponza, 'Enrico IV' and the Father into it, we were to start
with a phenomenology of characters, a kind of mammoth Cast of
Characters of the men, women and children that populate the world
of his narrative and drama, we would find how large and varied is the
part women play in it. They represent not only the other half of mankind, but are far less homogeneous as a group than Nicola Ciarletta
implies when, basing himself on a selective sample, he characterizes
Pirandello's women as 'without country – they could be equally well
Sicilian or German – stateless, without passport, tied to the power of
men who can construct or destroy them, raise them or debase them,
give them a name or take it away again'. In our discussion of single
works we have referred to some of them: *la vedova* Pescatore and
Adriana Paleari, Marta Ajala and Livia Arciani, Beatrice Fiorica and
signora Frola, signora Maddalena and her daughter Agata Renni,
Mita and Tuzza, Ersilia Drei and the landlady Onoria, Lillina Toti
and Rosaria Delisi, la Nestoroff and Silia Gala, the Stepdaughter and
the Mother, Matilde Spina and Frida. Though there are those that
are little more than part of a setting – signora Agazzi and her entourage in *Così è* (*se vi pare*), la Barbetti in *Tutto per bene*, zia Nifa and com-
are Gesa in *Liolà* – others have destiny, sometimes, as in the case of
signora Ponza, all the more rock firm for being so drastically under-
stated. In the plays that Pirandello wrote for Marta Abba – *La nuova
colonia* (1928), *Lazzaro* (1929), *Come tu mi vuoi* (1930), *Trovarsi* (1932),
Quando si è qualcuno (1933), in addition to those already mentioned –
and in those that she made hers through repeated performance, we
are of course not dealing with chorus figures but with protagonists,
protagonists who came on stage well after Pirandello had abandoned
the regional world of his early drama and had already created those
ambiguous female characters who, as in *La ragione degli altri*, proved
stumbling-blocks on the way to success. (The role of signora Perella
in *L'uomo, la bestia e la virtù* represents an exception in Abba's Pirandellian repertoire as just delineated, but she interpreted it with great
commitment when in 1929 she was invited to play it in French with
a French company in Paris.)

Of the first two plays that Pirandello wrote for Marta Abba,
L'amica delle mogli belongs to what are commonly thought of as the
minor works, while *Diana e la Tuda*, one of only three plays he
designated a tragedy, stood so high in his estimate that in the final
collection of *Maschere nude* he placed it immediately after the three
plays of the theatre-within-the-theatre and *Enrico IV*. There is one
structural feature that sets these two plays (as it does *La ragione degli*

altri for that matter) apart from the group we considered in connection with Ruggeri: the protagonist – to whom the title directs attention – appears on stage without elaborate preparation, without doubts or questions regarding her identity, which imposes itself instead with the incontrovertible evidence of a physical fact: 'Entra Marta', we read in the stage directions for *L'amica delle mogli*. 'È bellissima; fulva; occhi di mare, liquidi, pieni di luce. Ha ventiquattr'anni: contegno, non rigido, ma riserbatissimo, che non impedisce affatto però la pura espressione della più nobile grazia femminile' [Enter Martha. She is very beautiful, with tawny hair and sea-coloured dewy eyes, flooded with light. She is 24. She is reserved but not stiff, and her bearing does not in any way inhibit the purest expression of feminine grace and nobility]. And in the stage directions for *Diana e la Tuda*, as Tuda appears from behind the curtain which had shielded her from view while she was posing, we read: 'È giovanissima e di meravigliosa bellezza. Capelli fulvi, ricciuti, pettinati alla greca. Occhi verdi, lunghi, grandi e lucenti, che ora, nella passione, s'intorbidano come acqua di lago; ora nella serenità, si fermano a guardare limpidi e dolci come un'alba lunare; ora nella tristezza, hanno l'opacità dolente della turchese' [She is very young and marvellously beautiful. She has tawny curly hair dressed in Greek style. Long green eyes, large and shining. They grow cloudy like the waters of a lake, in passion; in peace and tranquillity, they are still, transparent and tender like the light of the rising moon; in sadness, they are mournfully lustreless like turquoise] (the second sentence appears in the original, Bemporad, edition but was later dropped).

Like *Enrico IV* (and *Il giuoco delle parti*), *Diana e la Tuda* ends with an act of murder. The murderer is Nono Giuncano, a sculptor who, in an impetus of rebellion and in his quest for the immediacy of life, gave up his art by smashing the statues in his study. When the play opens, he is trying to dissuade the much younger Sirio Dossi from continuing work on a statue of Diana for which the young, beautiful, and very much alive Tuda – she is holding a bunch of grapes in one hand and a sandwich in the other when she first appears – is posing. The stage directions describe Giuncano as in his sixties, gloomy and restless, with white dishevelled hair and beard but youthful, piercing eyes in contrast to a lined and wasted face. He has, in other words, the attributes of the troubled, divided Pirandellian hero. But as the title indicates, he is not the protagonist of the play. This creates an imbalance or a lack of focus absent from the plays written for Ruggeri. In comparison to those plays, *Diana e la Tuda* is simpler. In it, too, there is preceding action (Giuncano had befriended Siro when he was a boy and there is even a hint that the two are father and son), but its disclosure is not tortured and torturing as in those plays. *Diana e la Tuda* lacks their complicated time perspective, the revelation of time past, the searing *anagnorisis*. Our expectation of finding a protagonist-centred play is further disappointed when we discover that the title itself is misleading in this respect. It is the closest Pirandello has come to naming a play after a woman, an impression strengthened by its proximity to *Enrico IV* in the table of contents of *Maschere nude*. But the two female names refer one to the representation of the mytho-logical goddess as statue and the other, preceded by the familiar, almost condescending *la*, to the artist's model. Thus they stand not for two persons or even two things (Diana as an object and *la* Tuda as an object) but for a relationship: the relationship between the work of art and reality, or between Form and Life to use Tilgher's termino-logy, which is appropriate here. We are back with the more typical, epigrammatic Pirandellian titles which point to an underlying idea or express a gnomic judgement.

But in *Diana e la Tuda* story and idea do not merge as successfully as in *Cosí è (se vi pare)*, *Sei personaggi*, or *Vestire gli ignudi*. The untidi-ness of passion, which in Pirandello is never far beneath the surface of ratiocination, here bursts forth with particular virulence and sullies the stark monochrome of an extraordinary expressionistic setting: the studio's white walls, the black rug and furniture, the plaster casts of various Diana statues, the enormous, black shadow of the posing Tuda projected against the wall. Like 'Enrico IV' and Belcredi, Giuncano and Sirio are rivals (in both plays the word 'cimentare' [to provoke] recurs as the linguistic clue to the structural parallel just before the *dénouement*). While the old Giuncano, approaching the final and irreversible rigidity of death, opts for life, for the wonder of red poppies growing for no one but themselves on an abandoned field (a parallel to the dying Tommaso's vision of blades of grass in the early *Il dovere del medico*) or for Pygmalion's miracle which would discompose the statue into a living, moving woman (like others of Pirandello's protagonists Giuncano is looking for a 'remedy', an incandescent substance which could flow through marble like blood), Sirio is unrelenting in his pursuit of the completion and perfection of his work, after which he plans to commit suicide. (His mocking reply to Giuncano and Tuda's questioning of his resolve in Act I is a direct echo of 'Enrico IV''s 'in marsina e cravatta bianca' lines.) Tuda loves Sirio who, intent on his project, can love neither her nor anyone else, and she does not love Giuncano who both loves and understands her. (Twice she playfully kisses Giuncano in Act I, the consummate playwright's touch to hint at what the 'correct' pairing-off would be.) Worse still, Tuda loves Sirio the man, not Sirio the sculptor. The human sentiment with its unpredictable impulses, its rootedness in the world of everyday experience, thus deflects the direction of the play and introduces petty jealousies (Tuda's 'betrayal' of Sirio with the painter Caravani for whose grotesque, vulgar interpretation of Diana she also poses; the rivalry between Tuda and Sirio's mistress Sara Mendel) and the variegated activities connected with a successful model's life (a busy scene with dressmaker and milliner; an encounter with the 'witches', aged former models who come to warm themselves at the embers in Sirio's stove) into what is on another level the lonely Promethean struggle between artist and work. At the end, events accelerate and Giuncano, true to the model of 'Enrico', but without the added burden or illumination of insanity, kills his rival. Tuda is robbed of any possibility of self-realization, of 'consisting', to use a Pirandellian term, of having life, that is, as either woman or statue, person or character. In the bleak ending of the play, which finds Giuncano and Tuda separated, each in his own annihilation, Tuda, like Ersilia in *Vestire gli ignudi*, assumes responsibility for what has happened: 'Ucciso per me, per me che ho la colpa di tutto!' [He has been killed for (through) me who am to blame for everything]. Her failure has been one of compassionate understanding and self-sacrifice. The run-down, emaciated, prematurely aged woman into whom she has turned, with hard glassy eyes and clenched hands that she can no longer relax (a challenging interpretation for Abba the actress!) is an emblem parallel to that of the veiled signora Ponza at the end of *Così è (se vi pare)*: 'Io, io sì, di tutto – perchè non seppi essere quella per cui lui mi aveva voluto!' [Yes, I, I am to blame for everything because I was not able to be the one that he wanted]. Once more we hear that statement of supreme acquiescence and almost mystical merging by which the creature accepts the imprint of the maker, man accepts the will of God, which is one of the most powerful motifs in Pirandello's work and is the culturally conditioned underpinning of his yearning and straining for unity.

This brings us to the last area in Pirandello's production to which attention should be drawn: the plays that he designated as 'miti moderni' [modern myths]. In 1931 he published the first act of *I giganti della montagna* (left unfinished at his death) under the title of *I fantasmi*. In the introductory note he established the existence of a second trilogy in his work, a parallel to the theatre-within-the-theatre: *Lazzaro*, the religious myth; *La nuova colonia*, the social myth; *I giganti*, the art myth. What exactly Pirandello meant by myth is a moot point, although the reversed chronological order in which he cites the first two – *La nuova colonia* was actually conceived and executed before *Lazzaro* – would seem to indicate that he had in mind some global view of mankind's progress, probably derived from his early acquaintance with German Romantic thought and more recently reinforced by his contacts with theatrical and artistic life in France and Germany (Pitoëff and Reinhardt). 'Myth' is one of those 'very significant' and 'very difficult' words that Raymond Williams has written about in *Keywords* (Oxford UP, 1976). From what was once a negative term for a lie or an untruth, it has become a highly charged expression of approbation for the imaginative capacities of man, conceived not so much as the gift of an individual but of a whole people or race. While myth may be a story, it may also be a perspective or a mode of consciousness. In both instances, the primitive – whether cultural or psychological – is privileged. The world of myth is not only the world of fiction, but the world of archetypal images beneath and beyond the civilizing force of logic. In addressing an international meeting on the theatre in 1934, Pirandello showed how all-embracing his concept of theatre had become, encompassing not only the 'pantheatricalism' of Nikolaj Evreinov (1879–1953) but having recaptured also the original idea of theatre as public ritual and religious ceremonial. 'Il teatro propone', he said, 'quasi a vero e proprio giudizio pubblico le azioni umane quali veramente sono, nella realtà schietta e eterna che la fantasia dei poeti crea ad esempio ed ammonimento della vita naturale cotidiana e confusa: libero e umano giudizio che efficacemente richiama la coscienza degli stessi giudici a una vita morale sempre piú alta e esigente' (SPSV, 1007) [The theatre proposes, as though to true and proper judgement, human actions as they really are, in the genuine and eternal reality which is created by the imagination of poets to be example and admonition to natural life in its everydayness and confusion: a free and human judgement which effectively calls back the judges themselves to an ever higher and more exigent moral life].

The early spectators and reviewers of the myths – of *La nuova colonia* and *Lazzaro* to be precise, for *I giganti della montagna* had a different history – knew as little about nascent studies of myth as the spectators and reviewers who had first rejected *Sei personaggi* had known about a tradition of the play-within-the-play in the history of drama. Sandro D'Amico recalls that to the public that had just mastered Tilgher's interpretation, the 'new' Pirandello appeared to have undergone 'a kind of senile conversion', that his 'pervasive optimism' was as difficult to digest as his pessimism had been. Subsequent criticism, too, has maintained a negative view. Together with the rest of Pirandello's post-1923 production, the myths have been given short shrift. Once again, Pirandello's 'philosophy' – his ideas on nature, science, religion, morality, society, art (some of which were examined in chapter 1 of this study) – attracted more attention than his 'art'. Specifically, under Fascism the myths tended to be studied to determine whether or not they conformed to orthodox ideology while, since, Marxian criticism has used them to show how reactionary Pirandello's model of human progress is, inasmuch as he is deaf to the class struggle and depends on accommodation and illusion for whatever personal and social reconciliation he can envisage. The absence of any but the most meagre theatrical history for *La nuova colonia* and *Lazzaro* has made the situation particularly difficult for these two plays, by keeping occasions for a fresh view to a minimum. We must more or less accept on trust Bragaglia's opinion that *La nuova colonia* is 'an absolute masterpiece in Pirandello's theatre'. (Again the case of *I giganti* is different for its status of unfinished work has exercised a special fascination on directors and producers and it has been performed more frequently and under better conditions than the others.)

To come to *La nuova colonia* directly after *Diana e la Tuda* is to be struck by the vast world of difference between the two. Not only are the setting and the social class of the protagonists different, but it is as though the individual 'hero', the character seeking centre-stage to plead his 'reason', had been pushed back and almost completely reabsorbed into the chorus or crowd from which he had initially emerged. In terms of the social ladder sketched by Verga in the Preface to *I Malavoglia*, we are back 'in those lower spheres in which the mechanism of the passions is less complicated'. But *La nuova colonia* also differs from the more or less contemporary *Questa sera si recita a soggetto*, to which it is rarely related since the chronological proximity is lost sight of when the latter is grouped (as done by Pirandello himself) with the plays of the theatre-within-the-theatre. Franca Angelini has suggested that Pirandello's myths are to be placed in the context of Bontempelli's and of the latter's call for a theatre to educate the masses, to capture, as he wrote in 1933, that 'atmosphere of a beginning (*primordio* is his word) which fate has assigned to our time'.

There can be no doubt that Bontempelli is thinking of the new historical epoch ushered in by the Fascist revolution, but it is also true that the very words 'primordial' or 'primeval' carry with them a reference to origin: for Pirandello, his Sicilian origins.

In both *La nuova colonia* and *Questa sera* we find again, in contrast to *Diana e la Tuda*, Pirandello's well-known Sicilian subject-matter. Sicily provides the inner story of the play-within-the-play in *Questa sera*, and though this story is not set as precisely as *Liolà*'s had been (in the countryside of Agrigento, complete with the dialect that is spoken there and no where else), it is still a story of characters identifiable by their *état civil*, with recognizable names and documentable pedigrees. The distancing effect is supplied by the outer story – the plan for a performance based on improvisation rather than a script – and this outer 'story' is of course in the very vanguard of the theatrical experimentation of Modernism. In *La nuova colonia* the curtain rises on a tavern scene in a sea-faring town of the South; it might well be in Sicily but not necessarily so, for there is nothing geographically localized in the setting or the circumstances of the different characters who gather there. And the distancing effect achieved by this initial indeterminateness is reinforced when only one character (the tavern keeper) has the individual identity bestowed by a name and surname. All the others are known by given names, nicknames, and diminutives, differentiating them at the very primitive level of distinguishing characteristics perceived and verbalized in a closed and limited social environment. We are indeed in the world of myth and not of history, or to put it in terms of Pirandello's total production, we are in the world of *Sagra del Signore della nave*, *La favola del figlio cambiato*, *All'uscita*, and *I giganti della montagna*. In the first, the scene is a village festival and the people who congregate there are, with one exception, known only by their trade, profession, or status. In the second, the scene is a theatrical space with its possibility for changes in scenery, and the characters belong to the world of the fairy-tale: the prince and the changeling, the mother and the witch. In the third, we are on a country road against a cemetery wall, and the characters are 'Appearances' and 'Aspects of Life' – and it is not insignificant that the play, first written in 1916, should have been placed in *Maschere nude* (a collection arranged thematically and not chronologically) at the head of the last group of plays, immediately preceding *La nuova colonia*. In the fourth, finally, we are in an indeterminate place, 'al limite, fra la favola e la realtà' [at the boundary line, between fable and reality], and the characters are the Scalognati [the unlucky ones, ex-variety actors who have escaped from ordinary life], the members of the Countess's Acting Company (she is Ilse, 'la fata amica' [the fairy friend], who had already appeared fleetingly in *Arte e coscienza d'oggi*), and beings described simply as Apparitions, the angel Centuno, and puppets (*fantocci*) – a strange assortment indeed to appear on the stage that had through most of Pirandello's career been occupied by characters who 'imitated' men and women of the real world, even though they had often had, in their opposition to one another, an ontological function.

The later Pirandello is the most difficult one – difficult because he has not been studied enough, because he is unfamiliar, and especially because the many layers of his previous production, achieved step by step over a period of about fifty years, reappear and coexist in any one of the plays in an ever-changing configuration: recognizable character types and situations that ask to be understood anew both in spite of and because of their background. If we come to these plays by way of the earlier ones, we may be disturbed by similarities that yet do not conform to the familiar pattern. If we come to them directly, discounting the earlier ones, we risk finding ourselves faced by a shorthand – Pirandello's achieved personal self-expression – for which we lack the key. They represent a challenge which has barely begun to be taken up.

GENERAL NOTE. The standard edition of Pirandello's works is *Opere di Luigi Pirandello* (Milano, Mondadori), composed of *Novelle per un anno* (NA) 2 vols, 1956–7, new enl. ed. 1969; *Tutti i romanzi*, 1957, new ed. in 2 vols (TR) 1973; *Maschere nude* (MN) 2 vols, 1958; and *Saggi, poesie, scritti varii* (SPSV) 1960, 2nd enl. ed. 1965, 3rd enl. ed. 1973. All quotations are from this edition, indicated in the text by the abbreviations noted above, followed by volume and page number. The first edition of *Sei personaggi* (SÉ) (Florence, Bemporad 1921) is also cited.

Basic bibliographical works in chronological order

A.BARBINA, *Bibliografia della critica pirandelliana: 1889–1961* (Florence, Le Monnier 1967).

G.MARCHI, 'Dieci anni di critica pirandelliana' in *Pirandello negli anni sessanta* (Rome, Carucci 1973).

S.MONTI, *Pirandello* (Palermo, Palumbo 1974).

P.MENSI, *La lezione di Pirandello* (Florence, Le Monnier 1974).

A.ILLIANO, *Introduzione alla critica pirandelliana* (Verona, Fiorini 1976).

F.RAUHUT, *Der Junge Pirandello oder das Werden eines existentiellen Geistes* (Munich, Beck 1964) contains the most complete and accurate listing of Pirandello's works in their order of composition.

SPSV for different editions and translations.

F.MAY, sel. intro. trans. *Short Stories* (Oxford U P 1965) contains the most useful list of translations of Pirandello's short stories into English.

General Works

G.GIUDICE, *Luigi Pirandello* (Turin, U.T.E.T. 1963); Engl. tr. *Pirandello: A Biography* (Oxford U P 1975).

A.LEONE DE CASTRIS, *Storia di Pirandello* (Bari, Laterza 1962).

G.MACCHIA, 'Luigi Pirandello' in *Storia della letteratura italiana*, E.Cecchi and N.Sapego, eds, (Milan, Garzanti 1969) vol. IX: *Il Novecento*.

Atti del Congresso internazionale di studi pirandelliani. Venezia, Fondazione 'Giorgio Cini', Isola di San Giorgio Maggiore, 2–5 ottobre 1961 (Florence, Le Monnier 1967). Hereafter cited as ATTI.

INTRODUCTION

F.FERGUSSON, *The Idea of a Theater* (Princeton U P 1949).

R.BRUSTEIN, *The Theater of Revolt: An Approach to the Modern Drama* (Boston, Little Brown 1964).

S.D'AMICO, *Il teatro dei fantocci* (Florence, Vallecchi 1920).

B.CROCE, *La letteratura italiana per saggi storicamente disposti*, ed. M.Sansone (Bari, Laterza 1968). In vol. IV, pp.326–49, are conveniently brought together all of Croce's writings on Pirandello, which go from the 1909 review of *L'umorismo* to the 1948 review of A.Janner's *Luigi Pirandello*.

G.CONTINI, *La letteratura dell'Italia unita, 1861–1968* (Florence, Sansoni 1968), pp.607–27.

U.OJETTI, *Alla scoperta dei letterati*, ed. P.Pancrazi (Florence, Le Monnier 1946).

H.FURST, 'Popolarità all'estero', *Meridiano di Roma*, 20 Dec. 1936.

CHAPTER ONE: *World View and Theoretical Statements*
Most of Pirandello's essays and occasional writings are collected in
SPSV.

A.BARBINA, 'Sul primo Pirandello recensore e recensito' in *Pirandello negli
anni sessanta* (Rome, Carucci 1973) for recent additions to works by
and on the young Pirandello.

G.ANDERSSON, *Arte e teoria: Studi sulla poetica del giovane Luigi Pirandello*
(Stockholm, Almquist & Wiksell 1966)

M.POMILIO, *La formazione critico-estetica di Pirandello* (Napoli, Liguori
1966)

C.VICENTINI, *L'estetica di Pirandello* (Milan, Mursia 1970) – all three for
Pirandello's early theoretical works.

TR, I, 319–586, contains the critical edition of *Il fu Mattia Pascal*, ed.
G.Macchia with the assistance of M.Costanzo. For Pirandello and the
occult, see the notes in this edition as well as G.MACCHIA under
General Works above. See also

O.RAGUSA, 'Pirandello's Haunted House', *Studies in Short Fiction* (New-
berry, South Carolina) x (Summer 1973) and

A.ILLIANO, 'Pirandello dallo spiritismo alla teosofia: *Il fu Mattia Pascal*' in
Pirandello e il cinema (Agrigento, Centro Nazionale di Studi Pirandelliani 1978).

On Pirandello's indebtedness to his German experience, see F.RAUHUT and
G.MACCHIA above, and also

B.TECCHI, 'Pirandello siciliano ed europeo' in ATTI.

A.ILLIANO and D.P.TESTA, intro. trans. annot. *On Humor* [*L'umorismo*]
(U North Carolina P 1974).

H.EICHNER, ed. '*Romantic' and Its Cognates. The European History of a Word*
(U Toronto P 1972)

R.WELLEK, 'The Concept of Romanticism in Literary History' and
'Romanticism Re-examined', in his *Concepts of Criticism* (Yale U P
1963)

M.H.ABRAMS, *The Mirror and the Lamp: Romantic Theory and the Critical
Tradition* (Oxford U P 1953) – all three for some perspectives on
Romanticism.

W.C.BOOTH, *A Rhetoric of Irony* (U Chicago P 1974).

D.C.MUECKE, *The Compass of Irony* (London, Methuen 1969).

— *Irony* (London, Methuen 1970 'Critical Idiom Series').

O.BÜDEL, *Pirandello* (London, Bowes & Bowes 1966 'Studies in Modern
European Literature and Thought'), especially chs. on 'The Relativist'
and 'Humour as Pity'.

CHAPTER TWO: *Early Narrative and Drama*
N.CIARLETTA, 'Pirandello europeo e siciliano' in his *D'Annunzio, Piran-
dello* (L'Aquila, L.U.Japadre 1967) is especially good on Pirandello's
Sicilianism.

— 'Meridionalità ed europeismo nel teatro di Luigi Pirandello' in ATTI
is less comprehensive but more accessible.

L.SCIASCIA, *Pirandello e la Sicilia* (Caltanisetta-Rome, Salvatore Sciascia 1961), esp. chs. on 'Girgenti, Sicilia' and 'Il "borgese" e il "borghese"'.

W.STARKIE, *Luigi Pirandello 1867–1936*, 3rd ed. (U California P 1965), first published 1926, esp. ch. on 'Pirandello, the Sicilian' for an early English view.

O.RAGUSA, 'Pirandello and Verga' in her *Narrative and Drama* (The Hague, Mouton 1976) for Pirandello and *verismo*, including the speech on Verga and relevant bibliography.

P.M.SIPALA, *Capuana e Pirandello* (Catania, Bonanno 1974).

L.CAPUANA, *Scritti critici*, ed. E.Scuderi (Catania, Giannotta 1972) for the review of *Vita dei campi*.

R.BIGAZZI, *I colori del vero: Vent'anni di narrativa: 1860–1880* (Pisa, Nistri-Lischi 1969) is by far the best work on the formative period of *verismo*.

F.BONANNI, *Pirandello poeta* (*Motivi della poesia pirandelliana*) (Naples, Morano 1966).

A.DI PIETRO, 'Luigi Pirandello' in *I contemporanei* (Milan, Marzorati 1975), vol. I, esp. pp.46–57

L.LUGNANI, 'Genesi ed evoluzione del personaggio pirandelliano' in his *Pirandello: Letteratura e teatro* (Florence, La Nuova Italia 1970)

A.LEONE DE CASTRIS under General Works above – all three for *L'esclusa* and *Il turno*.

Romanzo, racconto, novella is not included in SPSV, but can be read in ANDERSSON, ch. I above.

B.TERRACINI, 'Le Novelle per un anno di Luigi Pirandello' in his *Analisi stilistica. Teoria, storia, problemi* (Milan, Feltrinelli 1966)

A.MOMIGLIANO, *Impressioni di un lettore contemporaneo* (Milan, Mondadori 1928), containing two articles on *Novelle per un anno* and *La mosca*

G.DEBENEDETTI, *Saggi critici. Nuova serie* (Rome, Edizioni del Secolo 1945), containing an article on *Una giornata*

G.PETRONIO, *Pirandello novelliere e la crisi del realismo* (Lucca, Lucentia 1950)

E.MIRMINA, *Pirandello novelliere* (Ravenna, Longo 1973) – all five, in addition to the works mentioned in the text, for Pirandello as a short story writer.

S.D'AMICO, 'Itinerario di Pirandello al teatro' in *Pirandello*, *Quaderni del Veltro* 8 (1968).

L.FERRANTE, *Pirandello* (Florence, Parenti 1958) for the text of the letter-preface to *Se non così*. . . .

A.BARBINA, ed. *Teatro verista siciliano* (Bologna, Cappelli 1970) for the text of the *La Tribuna* article referred to.

F.RAUHUT, 'Pirandello als sizilianischer Mundartdramatiker' in *Der Dramatiker Pirandello*, ed. F.N.Mennemeier (Cologne, Kiepenheuer & Wirsch 1965) is the best survey of Pirandello's dialect theatre.

L.BRAGAGLIA, *Interpreti pirandelliani* (Rome, Trevi 1969) provides a play by play discussion from the point of view of production history, bringing together information which would otherwise have to be sought in the newspapers and periodicals where the plays were first reviewed.

s.d'amico above for letter to Martoglio apropos Grasso and Musco. *Primato del teatro italiano* is not included in spsv and must be read in *Scenario*, iv (1935).

e.licastro, *Luigi Pirandello dalle novelle alle commedie* (Verona, Fiorini 1974) is the best comprehensive work on the relationship between short stories and plays, which is examined case by case within a framework of categories descriptive of the different uses made of the 'borrowed' material.

l.lugnani above (pp.98–9) for comment on *Liolà*.

l.ferrante above (p.101) for comment on *Il berretto a sonagli*.

o.ragusa, '*La patente*: Play and Story', in her *Narrative and Drama* above for a comparative analysis.

CHAPTER THREE: '*Teatro nuovo*'

g.livio, ed. intro. *Teatro grottesco del Novecento* (Milan, Mursia 1965), an anthology of four plays

l.ferrante, *Teatro italiano grottesco* (Bologna, Cappelli 1964)

c.terzi, 'Le poetiche del grottesco' in *L'idea del teatro e la crisi del naturalismo. Studi di poetica dello spettacolo*, ed. L.Anceschi (Bologna, Calderini 1971)

g.calendoli, *La suggestione del 'Grottesco'* (Padua, Delta Tre 1976) – all four fundamental for an understanding of the Theatre of the Grotesque.

l.lugnani, 'L'Italia e i problemi del teatro nel primo Novecento e il contributo pirandelliano', *Il Cristallo* (Bolzano) viii, 2 (1966)

— 'Pirandello e il teatro contemporaneo italiano', in his *Pirandello: Letteratura e teatro* above

g.livio, 'Il periodo grottesco del teatro pirandelliano', in his *Il teatro in rivolta: Futurismo, grottesco, Pirandello e pirandellismo* (Milan, Mursia 1976) – all three for Pirandello in context of the Theatre of the Grotesque.

a.tilgher, *Il problema centrale (Cronache teatrali 1914–1926)* ed. A.D'Amico (Edizioni del Teatro Stabile di Genova 1973) for his review of *La maschera e il volto*.

s.d'amico, *Cronache del teatro 1914–1928*, eds. E.F.Palmieri and S.D'Amico (Bari, Laterza 1936), vol. I, for his review of *Marionette, che passione!*.

l.pirandello, 'Lettere al figlio Stefano durante la grande guerra', *Almanacco letterario Bompiani* (1938).

u.leo, 'Luigi Pirandello zwischen zwei literarischen Gattungen', *Romanistisches Jahrbuch*, xiv (1963); trans. partially in

g.cambon, ed. *Pirandello. A Collection of Critical Essays* (Englewood Cliffs, N.J., Prentice-Hall 1967).

e.bentley, trans. intro. notes *Right You Are. A Stage Version* (New York, Columbia UP 1954) has 'blows' for *sciagure* and 'situation' for *disgrazia*, and though it preserves the word *sventura* ('misfortune') renders 'Chi ha una sventura come questa deve starsene appartato' in a particularly limp and unfortunate way as 'I know people should keep their misfortunes to themselves'.

R.BRUSTEIN under Introduction above.

E.LICASTRO above for a good review of criticism on *Cosí è*.

A.LEONE DE CASTRIS under General Works (p.160) for comment quoted.

G.CALENDOLI, *Luigi Pirandello* (Catania, La Navicella 1962) p.124 for comment quoted.

V.PANDOLFI, *Antologia del grande attore* (Bari, Laterza 1954) p.316 for Pirandello's letter to Talli, which also contains an extremely revealing remark documenting the basic incompatibility between Pirandello's dramatic intentions and contemporary stage practice. He admits that *Cosí è* does not have a part in the usual sense for the *prima attrice* (i.e., Maria Melato) of Talli's company, but he suggests that she might consider making the role of signora Ponza hers for she alone would know how to utter 'come nella mia intenzione andrebbero proferite, le ultime parole della commedia, ov'è racchiuso tutto il senso profondo di essa. . . .' Having already run foul of the expectations of a *prima attrice* in the case of *Se non cosí* . . ., Pirandello was in danger of doing so again, convinced as he was that the test of good acting is not the magnitude but the intensity of a role.

E.BENTLEY, *Right You Are* above (Introduction) for the expression 'drama of ideas'.

L.FERRANTE, *Rosso di San Secondo* (Bologna, Cappelli 1959) p.129 for the Rosso statement quoted.

R.SIMONI, *Trent'anni di cronaca drammatica* (Turin, Industria Libraria Tipografica Editrice 1951–60).

O.RAGUSA, 'Minor Pirandello: "*Ma non è una cosa seria* and *L'uomo, la bestia e la virtù*"' ATI (Association of Teachers of Italian Journal) Winter 1977.

G.PULLINI, *Teatro italiano del Novecento*, 2nd ed. (Bologna, Cappelli 1971).

L.BRAGAGLIA, *Ruggero Ruggeri in sessantacinque anni di storia del teatro rappresentato*, 2nd ed. (Rome, Trevi 1971).

L.RIDENTI, *Teatro italiano fra due guerre: 1915–1940* (Genoa, Dellacasa 1968).

L.PIRANDELLO, 'Lettere di Pirandello a Ruggeri', *Il dramma*, Aug.–Sept. 1955.

V.PANDOLFI above (pp.323–4) for Pirandello on *Il piacere dell'onestà*.

A.GRAMSCI, 'Virgilio Talli', now in *Letteratura e vita nazionale* (Rome, Editori Riuniti 1975) and in V.Pandolfi above (pp.313–15).

R.SIMONI above (I, 346–8) for the quoted remark on *Il giuoco delle parti*.

A.LEONE DE CASTRIS under General Works above (p.164) for the remark on Baldovino and Leone Gala.

R.ALONGE, *Pirandello tra realismo e mistificazione* (Naples, Guida 1972).

S.D'AMICO under Introduction above (p.100) for the passage quoted.

L.PIRANDELLO, *Théâtre complet* (P.Renucci, ed., Paris, Gallimard 1977) vol. I, pp.1305–17 for a comprehensive discussion of the problems connected with *Tutto per bene*, (mis)translated into French as *Tout finit comme il faut*.

S.D'AMICO above (pp.104–5) for the remark on Lori's despair.

Burke's remark is quoted in Diane U.Eisenberg 'A Conversation with Malcolm Cowley' *The Southern Review* XV (Spring 1979) p.290.

A.TILGHER, 'Enrico IV di Pirandello all'Argentina' Il mondo, 20 Oct. 1922, now in his Il problema centrale. Cronache teatrali (1914–1926) above.

B.CRÉMIEUX, 'Henry IV' et la Dramaturgie de Luigi Pirandello (Paris, Gallimard 1928).

G.STEINER, The Death of Tragedy (New York, Knopf 1961).

M.KRIEGER, The Tragic Vision (U of Chicago P 1960).

H.J.MULLER, The Spirit of Tragedy (New York, Knopf 1956).

R.J.DORIUS, in Encyclopedia of Poetry and Poetics, A.Preminger, ed. (Princeton U P 1965) p.860.

G.BÁRBERI SQUAROTTI, Le sorti del 'tragico' (Ravenna, Longo 1978).

E.BENTLEY, 'Il tragico imperatore', Tulane Drama Review X (Spring 1966).

K.S.GUTHKE, Modern Tragicomedy: An Investigation into the Nature of the Genre (New York, Random House 1966).

R.ALONGE, 'La tragedia astratta dell'Enrico IV' in Teatro di Pirandello. Convegno di studi, Asti, 27–8 maggio 1967 (Centro Nazionale di Studi Alfieriani n.d.).

F.DOGLIO, 'Appunti per una lettura dell'Enrico IV' in Pirandello negli anni sessanta (Rome, Carucci 1973).

S.D'AMICO, 'L'Enrico IV di Pirandello', L'idea nazionale, 20 Oct. 1922, now in his Cronache del teatro 1914–1928 (vol. II) under ch. 3 above.

The Verga statement can be found in his 25 February 1881 letter to Capuana.

CHAPTER FOUR: Sei personaggi

There are three easily accessible versions of Sei personaggi in English:
1) E.STORER's (based on the 1921 edition), used for both the London (26 February 1922) and the New York (30 October 1922) premières, published initially in L.Pirandello, Three Plays (New York, Dutton 1922; London, Dent 1923) and later in L.Pirandello, Naked Masks, E.Bentley, ed. (New York, Dutton 1952 and subsequently); 2) F.MAY's (based on the 1925 edition), used first for a production in Leeds in 1950, published by Heinemann in its Drama Library (London 1954); and 3) E.BENTLEY's (likewise based on the 1925 edition), included in his The Great Playwrights (New York, Doubleday 1970) 2 vols.

A.BARBINA under Bibliographical Works above for a listing of reviews.

L.BRAGAGLIA under chapter II above for productions in Italy.

R.LELIÈVRE, Le Théâtre dramatique italien en France, 1855–1940 (Paris, Colin 1959).

G.PITOËFF, Notre Théâtre (Paris, Messages 1949) – both for productions in France.

A.ILLIANO, 'Pirandello in England and the United States. A Chronological List of Criticism' Bulletin of the New York Public Library LXXI (1967)

— 'The New York Premiere of Six Characters: A Note with Excerpts from Reviews' Romance Notes (Chapel Hill, North Carolina) XIII (1971)

F.FIRTH, 'La fortuna dei Sei personaggi in cerca d'autore in Gran Bretagna' in Il teatro nel teatro di Pirandello (Agrigento, Centro Nazionale di Studi

Pirandelliani 1977) – all three for productions in England and the United States.

O.BÜDEL, 'Pirandello sulla scena tedesca' *Quaderni del Piccolo Teatro* I (1961) (trans. in *Der Dramatiker Pirandello* under ch. 2 above) for productions in Germany, Austria and Switzerland.

L.LUGNANI, 'L'Italia e i problemi del teatro . . .' under ch. 3 above

C.POMMER, *Luigi Pirandello als Direktor und Regisseur des Teatro d'Arte di Roma* (Munich, W. & J.M. Salzer 1973)

A.C.ALBERTI, ed. *Il teatro nel fascismo. Pirandello e Bragaglia: Documenti inediti negli archivi italiani* (Rome, Bulzoni 1974) – all three for Pirandello and the 'Teatro d'Arte'.

J.MOESTRUP, 'Le correzioni ai *Sei personaggi* e il Castelvetro di Pirandello' *Revue romane* (Copenhagen) II (1967) for the text.

O.VERGANI, 'L'ora dei *Sei personaggi*' *Corriere della sera*, 15 Dec. 1936

D.NICCODEMI, 'L'autore alla prova' in his *Tempo passato* (Milan, Treves 1929)

A.FRATEILI, 'La "prima" dei *Sei personaggi*' in ATTI under General Works above – all three for composition and early rehearsals.

A.LEONE DE CASTRIS, 'Ragione ideologica e proiezione drammatica del "Personaggio senza autore"' in ATTI

S.BATTAGLIA, 'Il personaggio in cerca d'autore' in his *Mitografia del personaggio* (Naples, Liguori 1967)

C.VICENTINI under ch. 1 above (pp.163–74) – all three for the concept of the character in search of an author.

A.TILGHER, 'Il teatro di Luigi Pirandello', in his *Studi sul teatro contemporaneo*, 2nd ed. (Rome, Libreria di Scienze e Lettere 1923), pp.207–13 esp. (trans. in G.CAMBON under ch. 3 above)

F.FERGUSSON, 'Action as Theatrical: *Six Characters in Search of an Author*' in his *The Idea of a Theatre* under Introduction above

G.GIUDICE, 'L'ambiguità nei *Sei personaggi in cerca d'autore*' in ATTI

E.BENTLEY, 'Father's Day' *The Drama Review* (1969) now in his *The Great Playwrights* above

L.LUGNANI, '*Sei personaggi in cerca d'autore*' in his *Pirandello: Letteratura e teatro* under ch. 2 above – all five for interpretations.

CHAPTER FIVE: *The Later Pirandello*

G.PULLINI, 'La critica militante nel teatro italiano del primo Novecento' in *Critica e storia letteraria. Studi offerti a Mario Fubini* (Padua, Liviana 1970).

G.GRANA, 'Tilgher critico' in *I critici* (G.Grana, ed., Milan, Marzorati 1969) vol. V.

A.ILLIANO, *Introduzione alla critica pirandelliana* under Basic bibliographical works above, pp.46–55.

G.RIZZO, 'Pirandello versus Pirandellism' *Cesare Barbieri Courier* (Spring 1967).

V.DEL LITTO, 'Les débuts de Pirandello en France. L'interprétation des Pitoëff' in ATTI.

G.ANTONUCCI, *Lo spettacolo futurista in Italia* (Rome, Nuova Universale Studium 1974).

A.C.ALBERTI, *Il teatro nel fascismo*, under ch. 4 above.

O.RAGUSA, 'Pirandello's "Teatro d'Arte" and a New Look at His Fascism' *Italica* (Summer 1978).

D.SCHNETZ, *Der moderne Einakter. Eine poetologische Untersuchung* (Berne/Munich, Francke Verlag 1967) for a general perspective on the one-act play as genre.

Gli atti unici di Pirandello, S.Milioto ed. (Agrigento, Edizioni del Centro Nazionale di Studi Pirandelliani 1978).

F.FIRTH, 'La fortuna degli atti unici di Pirandello in Gran Bretagna (con uno studio su *L'uomo dal fiore in bocca*)' in *Gli atti unici di Pirandello* above.

M.ABBA, 'La mia vita di attrice' *L'Italia letteraria* (22 Feb.–22 March 1936)

C.POMMER, *Luigi Pirandello als Direktor und Regisseur* . . . under ch. 4 above, pp.127–39 and

G.GIUDICE, *Luigi Pirandello* under General Works above – are the three best sources for information on the relationship between Pirandello and Marta Abba.

M.PRAGA's review of *The Seagull* appeared in *L'Illustrazione italiana*; now in his *Cronache teatrali 1924* (Milan, Treves 1925) p.103.

V.CARDARELLI, '*Paulette* di Eugenio Giovannetti al Teatro d'Arte' now in his *La poltrona vuota* (Milan, Rizzoli 1969).

M.BONTEMPELLI, 'Il Teatro degli undici o dei dodici' *Scenario* (Rome) Feb. 1933, p.63.

The London *Times* review is quoted in C.POMMER, p.132.

S.D'AMICO, '*Nostra Dea* di Bontempelli' *L'Idea nazionale*, 24 April 1925; now in his *Cronache del teatro* (Bari, Laterza 1963) vol. 1, pp.502–6.

N.CIARLETTA, 'Meridionalità ed europeismo nel teatro di Luigi Pirandello' under ch. 2 above, p.348 for the passage cited.

A.SPAINI, 'Il Pirandello autore drammatico' in *Enciclopedia dello spettecolo* (Rome, Le Maschere 1961) is especially good on *Diana e la Tuda*, a play on which there is little bibliography.

S.D'AMICO, 'Appunti per una diversa lettura critica e teatrale dei miti' in *I miti di Pirandello* (E.Lauretta, ed., Palermo, Palumbo 1975).

L.BRAGAGLIA, *Interpreti pirandelliani* under ch. 2 above. The passage quoted is in the 'Aggiornamento critico delle rappresentazioni pirandelliane in Italia 1971–72–73' which was added to later reprints.

F.ANGELINI, *Il teatro del Novecento da Pirandello a Fo* (Bari, Laterza 1976); also in vol. IX of *Letteratura italiana Laterza* (C.Muscetta, ed.).